AS WE HAVE ALWAYS DONE

INDIGENOUS AMERICAS
Robert Warrior, Series Editor

AS WE HAVE ALWAYS DONE

Indigenous Freedom through Radical Resistance

LEANNE BETASAMOSAKE SIMPSON

INDIGENOUS AMERICAS

University of Minnesota Press | Minneapolis | London

The publication of this book was assisted by a bequest from Josiah H. Chase to honor his parents, Ellen Rankin Chase and Josiah Hook Chase.

Title page art copyright Lianne Marie Leda Charlie

"Our Treaty with the Hoof Nation" and "Binoojiinh Makes a Lovely Discovery" were previously published in Leanne Betasamosake Simpson, *The Gift Is in the Making,* from the Debwe Series published by HighWater Press, 2013. Reprinted with permission.

The interview by Naomi Klein was previously published as "Dancing the World into Being: A Conversation with Idle No More's Leanne Simpson," *Yes! Magazine,* March 5, 2013. http://www.yesmagazine.org/peace-justice/ dancing-the-world-into-being-a-conversation-with-idle-no-more-leanne -simpson.

Billy-Ray Bellcourt, "sacred," was previously published at https:// nakinisowin.wordpress.com/2016/02/26/sacred/. Reprinted with permission of the author.

Published by the University of Minnesota Press
111 Third Avenue South, Suite 290
Minneapolis, MN 55401-2520
http://www.upress.umn.edu

ISBN 978-1-5179-0387-9 (pb)
A Cataloging-in-Publication record for this book is available from the Library of Congress.

Printed in the United States of America on acid-free paper

The University of Minnesota is an equal-opportunity educator and employer.

28 27 26 25 24 23   10 9 8 7 6 5 4 3 2

CONTENTS

INTRODUCTION
MY RADICAL RESURGENT PRESENT

I AM WRITING THIS CHAPTER on a gray, wet winter day, in the café in the sports complex at Trent University as my two kids attend swimming lessons.[1] The doors of the complex have Trent's logo on them—the French "explorer" Champlain's sword, jutting into waves, or as my elder Doug Williams often cynically jokes, "the heart of the Michi Saagiig Nishnaabeg."[2] My kids pass the symbol with a casual "they should change that" and "don't have a fit, Mom." They have grown up in their territory, learning with a community of artists, makers, and elders, a luxury that not all of us, including myself, have had. Because of that, I see a strength in them that I don't see in myself. I see an ability to point out and name colonialism, resist and even mobilize to change it. They know more about what it means to be Nishnaabeg in their first decades than I did in my third. This intimate resurgence in my family makes me happy.

Over a decade ago, I was listening to Doug speak to a group of Canadians in a coffee shop in downtown Peterborough, a city in central Ontario between Toronto and Ottawa. Peterborough is known to be a conservative hockey town (really, a small city) on the edge of cottage country. Doug wanted his audience to know where they were, and he began by telling them what the land used to look like. The non-Native audience was nearly silent, transfixed by each sentence he spoke. So was I, because as he was speaking, I was recognizing that the land I know as my home has been devastated by settlement, industrial development, the construction of highways and roads, the Trent-Severn Waterway, and four centuries of dispossession. I understood that the landscape I knew as home would be almost unrecognizable to my Ancestors, and I hadn't known previously that I could barely even imagine the worlds that had already been lost. In the weeks after that talk, I spoke with Doug about what he had shared. As we drove around our territory in the months that followed, he pointed out where the Wendat (Huron) villages used to be, where hunting grounds were located, the former locations of black oak savannas and tallgrass prairies. I began to start my own talks with a narrative of what our land used to look like as a quick glimpse, albeit a generalized one, of what was lost—not as a mourning of loss but as a way of living in an Nishnaabeg present that collapses both the past and the future and as a way of positioning myself in relation to my Ancestors and my relations. I want to do the same here in this book.

Nogojiwanong (the place at the end of the rapids, or Peterborough) is in the heart of the Michi Saagiig part of the Nishnaabeg nation, and we call our nation "Kina Gchi Nishnaabeg-ogamig— the place where we all live and work together."[3] Michi Saagiig Nishnaabeg territory is along the north shore of Chi'Niibish, or Lake Ontario. Chi'Niibish literally means "big water," and we share this lake with the Rotinonhseshá:ka.[4] Michi Saagiig means "at the mouth of the rivers," and that name comes from our history as people that spent time at the mouths of the rivers draining into Lake Ontario.[5] We are travelers, moving throughout our lands rather than settling in one place. We are the eastern doorway of the Nishnaabeg nation, and we have responsibilities to take care of our relationship with the Rotinonhseshá:ka. We also have diplomacy with the Rotinonhseshá:ka Confederacy; there are at least four wampum belts (treaties) that remind us of those responsibilities as well.[6] There is also a wait-in-the-woods ceremony between the Kanien'kehá:ka (Mohawk) and the Michi Saagiig Nishnaabeg. Diplomatically, we have always had close ties to the Wendat. They asked to live in our territory at different points in history, and we made agreements with them so they could. There are wampum belts made, and the oral tradition has a lot of evidence that we lived together quite well: they lived in longhouses and farmed, and we were hunting and fishing, ricing and sugaring, traveling by the waterways.

Michi Saagiig Nishinaabeg are salmon people. Doug tells me Chi'Niibish had its own resident population of salmon that migrated all the way to Stoney Lake to spawn. We drank directly from the lakes, and that was a good, healthy thing to do. There was a large population of eels that also migrated to Stoney Lake each year from the Atlantic Ocean. There was an ancient old-growth forest of white pine that stretched from Curve Lake down to the shore of Lake Ontario, which had virtually no understory except for a bed of pine needles. There were tallgrass prairies and black oak savannas where Peterborough stands today. The lakes were teeming with minomiin, or wild rice. The land was dotted with sugar bushes, the lakes were full of fish.

It sounds idyllic, because compared to now it was idyllic. Our knowledge system, the education system, the economic system, and the political system of the Michi Saagiig Nishinaabeg were designed to promote more life. Our way of living was designed to generate life—not just human life but the life of all living things. Michi Saagiig Nishnaabeg were travelers; we rarely settled, and this was reflected in our politics and governance, in our diplomacy with other nations, and even in the protection of our land. Stable governing structures emerged when necessary and dissolved when no longer needed. Leaders were also recognized (not self-appointed) and then disengaged when no longer needed. It was an emergent system reflective of the relationality of the local landscape. I think of our system of governance as breathing—a rhythm of contraction and release.

There was a high degree of individual self-determination in Michi Saagiig Nishnaabeg society. Children were full citizens with the same rights and responsibilities as adults. They were raised in a nest of freedom and self-determination. Authoritarian power—aggressive power that comes from coercion and hierarchy—wasn't a part of the fabric of Michi Saagiig Nishnaabeg philosophy or governance, and so it wasn't a part of our families.

People were expected to figure out their gifts and their responsibilities through ceremony and reflection and self-actualization, and that process was really the most important governing process on an individual level—more important than the gender you were born into. In the context of gender fluidity and sexualities and relationship orientations outside of colonial conceptualizations, I see this idea of freedom as one that permeated the fabric of precolonial Nishnaabeg society.

When Champlain visits us and refers to the freedom our children have within our society, and our nonpunitive, attachment-based parenting, it's his white male way of acknowledging that freedom and authentic power.[7] His sword did not pierce the hearts of the Michi Saagiig Nishnaabeg. We are still here.

Over the past two hundred years, without our permission and without our consent, we have been systemically removed and dispossessed from most of our territory. We have fought back as our homeland has been stolen, clear-cut, subdivided, and sold to settlers from Europe and later cottagers from Toronto. The last eels and salmon navigated our waters about a hundred years ago. We no longer have old-growth white pine forests in our territory. Our rice beds were nearly destroyed. All but one tiny piece of prairie in Alderville has been destroyed. Most of our sugar bushes are under private, non-Native ownership.

Our most sacred places have been made into provincial parks for tourists, where concrete buildings cover our teaching rocks. Our burial grounds have cottages built on top of them. The rivers have lift locks blocking them. The shores of every one of our lakes and rivers have cottages or homes on them, making it nearly impossible for us to launch a canoe. Our rice beds have been nearly destroyed by raised water levels from the Trent-Severn Waterway, boat traffic, and sewage from cottages.

We live with the ongoing trauma of the Indian Act, residential schools, day schools, sanatoriums, child welfare, and now an education system that refuses to acknowledge our culture, our knowledge, our histories, and experience. At the beginning of the colonial period, we signed early treaties as international diplomatic agreements with the crown to protect the land and to ensure our sovereignty, nationhood, and way of life.[8] We have fought against the gross and blatant injustice of the 1923 Williams Treaty and its "basket clause" for nearly one hundred years, a treaty that wasn't a treaty at all within our political practices but another termination plan.

Heralded as the "first modern-day treaty," it resulted in eighty-nine years without hunting and fishing rights. My grandmother grew up eating squirrel and groundhogs because if her parents were caught hunting deer or fishing, they were criminalized. In the fall of 2012, as a result of a civil suit, the province of Ontario sent us a letter indicating that it will recognize our treaty rights secured in the earlier, 1818 treaty over a hundred thousand acres in southern Ontario. We will see. We have been living our understanding of our rights, and nearly every year since the treaty was signed, people are charged by conservation officers for hunting and fishing "out of season."[9]

This is the context within which I experience resurgence. This is the very real urgency of resurgence. Michi Saagiig Nishnaabeg, like other Indigenous peoples living in the most urban and industrialized parts of Canada, have virtually no land left to be Michi Saagiig Nishnaabeg. There are very few places to retreat to the bush, and almost none where you can't hear the rumble of traffic or run into a cottager or tourist. My kids regularly remind me of this. On their first visit to Yellowknives Dene First Nation territory, they remarked that they could be more Nishnaabeg in Dene territory than in their own. They asked why there were no police or white people watching us fish, a hundred kilometers off grid outside of Sombe'ke (Yellowknife). Settler surveillance for them is a normalized part of being on the land. They expect it.

They also expect that we will be there anyway, in spite of environmental destruction, despite the violence of surveillance culture, because they were born into a centuries-old legacy of resistance, persistence, and profound love that ties our struggle to other Indigenous peoples in the Americas and throughout the world. It is not happenstance or luck that Indigenous peoples and our lands still exist after centuries of attack. This is our strategic brilliance. Our presence is our weapon, and this is visible to me at every protest, every mobilization, every time a Two Spirit person gifts us with a dance at our powwows, every time we speak our truths, every time we embody Indigenous life. It is visible to me in the Unist'ot'en camp, in the hearts of Mooseside Tanners Against Fascism in Denendeh, in the work of the Native Youth Sexual Health Network, in the forty years of mobilization against mercury contamination and deforestation at Grassy Narrows First Nation, in Elsipogtog, Kanehsatà:ke, Listuguj, and of course in the phenomenal mobilization against the Dakota Access pipeline in Standing Rock, North Dakota, by the Standing Rock Sioux Tribe and the Oceti Sakowin (The Great Sioux Nation).[10] It is visible to me when we refuse to replicate transphobia and anti-Blackness in our territories. It is our Ancestors working to ensure we exist as Indigenous peoples, as they have always done.

From this standpoint, it doesn't matter who is president or prime minister, because our most important work is internal, and the kinds of transformations we are compelled to make, the kinds of alternatives we are compelled to embody are profoundly systemic. I am strongly interested in building an Nishnaabeg presence, an Nishnaabeg present, that embodies and operationalizes the very best of our nation because this is what we have always done. My Ancestors struggled, sacrificed, and fought much worse than I have to get me here, and I have the same responsibility to my future relations.

I Am Not a Nation-State

During the winter of 2013, Idle No More organizers in Toronto recognized that although Indigenous peoples have been talking about nationhood for years, the idea of Indigenous nationhood is a concept still very misunderstood by Canadians.[11]

In response, the Toronto organizers launched a dialogue called "Nation to Nation Now—The Conversations," which took place at the end of March in Toronto. They invited speakers from both the Rotinonhseshá:ka Confederacy and the Nishnaabeg nation to come together and share about what nationhood means to us from within our own political practices. Nishnaabeg curator and artist Wanda Nanibush moderated a discussion between myself and Nishnaabeg elder/artist and language speaker Robert Houle.

Robert and I were on first. I got up very early and drove into the city on the 401, following the north shore of Lake Ontario. I remembered our old stories of what the land used to look like, and I wondered if my great-great-grandmother would even recognize her homeland with the nuclear plant, the condos, and the six lanes of traffic that never stop day or night. I wondered if she were here with me, in the car, driving as the sun came up, if she would feel home. It struck me at that moment that our nationhood, my nationhood, by its very nature calls into question this system of settler colonialism, a system that is such an overwhelming, violent, normalized, and dishonest reality in Canada and so many other places. It is the force that has removed me from my land, it has erased me from my history and from contemporary life, and it is the reason we currently have thousands of missing and murdered Indigenous women and Two Spirit/queer people in Canada.

When I arrived at the conference venue several cups of coffee and two traffic jams later, I wasn't thinking about my grandmothers anymore. I was thinking about what I wanted for my own great-grandchildren. It was very simple. It is very simple. Indigenous freedom. I include it here because Indigenous freedom is a guiding vision or manifesto for what follows, and it starts with being very clear about what I want out of the present and what I expect from the future. What does it mean for me, as an Nishnaabekwe, to live freedom? I want my great-grandchildren to be able to fall in love with every piece of our territory. I want their bodies to carry with them every story, every song, every piece of poetry hidden in our Nishnaabeg language. I want them to be able to dance through their lives with joy. I want them to live without fear because they know respect, because they know in their bones what respect feels like. I want them to live without fear because they have a pristine environment with clean waterways that will provide them with the physical and emotional sustenance to uphold their responsibilities to the land, their families, their communities, and their nations. I want them to be valued, heard, and cherished by our communities.

I want my great-great-grandchildren and their great-great-grandchildren to be able to live as Michi Saagiig Nishnaabeg unharassed and undeterred in our homeland.

The idea of my arms embracing my grandchildren, and their arms embracing their grandchildren is communicated in the Nishnaabeg word *kobade*. According to elder Edna Manitowabi, kobade is a word we use to refer to our great-grandparents and our great-grandchildren. It means a link in a chain—a link in the chain between generations, between nations, between states of being, between individuals. I am a link in a chain. We are all links in a chain.

Doug calls our nation Kina Gchi Nishnaabeg-ogamig, the place where we all live and work together. Where Nishnaabeg are in deep relationship with each other. Our nation is a hub of Nishnaabeg networks. It is a long kobade, cycling through time. It is a web of connections to each other, to the plant nations, the animal nations, the rivers and lakes, the cosmos, and our neighboring Indigenous nations.

Kina Gchi Nishnaabeg-ogamig is an ecology of intimacy.

It is an ecology of relationships in the absence of coercion, hierarchy, or authoritarian power.

Kina Gchi Nishnaabeg-ogamig is connectivity based on the sanctity of the land, the love we have for our families, our language, our way of life. It is relationships based on deep reciprocity, respect, noninterference, self-determination, and freedom.

Our nationhood is based on the idea that the earth gives and sustains all life, that "natural resources" are not "natural resources" at all, but gifts from Aki, the land. Our nationhood is based on the foundational concept that we should give up what we can to support the integrity of our homelands for the coming generations. We should give more than we take.[12]

It is nationhood based on a series of radiating responsibilities.

This is what I understand our diplomats were negotiating when settlers first arrived in our territory. This was the impetus for those very first treaties—Nishnaabeg freedom, protection for the land and the environment, a space—an intellectual, political, spiritual, artistic, creative, and physical space where we could live as Nishnaabeg and where our kobade could do the same.

This is what my Ancestors wanted for me, for us. They wanted for our generation to practice Nishnaabeg governance over our homeland, to partner with other governments over shared lands, to have the ability to make decisions about how the gifts of our parent would be used for the benefit of our people and in a manner to promote her sanctity for coming generations. I believe my Ancestors expected the settler state to recognize my nation, our lands, and the political and cultural norms in our territory.

My nationhood doesn't just radiate outwards, it also radiates inwards. It is my physical body, my mind, and my spirit. It is our families—not the nuclear family that has been normalized in settler society, but big, beautiful, diverse, extended multiracial families of relatives and friends that care very deeply for each other.

This is the intense love of land, of family, and of our nations that has always been the spine of Indigenous resistance. The fact that I am here today is a miracle, because it means my family, like every Indigenous family, did whatever they could to ensure that I survived the past four hundred years of violence. For my kobade to survive and flourish the next four hundred years, we need to join together in a rebellion of love, persistence, commitment, and profound caring and create constellations of coresistance, working together toward a radical alternative present based on deep reciprocity and the gorgeous generative refusal of colonial recognition.

This vision for a present has the potential to create Nish-naabeg futures that categorically refuse and reject dispossession and settler colonialism and the violence of capitalism, hetero-patriarchy, white supremacy, and anti-Blackness that maintains them.[13] To me, Indigenous nationhood is a radical and com-plete overturning of the nation-state's political formations. It is a vision that centers our lives around our responsibility to work with our Ancestors and those yet unborn to continuously give birth to a spectacular Nishnaabeg present. This is a manifesto to create networks of reciprocal resurgent movements with other humans and nonhumans radically imagining their ways out of domination, who are not afraid to let those imaginings destroy the pillars of settler colonialism.

This is my beginning. This is my radical resurgent present.

ONE
NISHNAABEG BRILLIANCE AS RADICAL RESURGENCE THEORY

GILBERT DROVE THE KIDS from the reserve into town for school every morning, and sometimes when we would come to visit, he would drive another lap around the reserve to pick up all the Elders in his yellow and black bus, driving us to the treatment center or out to the community trapline on the edge of the reserve. I was in my midtwenties. Young. I didn't yet know which things in life are rare and which things happen all the time if you remain open and happen to be in the right place at the right time. Over two years, spending time with a group of twenty-five Elders who had known each other and their land for their entire lives was an extremely rare situation. One that in the next twenty years of my life wouldn't be repeated with the same depth.

I've gone back to this experience over and over again in my head and in my writing because it changed the way I think in a fundamental way. It changed the way I am in the world. I want to reconsider it here because this experience is foundational to my work on resurgence and to who I have become. I considered parts of this story in the short story "lost in the world where he was always the only one," published in *Islands of Decolonial Love,* although somewhat fictionalized, as a way of linking our current reality to the Nishnaabeg sacred story of a little boy who is taken to the skyworld to learn from seven Elders and then returned to the earth to share his new knowledge with the Nishnaabeg.[1] Meaning, we all have to be, in some way, that little boy. Like that boy, those Elders that I learned from for those two years actually gave me something that has propelled my writing and thinking ever since. It was the greatest gift.

I was working with Professor Paul Driben, an anthropologist from Lakehead University at the time. We had been hired by the Effects on Aboriginals from the Great Lakes Environment (EAGLE) project of the Assembly of First Nations (AFN) to work with the Anishinaabeg reserve community of Long Lake #58, located in the boreal forest of northern Ontario, about three hundred kilometers northeast of Thunder Bay, to create a land-use atlas. The band council sent us to the Elders. This was not a unique project in the 1980s and 1990s. Traditional Ecological Knowledge was in its heyday in the eyes of white policy makers, academics, and even Aboriginal organizations. The idea was that if we documented on paper the ways that we use the land, policy makers would then use the information to minimize the impacts of development on our lands and ways of life. The idea was that clearly documented land use would bring about less dispossession, as if dispossession occurs by accident or out of not knowing, rather than being the strategic structure it is. The project was to gather the individual cognitive, territorial maps Elders held in their heads into a collective, a visual re-mapping and translation of some aspects of Indigenous Knowledge into a form that would be *recognized* by industry and the state.

Of course, I don't think the Elders involved in these studies were naive. I think what I saw, and perhaps what they saw, was a process that could be used as a tool to generate cohesion, pride, and rebuilding within our own communities when our own people saw visually and so clearly what dispossession, displacement, encroachment, and industrial extractivism look like over our territories across time. Laid out in a visual way, the magnitude of the loss cannot be explained away, the strategic nature of colonialism cannot be ignored. The driving force of capitalism in our dispossession cannot be denied.

I was suspicious of Dr. Driben in the beginning. He wasn't Native, he was an anthropologist of all things, but he had created these maps before with other Nishnaabeg communities. Sitting in his windowless cement office in the basement of a building at Lakehead University eating subs, I could tell by the details on the maps that Elders trusted him. I could tell by the bunker-like nature of his office far removed from the upper echelons of the university that perhaps the university didn't. This boded well for our relationship.

Paul did something that has stayed with me and has always informed my approach to working with communities and to research. He was invited into the community to do a specific task, which in the end he delivered, but he actively and continually divested himself of the false power the academy bestowed upon him when he drove onto the reserve. He asked the Elders if they thought the project was a good idea. They said it was. He asked them how best to proceed. They told him. He asked them if they would be the decision makers. They agreed, and then they were, and he got out of their way.

This was an overwhelmingly different way of conducting research than I had experienced in two biology degrees. At the time, I could only frame it within collaborative or participatory or community-based methodologies, but it was really none of those. Those kinds of methodologies to some degree privileged Western theories, epistemologies, or knowledge systems, and the process that emerged in this situation was Nishnaabeg to the core. These methodologies assume there is a role for the academic. Paul did not. He came into their circle on the terms of the experts, the Nishnaabeg Elders, not the other way around.

Which enabled me to come into their circle, as a young Nishnaabeg person with very few useful skills to them other than youth. Western education does not produce in us the kinds of effects we like to think it does when we say things like *education is the new buffalo.* We learn how to type and how to write. We learn how to think within the confines of Western thought. We learn how to pass tests and get jobs within the city of capitalism. If we're lucky and we fall into the right programs, we might learn to think critically about colonialism. But postsecondary education provides few useful skill sets to those of us who want to fundamentally change the relationship between the Canadian state and Indigenous peoples, because that requires a sustained, collective, strategic long-term movement, a movement the Canadian state has a vested interest in preventing, destroying, and dividing. Postsecondary education provides very few skill sets to those who want to learn to think in the most complex ways possible within the networked system of Indigenous intelligence. In fact, I needed to leave all of that kind of education behind in order to come into this with hesitation and an open heart. The parts of me that I drew on in this circle of Elders were liabilities at university—gentleness, humility, carefulness, and the ability to proceed slowly.

During the next two years, the Elders, who in my memory are now eagles, took me under their wing. I wrote down on large topographical maps every place-name for every beach, bay, peninsula, and island they could remember—hundreds and hundreds of names. We marked down all of their traplines, and the ones before that and the ones before that. We marked down hunting grounds and fishing sites, berry patches, ricing camps, and medicines spots. We marked down birthplaces and graves. We marked down places where stories happened. We marked down ceremonial sites, places where they lived, places where life happened. We also marked down the homes of their relatives—places where moose and bears lived, nesting spots and breeding grounds. We marked down travel routes, spring water spots, songs and prayers. Places where feet touched the earth for the first time. Places where promises were made. The place where they blocked the tracks during the summer of the so-called Oka Crisis.[2]

We also recorded pain. The prisoner-of-war camp, the in-

ternment camp, and its school that some Nishnaabeg kids at-
tended so they could continue to live with their families and not
go to residential school. The 150 years of clear-cuts. The hydro-
electric dams, the direction the lake was supposed to flow. The
flood, the road, the railway tracks, the mines, the pipeline, the
hydrolines. The chemical sprays, the white people parks and
campgrounds. Deaths.

The overlays showed decade after decade of loss. They
showed the why.

Standing at the foot of a map of loss is clarity.

Colonialism or settler colonialism or dispossession or displacement or capitalism didn't seem complicated anymore.
The mess I was wrapped in at birth didn't seem so inevitable.
It seemed simple. Colonizers wanted the land. Everything else,
whether it is legal or policy or economic or social, whether it
was the Indian Act or residential schools or gender violence,
was part of the machinery that was designed to create a perfect
crime—a crime where the victims are unable to see or name the
crime *as a crime*.[3]

But this isn't even the most important thing I learned from
the Elders of Long Lake #58 in the middle of the 1990s. They
gifted me with my first substantial experience with Nishnaabeg
thought, theory, and methodology in a research context, and
Nishnaabeg intelligence in life context. Paul showed me the
kind of researcher I thought I wanted to be, but in reality I
wanted to be able to think like those Elders, not him. By taking such a radically different approach to both community and
research, Paul divested his power and authority as an academic
that had been placed on him by the academy and then by an
Aboriginal organization and placed that responsibility where it
belonged: with the leaders and the intellectuals of the community. Paul was a holder of space. He created the space for Elders
to not just say the prayer and smudge us off at the beginning of
the meeting but to be the meeting. He created the space to put
Nishnaabeg intelligence at the center and to use its energy to
drive the project. Those Elders gave me my first glimpse of Nishnaabeg brilliance—theory, methodology, story, ethics, values all

enmeshed in Nishnaabeg politics and encircled by the profound influence of the world. They pulled me into an alternative Nishnaabeg world existing alongside the colonial reality I knew so well. This has propelled my life.

This experience more than anything else opened my mind and heart to the brilliance and complexity of Nishnaabeg embodied thought. It resonated in a profound way in me and has driven two decades of living, making, writing, and research. Sometimes it is the only thing I am absolutely sure of, and more than that, I am absolutely sure that we as Nishnaabeg cannot survive as a people without creating generations of artists, thinkers, makers, and doers that live in Nishnaabeg worlds, that are in respectful relationship with each other, that create a movement that joins us to other Indigenous nations to protect the land and bodies. We need to live deliberately and with meaning.

I think about the maps those Elders carried in their bodies as two-dimensional representations of the networks they live and their parents and grandparents lived. I think about the maps my generation carries in our heads or maybe in our phones. I think about the networks the next generation will carry in their bodies. I think about how the networks we have in our heads today create the networks our children have in their heads as adults. It is this experience more than any others that has led me to center Nishnaabeg intelligence in my life, in my work, and in my thinking about resurgence.

Years later, when I would begin thinking and writing about Indigenous resurgence as a set of practices through which the regeneration and reestablishment of Indigenous nations could be achieved, the seeds those Elders planted in me would start to grow with a strong *feeling*, more than thinking, that the intellectual and theoretical home of resurgence had to come from within Indigenous thought systems, intelligence systems that are continually generated in relationship to place. I realized that the Elders of Long Lake #58 had pulled me into an Nishnaabeg world, and that this world was a very fertile place for dreaming, visioning, thinking, and remembering the affirmative Indigenous worlds that continue to exist right alongside the colonial worlds. I got a strong sense from them that our intellectual systems are our responsibilities, that they are an extension of our bodies and an expression of our freedom. There was no room in their Nishnaabeg world for the desire to be recognized and affirmed by the colonizer. There was no room in their Nishnaabeg world to accommodate or center whiteness.

The Nishnaabeg brilliance those Elders pulled me into was profound. Their world—a cognitive, spiritual, emotional, land-based space—didn't recognize or endlessly accommodate whiteness, it didn't accept the inevitability of capitalism, and it was a disruption to the hierarchy of heteropatriarchy.[4] Thinking about it now, I see that it was my first flight path out of settler colonialism. In their very quiet, nondemonstrative, and profoundly gentle way, those Elders refused settler colonialism, driving along the TransCanada in a children's school bus, laughing all the way to their trapline. They refused and generated something different. Everyday. Just like their Ancestors and their Ancestor's Ancestors.

Biiskabiyang and Flight

Biiskabiyang—the process of returning to ourselves, a reengagement with the things we have left behind, a reemergence, an unfolding from the inside out—is a concept, an individual and collective process of decolonization and resurgence.[5] To me, it is the embodied processes as freedom. It is a flight out of the structure of settler colonialism and into the processes and relationships of freedom and self-determination encoded and practiced within Nishnaabewin or grounded normativity. In this way, it is a form of marronage.[6] Scholar Neil Roberts describes the concept of marronage (derived from Awawak and Taínos thought) in his book *Freedom as Marronage* "as a group of persons isolating themselves from a surrounding society in order to create a fully autonomous community,"[7] like the act of retreating to the bush, or resurgence itself. Breaking from contemporary political theory's vocabulary to describe this flight, Roberts writes, "marronage is a multidimensional, constant act of flight that involves what I ascertain to be four interrelated pillars: distance, movement, property, and purpose. Distance denotes a spatial quality separating an individual or individuals in a current location or condition from a future location or condition. Movement refers to the ability of agents to have control over motion and the intended directions of their actions. Flight, therefore, is directional movement in the domain of physical environment, embodied cognition, and/or the metaphysical."[8] It necessarily, then, must be rooted in the present. Black feminist theorist and poet Alexis Pauline Gumbs, in an interview about her book *Spill: Scenes of Black Feminist Fugitivity,* says, "I am interested in presence and the present tense. I think fugitivity requires being present and being *with,* which are both challenges."[9]

Those Elders of Long Lake #58 knew present and being with, they knew flight—distance, movement, land as relationship, purpose. They watched the freedom of eagles, our messengers, moving effortlessly between worlds as expert communicators. Through ceremony, they shifted through physical realities to heightened spiritual ones. They constructed the world according to the structures, the processes, and the relationships Nishnaabewin illuminates. To me, they were marronage. My flight to escape colonial reality was a flight into Nishnaabewin. It was a returning, in the present, to myself. It was an unfolding of a different present. It was freedom as a way of being as a constellation of relationship, freedom as world making, freedom as a practice. It was biiskabiyang.

No matter what we were doing together, those Elders always carried their Ancestors with them. They were in constant communication with them as they went about their daily lives engaged in practices that continually communicated to the spiritual world that they were Nishnaabeg. I didn't understand this. I kept asking them about governance, and they would talk about trapping. I would ask them about treaties, and they would take me fishing. I'd ask them what we should do about the mess of colonialism, and they would tell me stories about how well they used to live on the land. I loved all of it, but I didn't think they were answering my questions. I could see only *practice.* I couldn't see their *theory* until decades later. I couldn't see intelligence until I learned *how* to see it by engaging in Nishnaabeg practices for the next two decades.

It would be fifteen more years after my experiences at Long Lake #58 before I would sit down and begin to write what would become *Dancing on Our Turtle's Back*. I had completed a PhD at the University of Manitoba and was spending a good deal of time with Robin Greene-ba, a Treaty 3 Elder, and Elder Garry Raven-ba, and the community of Hollow Water First Nation on the east side of Lake Winnipeg. I had moved home to Michi Saagiig Nishnaabeg territory to learn from my own Elders and had connected with Curve Lake Elder Doug Williams, as well as Wikwemikong Elder Edna Manitowabi. They all confirmed my experiences in Long Lake #58: that centering ourselves in this Nishnaabeg process of living is both the instrument and the song.

I set out initially in *Dancing on Our Turtle's Back* to find Nishnaabeg knowledge of how to rebuild from within after devastation because I thought this knowledge would be instructive about how to continue to resist and resurge in the face of ongoing colonialism. I did this not so much through discussion, although there was discussion, but through deep engagement with the Nishnaabeg systems inherent in Nishnaabewin all of the Nishnaabeg practices and ethical processes that make us Nishnaabeg—including story or theory, language learning, ceremony, hunting, fishing, ricing, sugar making, medicine making, politics, and governance. Through this engagement, a different understanding emerged. This is entirely consistent with Nishnaabeg thought, although I did not appreciate it at the time.[10] It became clear to me that *how* we live, *how* we organize, *how* we engage in the world—the process—not only frames the outcome, it is the transformation. *How* molds and then gives birth to the present. The *how* changes us. *How* is the theoretical intervention. Engaging in deep and reciprocal Indigeneity is a transformative act because it fundamentally changes modes of production of our lives. It changes the relationships that house our bodies and our thinking. It changes how we conceptualize nationhood. Indigenous intelligence systems set up, maintain, and regenerate the neuropathways for Indigenous living both inside our bodies and the web of connections that structure our nationhood outside our bodies.[11] Engagement changes us because it constructs a different world within which we live. We live fused to land in a vital way. If we want to create a different future, we need to live a different present, so that present can fully marinate, influence, and create different futurities. If we want to live in a different present, we have to center Indigeneity and allow it to change us.[12]

I talk about this in *Dancing on Our Turtle's Back* as emergence, but emergence isn't quite the right concept because it isn't just a recognition of the complexity and multidimensionality that we might not fully understand at work. It is also a strategic, thoughtful process in the present as an agent of change—a *presencing of the present* that generates a particular kind of emergence that is resurgence. Kinetics, the act of doing, isn't just praxis; it also generates and animates theory within Indigenous contexts, and it is the crucial intellectual mode for generating knowledge. Theory and praxis, story and practice are interdependent, cogenerators of knowledge. Practices are politics. Processes are governance. Doing produces more knowledge. This idea is repeated over and over again in Nishnaabeg story and for me ultimately comes from the Seven Fires creation story as told to me by spiritual leader Edna Manitowabi and recorded in *Dancing on Our Turtle's Back*.[13] Through this story, she taught me that knowledge or existence itself is a function of intellectual thought, emotional knowledge, and kinetics or movement. Gzhwe Manidoo (The Creator, the one who loves us unconditionally) didn't research about creating the world or think about creating the world. Gzhwe Manidoo created the world by struggling, failing, and by trying again and again in some of our stories.[14] Mistakes produce knowledge. Failure produces knowledge because engagement in the process changes the actors embedded in process and aligns bodies with the implicate order. The only thing that doesn't produce knowledge is thinking in and of itself, because it is data created in dislocation and isolation and without movement.

The Seven Fires creation story confirmed to me in an epic way that the original knowledge, coded and transmitted through complex networks, says that everything we need to know about everything in the world is contained within Indigenous bodies, and that these same Indigenous bodies exist as networked vessels, or constellations across time and space intimately connected to a universe of nations and beings. All of our origin stories do this, and, really, in the complex reality networked emergence generates, Nishnaabewin itself is a continual generation and iteration of these stories and principles.

The Seven Fires creation story sets the parameters for Nishnaabeg intelligence: the commingling of emotional and intellectual knowledge combined in motion or movement, and the making and remaking of the world in a generative fashion within Indigenous bodies that are engaged in accountable relationships with other beings. This is propelled by the diversity of Indigenous bodies of all ages, genders, races, and abilities in attached correlations with all aspects of creation. This is the exact opposite of the white supremacist, masculine, heteropatriarchal theory and research process in the academy, which I think likely nearly every Indigenous body that has walked into the academy in some way has felt. We need (to continue) to refuse that system or refuse to let our presence in that system change who we are as Indigenous peoples.[15] We need to continue and expand rooting the practice of our lives in our homelands and within our intelligence systems in the ways that our diverse and unique Indigenous thought systems inspire us to do, as the primary mechanism for our decolonial present, as the primary political intervention of our times. This means struggle. Struggle because we are occupied, erased, displaced, and disconnected. Struggle because our bodies are still targets for settler colonial violence. Struggle because this is the mechanism our Ancestors engaged in to continuously rebirth the world. And our struggle is a beautiful, righteous struggle that is our collective gift to Indigenous worlds, because this way of living necessarily continually gives birth to ancient *Indigenous* futures in the present.

Nishnaabewin as Grounded Normativity

What I learned from *Dancing on Our Turtle's Back,* from the process that created it and through the process of engaging in conversations about it over the past five years, is that although I found lots of stories within Nishnaabeg thought about rebuilding, struggle, and self-determination, these were not all crisis-based narratives, and they certainly were not victim-based narratives, nor were they about mere survival. These stories relied upon a return to self-determination and change from within rather than recognition from the outside. They all pointed to invigorating a particular way of living. A way of living that was full of community. A way of living that was thoughtful and profoundly empathetic. A way of living that considered, in a deep profound way, relationality. When I look back at it now, my experience with the Elders of Long Lake #58 was my first substantive experience of Nishnaabewin, or what Dene political theorist Glen Coulthard, author of *Red Skin, White Masks: Rejecting the Colonial Politics of Recognition,* calls "grounded normativity," ethical frameworks generated by these place-based practices and associated knowledges.[16] In academic circles, particularly theoretical ones, this is an important intervention because grounded normativity is the base of our political systems, economy, and nationhood, and it creates process-centered modes of living that generate profoundly different conceptualizations of nationhood and governmentality—ones that aren't based on enclosure, authoritarian power, and hierarchy. The term itself is far less important in Indigenous circles; we've always known our way of life comes from the place or land through the practice of our modes of intelligence. We know that place includes land and waters, plants and animals, and the spiritual world—a peopled cosmos of influencing powers. We know that our practices code and reveal knowledge, and our knowledge codes and reveals practices. We know the individual values we animate in those lives in turn create intimate relationships with our family and all aspects of creation, which in turn create a fluid and collective ethical framework that we in turn practice. I think in the context of my own nation, the term Nishnaabewin—all of the associated practices, knowledge, and ethics that make us Nishnaabeg and construct the Nishnaabeg world—is the closest thing to Coulthard's grounded normativity. I use the term interchangeably with Nishnaabeg intelligence, like Coulthard, as a strategic intervention into how the colonial world and the academy position, construct, contain, and shrink Indigenous knowledge systems.

In this sense, in the past, Nishnaabeg woke up each morning and built Nishnaabeg life every day, using our knowledge and practices because this is what we are encouraged to do in our creation stories; these are our original instructions. This *procedure* or practice of living, theory and praxis intertwined, is generated through relations with Michi Saagiig Nishnaabeg land, land that is constructed and defined by our intimate spiritual, emotional, and physical relationship with it. The procedure is our grounded normativity. Living is a creative act, with self-determined making or producing at its core. Colonized life is so intensely about consumption that the idea of making is reserved for artists at best and hobbies at worst. Making is not seen as the material basis for experiencing and influencing the world. Yet, Nishnaabeg life didn't rely on institutionality to hold the structure of life. We relied upon process that created networked relationship. Our intelligence system is a series of interconnected and overlapping algorithms—stories, ceremonies, and the land itself are procedures for solving the problems of life. Networked because the modes of communication and interaction between beings occur in complex nonlinear forms, across time and space. There is necessarily substantial overlap in networked responsibilities, such that the loss of a component of the network can self-correct and rebalance.

Governance was *made* every day. Leadership was embodied and acted out every day. Grounded normativity isn't a thing; it is generated structure born and maintained from deep engagement with Indigenous processes that are inherently physical, emotional, intellectual, and spiritual. Processes were created and practiced. Daily life involved making politics, education, health care, food systems, and economy on micro- and macro-scales. I didn't need to look for catastrophe or crisis-based stories to learn how to rebuild. The Nishnaabeg conceptualizations of life I found were cycles of creative energies, continual processes that bring forth more life and more creation and more thinking. These are the systems we need to re-create. The structural and material basis of Nishnaabeg life was and is process and relationship—again, resurgence is our original instruction.

What does Nishnaabeg grounded normativity look like? What is the ethical framework that is provided to me living my life on the north shore of Lake Ontario? What are these practices and associated forms of knowing? Nishnaabeg political systems begin in individuals and our relationships to the implicate order or the spiritual world. The ethics and values that individuals use to make decisions in their personal lives are the same ethics and values that families, communities, and nations use to make decisions about how to live collectively. Our ethical intelligence is ongoing; it is not a series of teachings or laws or protocols; it is a series of practices that are adaptable and to some degree fluid. I don't know it so much as an "ethical framework" but as a series of complex, interconnected cycling processes that make up a nonlinear, overlapping emergent and responsive network of relationships of deep reciprocity, intimate and global interconnection and interdependence, that spirals across time and space. I know it as the algorithm of the Nishnaabeg world. I wrote about many of these in *Dancing on Our Turtle's Back*—the seven grandmother teachings, ethics of noninterference and the practice of self-determination, the practice of consent, the art of honesty, empathy, caring, sharing, and self-sufficiency, for example. Our economy, fully integrated with spirituality and politics, was intensely local within a network of Indigenous internationalism (discussed in chapter 4) that included plant and animal nations, the Great Lakes, the St. Lawrence River, and nonhuman beings and other Indigenous nations. Its strength is measured by its ability to take care of the needs of the people, all the peoples that make up the Nishnaabeg cosmos. Colonialism has strangulated grounded normativity. It has attacked and tried to eliminate or confine the practice of grounded normativ-ity to the realm of neoliberalism so that it isn't so much a way of being in the world but a quaint cultural difference that makes one interesting. When colonialism could not eliminate ground-ed normativity, it tried to contain it so that it exists only to the degree that it does not impede land acquisition, settlement, and resource extraction. It is this situation, the dispossession of Indigenous peoples from our grounded normativities through the processes of colonialism and now settler colonialism, that has set up the circumstances that require a radical Indigenous resurgence as a mechanism for our continuance as Indigenous peoples.

I feel grateful, looking back, that I was able to interact with the Elders of Long Lake #58, these Nishnaabewin theorists, on their own terms, as opposed to as a graduate student. Had I gone into their community as a student, I would have inevitably writ-ten about this project within the confines of the academic litera-ture and thinking of the academy in the 1990s, and this perhaps would have become my record of these events. Instead, I didn't write about this experience until now, but I held it as a seed that in the right Nishnaabeg context grew and gives credence to the idea that the fuel for our radical resurgence must come from within our own nation-based grounded normativities because these are the intelligence systems that hold the potential, the theory as practice, for making ethical, sustainable Indigenous worlds.

I believe our responsibility as Indigenous peoples is to work alongside our Ancestors and those not yet born to continually give birth to an Indigenous present that generates Indigenous freedom, and this means creating generations that are in love with, attached to, and committed to their land. It also means that the intellectual and theoretical home for our nation-based resurgences must be within grounded normativity and, for me specifically, within Nishnaabewin, our lived expression of Nish-naabeg intelligence.

TWO
KWE AS RESURGENT METHOD

WHILE THE FEW YEARS I spent with the elders of Long Lake #58 are responsible for me falling deeply in love with Nishnaabewin, they are also the beginning of me being able to link the experiences of my life with a critique and analysis of colonialism. As an instructor in many different Indigenous land-based programs, I often have the honor of witnessing our people link the circumstances of their lives—that is, how they experience the personal trauma of colonialism through the child welfare system, the state education system, gender violence, addictions, poverty, the prison system, or mental health issues—to the larger structures and process of settler colonialism. These are powerful moments to witness, and in my own person these moments have been the most theoretically generative, particularly if these moments are housed and nurtured within grounded normativities.

Like *Dancing on Our Turtle's Back* and "Land as Pedagogy," this book was generated from within Nishnaabeg intelligence—Nishnaabeg intellectual practices or, more broadly, Nishnaabewin—rather than the traditional theoretical and

methodological orientations of the Western academy.[1] It is anchored theoretically within the ways my people generate knowledge, through deep reciprocal embodied engagement with Aki,
and by participating with full presence in embedded practices—
inherent processes that occur within a series of ethical frameworks that, when adhered to, continually generate consent.[2]

In *Dancing on Our Turtle's Back*, I used the Seven Fires
Nishnaabeg creation story, as told to me by elder Edna Manitowabi, to demonstrate the nature of knowledge from within
Nishnaabewin, and this is also an important theoretical anchor
in this book.[3] In *Dancing on Our Turtle's Back*, I emphasized in
my analysis of this story that knowledge within the Nishnaabeg
universe comes from the spiritual world and flows to humans
through intimate relationships with human and nonhuman entities. I discussed how knowledge is created through the combination of heart knowledge or emotion, and thought or intellect.
I explained how the transformative power of knowledge is un-
leashed through movement, kinetics or action, our embedded
practices and processes of life; that is, one has to be fully present
and engaged in Nishnaabeg ways of living in order to generate
knowledge, in order to generate theory. In this way theory is
generated from the ground up, and it necessarily then has to be
accessible to all Nishnaabeg so we each have the opportunity to
develop our own intimate meaning. I talked about how Gzhwe
Manidoo transferred all the knowledge that went into the creation of the universe to Nishnaabeg bodies, but that the knowledge was so vast it didn't just stay in our heads, it spilled into
every aspect of our beings.[4] I stressed that knowledge is intimate
within Nishnaabewin: individuals have the responsibility for
generating meaning in their lives, for discovering their place in
the world with the guidance of their names, spiritual relations,
clan affiliations, their own gifts, desires, talents, and skills sets
and by actively engaging the world. I emphasized it was the responsibility of families and communities to support individuals
and their diverse life paths, as opposed to judging and discour-
aging individual growth and actualization, and that this creates
agency and self-determination, variance and diversity. I went

on to talk about how Nanabush's early trips around the world (discussed in more detail in chapter 4 of this volume) outline Nishnaabeg ways of knowing or generating knowledge, including visiting, ceremony, singing, dancing, storytelling, hunting, fishing, gathering, observing, reflecting, experimenting, visioning, dreaming, ricing, and sugaring, for example.[5] Chapter 4 also explains how Nishnaabeg internationalism allows for the engagement of other theoretical traditions within the frame of Nishnaabewin. Edna says, "wear your teachings," and what she is telling us when she does, is that you can't study or read about this system to understand it. One has to animate our practices of living over several decades. One has to be the intervention, one has to not only wear the theories but use them to navigate life.

As much as this book is about my own deepening understandings of these theories within my life, these intellectual practices are also the mechanism through which I have generated my understanding of the theories, concepts, and ideas in this book. This book comes then from a different set of intellectual practices than the ones privileged in the academy. It adheres to a different set of theories on how knowledge is constructed, generated, and communicated. It uses a different set of methodologies to generate those ideas. I understand the word *kwe* to mean woman within the spectrum of genders in Nishnaabemowin, or the Nishnaabe language. Kwe is not a commodity. Kwe is not capital. It is different than the word *woman* because it recognizes a spectrum of gender expressions and it exists embedded in grounded normativity. Kwe cannot be exploited. There is a fluidity to my use of the term kwe that gestures to the gender variance within Nishnaabewin. Kwe does not conform to the rigidity of the colonial gender binary, nor is kwe essentialized. In my mind, kwe has the capacity to be inclusive of both cis and trans experiences, but this is not my decision to make, because I do not write from that positionality.

My life as a kwe within Nishnaabewin is *method* because my people have always generated knowledge through the combination of emotion and intellectual knowledge within the kinetics of our placed-based practices, as mitigated through our bodies, minds, and spirits. In fact, within Nishnaabewin, I am fully responsible for generating meaning about my life through the way I think and live. This internal work is a necessary and vital part of living responsibly and ethically within our grounded normativity. It is my sovereignty. Within this larger process, on the land I've engaged in Nishnaabeg practices of hunting, fishing, harvesting rice and medicines, ceremony, language learning, singing, dancing, making maple syrup, parenting, and storytelling, and I've spent over a decade learning from elder Doug Williams. I've paid great attention to my thoughts, emotions, and experiences as a kwe living at this particular point in time, and I've used this to critique settler colonialism and to generate thoughts on radical resurgent responses.[6] I have not reacted to these emotional responses uncritically but explored and processed them through ceremony, discussions, artistic practice, and therapeutic contexts and with elders. This is an act of resurgence itself: centering Nishnaabeg intellect and thought through the embodiment of Nishnaabeg practices, and using the theory and knowledge generated to critique my current reality.

This is not just experiential knowledge or embodied knowledge. It is not just individual knowledge rooted in my own perspectives and experiences with the abusive power of colonialism, because it is theoretically anchored to and generated through Nishnaabeg intelligence and because it takes place entirely within grounded normativity—perhaps a strangulated grounded normativity but grounded normativity nevertheless. In an entirely Nishnaabeg intellectual context, I wouldn't have to explain this at all. This would be understood because it is how our knowledge system has always worked.

This is kwe as method generating kwe as theorist.

This is kwe as method generating kwe as theorist, *as we have always done*.

To this end, this isn't an academic book in a Western sense, because in many ways it does not conform to and reproduce straight, white, cisgendered, masculinist academic conventions, theories, and citational practices, and therefore knowledge, despite the fact these are normalized within the academy.[7] Indigenous peoples, particularly children, women, and Two Spirit and queer (2SQ) people, can choose to use the conventions of the academy to critique the system of settler colonialism and advance Indigenous liberation, and I believe this is valuable work.[8] We can also choose to continue to produce knowledge and theory in opposition to the academy as resistance, resurgence, and sustenance through our own systems of knowledge, and I believe this is also vital work.[9] Many of us do both at the same time. However, the knowledge our bodies and our practices generate, that our theories and methodologies produce, has never been considered valid knowledge within the academy and therefore often exists on the margins.[10] As a result of this gatekeeping, the academy cannot account for nor explain what has happened to me as a kwe under the system of colonialism in a manner that I can wholeheartedly embrace, and without the knowledge, analysis, and critique produced by Indigenous people, particularly women and 2SQ people on our own terms, the academy cannot have a full understanding of colonialism as a process nor can it fully understand Indigenous resurgence.[11] As political orders, our bodies, minds, emotions, and spirits produce theory and knowledge on a daily basis without conforming to the conventions of the academy, and I believe this has not only sustained our peoples, but it has always propelled Indigenous intellectual rigor and propelled our resurgent practices.[12] This is Indigenous excellence.

Following Nishnaabeg intellectual practices, you will find me citing Indigenous scholars and writers that resonate most profoundly in my head and in my heart, as the practice of debwewin, or the process of producing truths.[13] You will find me relying on Nishnaabeg practices as theory, highlighting my own personal practice of Nishnaabeg intelligence and privileging the often painful and uncomfortable knowledge I carry that has been generated from existing as an Indigenous woman in the context of settler colonialism. My body and my life are part of my research, and I use this knowledge to critique and analyze. I will not separate this from my engagement with academic literature, because in my life these things are not compartmentalized.

I write from the first person, because within Nishnaabewin, this is a mechanism of accountability for my own thoughts, critique, and analysis, and a recognition that these will necessarily vary from other Nishnaabeg thinkers. I use Nishnaabewin as theory because that is what my people have always done, although there are many other conceptual windows into our thought system. I tell stories, both sacred stories (aandisokaanan) and personal stories (dibajimowinan), as a way of communicating ideas and concepts because that is how my people express themselves, and I rely on Nishnaabeg aesthetics to communicate meaning through story (see chapter 11 for a detailed explanation). Some concepts are introduced early in this book and then repeated later in the work as a mechanism for deepening understandings because in Nishnaabeg intellectual practices meaning is derived from both repetition and context.

There are those who will not see this as an expression of the complex system of Nishnaabeg intelligence, as theory or intellect, or as a valid form of knowledge production. I will not apologize for this, or qualify this, or defend this, nor will I write this book in a way that might be more palatable to whiteness. There are those who will therefore position this work not as theory or an academic contribution but as a soft intellectual work or narrative or creative nonfiction. The latter positioning is both racialized and gendered, and I have no desire to center whiteness and answer to their positioning. This work has already been done by several scholars and students in Indigenous academic circles. I believe my job as an Indigenous thinker and writer is to use the work of my colleagues to expand us, challenge us, and to hold us all up, as this community continually does for me.[14]

This book builds upon the thinking and action of countless Indigenous peoples I am in relationship with in the present and with those who have engaged the same ideas and thinking in the past. My writing and thinking is (still) highly influenced by the unapologetic work of Lee Maracle in general and *I Am Woman* in particular. When I read this book, it feels like she wrote it *to me*.[15] It feels truthful. It feels real because it is. She wrote about what it was like to be an Indigenous woman, and she used it to formulate a scathing critique of the colonial system. She didn't back it up with academic references. She didn't qualify it. She didn't say maybe it isn't like this for everyone. She didn't dance around being a victim. She didn't beg for the colonizer to recognize her pain. She hit gender violence, capitalism, heteropatriarchy, and colonialism hard. She just spoke her truth, without apologies. And then she published it herself. As if this is normal, as if it is her birthright, because, as she demonstrates to us, it is. Here we are, over twenty years later. It is still in print. It's still being used in courses. There is still nothing like it. To a large extent, I learned *kwe as method* from her, scholars like Trish Monture, and community organizers like Judy DaSilva and from so many Indigenous women like them, working in their communities, in cities, and in their families with zero fanfare and little recognition. I think the first time I saw kwe as method in action was during the summer of 1990, when I watched Mohawk activist from Kanehsatà:ke Ellen Gabriel on the nightly news act as spokesperson for her people during the "Oka Crisis." The same unapologetic grounded truth that emanated from her during the summer of 1990 she carries with her to this day, not as a celebrity, but as a committed educator and language activist in her community.

At its core, kwe as method is about refusal.[16] It is about refusing colonial domination, refusing heteropatriarchy, and refusing to be tamed by whiteness or the academy. I understand this refusal in the context of Nishnaabewin and Michi Saagiig grounded normativity because I have come to know refusal most intimately in this context. Within Nishnaabewin, refusal is an appropriate response to oppression, and within this context it is always generative; that is, it is always the living alternative. When the Nishnaabeg were exploiting the deer by overharvesting, the deer refused and left the territory.[17] After the state believed we could no longer hunt and fish in our territory as a result of the Williams Treaty, many hunters and fishers refused and continued to do so. When Michi Saagiig Nishnaabeg women were told they were not Status Indians because of whom they married, many refused and continued to live as Nishnaabeg.

Earlier this year, when white cottagers demanded James Whetung stop harvesting wild rice on Pigeon Lake, he refused, and
then the wider community also refused.[18] I exist as a kwe because of the continual refusal of countless generations to disappear from the north shore of Lake Ontario. I am interested in
all the ways the Nishnaabeg refuse colonial authority, domination, and heteropatriarchy throughout time while generating
Nishnaabewin.

I am often reminded of this when I think of Kiizhigo, and I
think of Kiizhigo when I'm refusing to be confined to the city
and when I am out on our lakes. Kiizhigo was a Michi Saagiig
Nishnaabeg who lived in Curve Lake. He did not like the way
the government was constantly interfering in the life of the community, so he left and went to live on an island by himself. He
refused colonial domination and reembedded himself in Nishnaabewin, taking care of himself with his bush skills and knowledge of the land. Kiizhigo lived there by himself for many years
until he died, and the island is now named after him.[19] Everyone
thinks of Kiizhigo and his refusal when we drive or paddle by his
island. His refusal is now encoded on the land.

The Radical Resurgence Project

The Radical Resurgence Project uses Indigenous interrogation, critique, and theory, and the grounded normativity these
systems generate, as the intelligence system that instigates resurgence and is the process from which grounded, real world,
Indigenous alternatives are manifest and realized. It employs
Nishnaabeg story as algorithm, as coded processes that generate solutions to the problems of occupation and erasure and to
life on earth. It begins from a place of refusal of colonialism and
its current settler colonial structural manifestation. It refuses
dispossession of both Indigenous bodies and land as the focal
point of resurgent thinking and action. It continues the work of
dismantling heteropatriarchy as a dispossessive force. It calls for
the formation of networks of constellations of radical resurgent
organizing as direct action within grounded normativities and
against the dispossessive forces of capitalism, heteropatriarchy,

and white supremacy. These are actions that engage in a generative refusal of an aspect of state control, so they don't just refuse, they also embody an Indigenous alternative. This in my mind is not up for debate. I simply cannot see how Indigenous peoples can continue to exist as *Indigenous* if we are willing to replicate the logics of colonialism, because to do so is to actively engage in self-dispossession from the relationships that make us Indigenous in the first place.

As I do in all my writing, I write first and foremost for my own people. There are many different diverse interpretations and philosophical standpoints within Nishnaabewin, and as communities of thinkers, I know we will continue to engage very deeply with our knowledge in our Nishnaabeg lives. My favorite thing is discussions where Indigenous intellectuals engage with my work from within their own nations' thought system. These conversations are so rich and affirmative to me. I look forward to this Indigenous internationalism. I look forward also to continuing to build this internationalism with the brilliance of Black theorists, artists, activists, revolutionaries, and radical imaginaries and their communities both within my territory and beyond with the hope that we can become mutual coresistors in our flight to freedom.

At this point, I've made a series of basic, necessary interventions to set the stage for my discussion of the Radical Resurgence Project. I've made the case for centering this work in the theoretical home of Indigenous intelligence and grounded normativity, and that this book itself is conceptualized and communicated through Nishnaabewin. I use kwe as method to refuse and to analyze colonialism as a *structure of processes,* and I've placed the eradication of gender violence as a central project of radical resurgence. These interventions continue and are expanded over the course of the book. In chapter 3, I put forth a more expansive nonhierarchical conceptualization of dispossession to include land and bodies as the meta-relationship Indigenous peoples have with the state. I also use kwe as method to discuss settler colonialism as a structure of processes. My discussion of Indigenous intelligence or grounded normativity as the theoretical fuel for radical resurgence is deepened in chapter 4 with my discussion of place-based Nishnaabeg internationalism. I then turn to another crucial intervention in resurgence theory with a consideration of Nishnaabeg practices of anticapitalism in chapter 5. Chapters 6, 7, and 8 take on heteropatriarchy as an impediment to Indigenous nation building and radical resurgence, and queer Indigeneity as a crucial expression of Indigenous intelligence. Chapter 9 explores place-based resurgent education that centers children in Nishnaabewin. Chapter 10 considers resurgent struggle, recognition, and generative refusal within Indigenous movement building. This leads to my consideration in chapters 11 and 12 of constellating everyday acts of resurgence into collective action through everyday decolonization and living a decolonizing queer politics, drawing on work by Kwagiulth (Kwakwaka'wakw) scholar and resurgence theorist Sarah Hunt along with non-Indigenous scholar Cindy Holmes. I also examine Cree/Dene scholar Jarrett Martineau's work on resurgence in artistic practice and the creation of constellations as flight paths to Indigenous freedom. The Radical Resurgence Project concludes in the final chapter by considering resurgent mobilization.

These interventions are explored through engagement with my own understandings of Nishnaabeg intelligence, Indigenous scholarship, and kwe as resurgent method. They are reoccurring themes that are introduced in various forms and then deepened as the book progresses. These interventive themes are explored from the starting point that radical resurgent mobilizing must refuse dispossession in all forms and take on, in a deeply critical way, the forces of capitalism, white supremacy, and heteropatriarchy, and that in these refusals, we center ourselves in generating the alternatives.

As for *Dancing on Our Turtle's Back*, the vast majority of thinking and research for this book has taken place in community and on the land. My thinking is highly influenced through conversations and interactions with several Indigenous theorists, including elders Doug Williams and Edna Manitowabi, my children, Minowewebeneshiihn and Nishna, and the col lective work of the Dechinta Centre for Research and Learning, particularly Dene elders and land users. Some of the theorists cited in these pages practice within Indigenous intelligence systems, some within Western systems, and some carry and practice both. They are all concerned with Indigenous excellence regardless of where their practices are based, and their work is rigorous. I have thought a great deal about the important discussions around citational politics in Indigenous Studies, and for me this discussion moves beyond just citations; for me these are complex questions that relate to the construction of knowledge itself. Those who think and live within Indigenous intelligence systems are marginalized within the academia and are not positioned as theorists or thinkers. For those of us trained within the academy, the parts of us that embody Indigenous intelligence are also marginalized and often invisible to the academy but visible to our families and communities. Following Nishnaabeg practices, I have cited the source where I first learned the concept—not necessarily where I first heard the concept, but where I first paid attention to it. The idea of *thinking in formation* or *thinking with*, for me, comes from Indigenous intellectual practices and is also parallel to the intellectual work and brilliance of Black feminist theorists and is central to this work.[20] In this book, I am thinking and writing deeply about the challenges Black feminist theorist Alexis Pauline Gumbs asked of herself in writing *The Spill*. I am asking myself, what does it mean to write *with* Indigenous theory? What does it mean to "prioritize being with each other, being with the work, being with the possibilities, more than they prioritize the gymnastics of trying to get it right in a structure built on wrongness?"[21] To Gumbs, this meant not citing white people or men in her book. To me, it has come to mean thinking critically about the emerging canon in Indigenous Studies, noticing whose voices are centered and whose are marginalized, prioritizing Indigenous intellectual practices and theories, embedding myself in a formation with other Indigenous thinkers, and citing the works necessary to bring about interventions of the highest caliber as I strive for excellence within these Indigenous spaces on Indigenous terms.

THREE
THE ATTEMPTED
DISPOSSESSION OF KWE

A FEW YEARS AGO, the Ontario government recognized the hunting and fishing rights promised to the Michi Saagiig Nishnaabeg in the 1818 treaty, after refusing to do so for eighty-nine years.[1] This made me happy. I am now able to hunt and fish in my territory without worrying that constant settler surveillance will lead to my criminalization for violating provincial fish and gaming regulations. But there is also a problem. It seems like the state is recognizing our hunting and fishing rights, on one hand, because we legally forced them to do so (using their legal system), and on the other hand, because our hunting and fishing rights no longer pose a threat to the state and to settler society. They pose no threat to cottage life in the Kawarthas, to either the family farms or the industrialized farming in the southern part of our territory, or to the cabin cruisers on the Trent-Severn Waterway. They pose no threat to the golfers in the multiple pesticide-laden courses throughout Kina Gchi Nishnaabeg-ogamig, to the sport hunters jammed onto the fragments of crown land on opening day, or to the anglers on the lakes and rivers following the regulatory seasons of the Ministry of Natural Resources.[2] They pose no threat to settler land acquisition. Harvesting is no longer the economic fabric of our nation. Dispossession in our territory is now so complete that there is almost no place to hunt. The recognition of these rights seemingly poses no economic or political threat to settlers, because hunting and fishing can now really be practiced in this territory only on a microscale, as a hobby. And to keep it that way, the provincial recognition of these rights did not come with a return of land upon which these rights could be exercised.

I hunt anyway. We hunt anyway—on the small patches of "crown" land, with permission on private land, without permission on "private land," and in the places where our people have always hunted. Just like we do ceremony in campgrounds, in interpretive centers, and in church basements, in the places our people have always done ceremony. Just like we pick medicine in ditches, in farmers' fields, and in tiny forests, where our people have always picked medicines. Just like we rice, launch canoes on the sides of roads or from private docks or lawns, and spearfish in the spring, in the places we always have.

While being out on the land in my territory can be wonderful, it is also heartbreaking because my primary experience of being a Michi Saagiig Nishnaabekwe in my territory is one of continual dispossession. I am constantly reminded of this through the physical destruction of terrestrial and aquatic ecosystems, by the construction of monster cottages in our campsites and sacred places, by the physical barriers of roads, lift locks, farms, and golf courses, by the sheer volume of boat traffic, jet skis, and leaf blowers in the summer, and by the settler erasure and surveillance that reminds me, according to them, I am not supposed to be here. I grew up physically disconnected from my territory. I grew up cognitively disconnected from Nishnaabeg thought and language. I grew up, like other Michi Saagiig Nishnaabeg, in the United Church as opposed to our own spiritual practices. I grew up disconnected from my own power as a kwezens and later as a kwe. I grew up disconnected from the practices of Nishnaabewin. I also refuse that reality.

Expansive Dispossession

The removal of Michi Saagiig Nishnaabeg bodies from the land, from the present, and from all of the relationships that are meaningful to us, politically and otherwise, is the meta-relationship my Ancestors and I have with Canada. This was accomplished and is maintained through land theft as a result of unethical treaty making and the murdering, disappearing, assimilating, and erasing of Michi Saagiig Nishnaabeg bodies and presence from the north shore of Lake Ontario.[3] A great deal of the colonizer's energy has gone into breaking the intimate connection of Nishnaabeg bodies (and minds and spirits) to each other and to the practices and associated knowledges that connect us to land, because this is the base of our power. This means land and bodies are commodified as capital under settler colonialism and are naturalized as objects for exploitation. This has always been extremely clear to Indigenous women and 2SQ people, and it's why sexual and gender violence has to be theorized and analyzed as vital, not supplemental, to discussions of colonial dispossession.[4]

Indigenous bodies, particularly the bodies of 2SQ people, children, and women, represented the lived alternative to heteronormative constructions of gender, political systems, and rules of descent. They are political orders. They represent alternative Indigenous political systems that refuse to replicate capitalism, heteropatriarchy, and whiteness. They are the embodied representation in the eyes of the colonizers of land, reproduction, Indigenous governance, and political systems.[5] They reproduce and amplify Indigeneity, and so it is these bodies that must be eradicated—disappeared and erased into Canadian society, outright murdered, or damaged to the point where we can no longer reproduce Indigeneity.[6] The attack on our bodies, minds, and spirits, and the intimate trauma this encodes is how dispossession is maintained. This is why the bodies of children and the structure of our families were attacked through the residential and day school system and continue to be targeted through the state's child welfare system and state-run education system. This is why the bodies of women and 2SQ people as well as men are attacked through outright murder, imposed poverty, criminalization, assimilation, addictions, physical and mental illness, legislative disappearance, ongoing cognitive imperialism, racisms, and the heteropatriarchy of Canadian society. Our bodies are taken from us, and if they are handed back to us at all, they are battered, bruised, neglected, and broken. So Indigenous bodies have to work very hard first to be alive and second to exist *as Indigenous peoples*. The "social ills" in our communities Canadians so love to talk about are simply manifestations of the hurt and trauma from the ongoing violence of dispossession. They are the symptoms, not the disease. "Fixing" the "social ills" without addressing the politics of land and body dispossession serves only to reinforce settler colonialism, because it doesn't stop the system that causes the harm in the first place while also creating the opportunity for neoliberalism to benevolently provide just enough ill-conceived programming and "funding" to keep us in a constant state of crisis, which inevitably they market as our fault.

The Canadian state has always been primarily interested in acquiring the "legal" rights to our land for settlement and for the extraction of natural resources. The removal and erasure of Michi Saagiig Nishnaabeg bodies from land make it easier for the state to acquire and maintain sovereignty over land because this not only removes physical resistance to dispossession, it also erases the political orders and relationships housed within Indigenous bodies that attach our bodies to our land. The results are always the same: the fictitious creation of the Canadian mythology that if Indigenous nations existed, they did so in politically primitive forms in the distant past; that if Canada has any colonial baggage, it is also firmly in the past; and that while some unfortunate things might have happened, again in the past, it is time to put that aside and start a new relationship where we are now; that is, with Canada having full and unchallenged jurisdiction over all the land within its borders; that is, in this new relationship, we will not be talking about land, and we will certainly not be talking about land restitution.

Dispossession for kwe is not just about the removal of my body from the land. It is the removal of my body from Michi Saagiig Nishnaabeg intelligence or grounded normativity, and then the attempted destruction of grounded normativity itself. It is the Christianization of my spirit. It is the theft of my sexuality. It is the theft of my emotional life, which is now overwhelmed processing a backlog of trauma and the ongoing daily violence of being Indigenous in Canada. It is the violent extraction of my body, mind, emotions, and spirit and the relationships they house from Nishnaabewin, the relational structure that attaches me to Aki.

Aki is not capital. It is not a commodity. Kwe is not capital. Kwe is not a commodity.

Throughout my life, the land-based people I have come in contact with categorically refuse this expansive dispossession. In some ways, this refusal is acute in my homeland because we have so little Nishnaabeg space left. My people are out on the land, even if we are criminalized, even if we have to ask settlers for false permission, even though the land is not pristine, even though, even though.[7] This is in part because within Nishnaabeg thought, the opposite of dispossession is not possession, it is deep, reciprocal, consensual *attachment*. Indigenous bodies don't relate to the land by possessing or owning it or having control over it. We relate to land through connection—generative, affirmative, complex, overlapping, and nonlinear *relationship*. The reverse process of dispossession within Indigenous thought then is Nishnaabeg intelligence, Nishnaabewin. The opposite of dispossession within Indigenous thought is grounded normativity.[8] This is our power.

What does all of this mean in terms of building radical Indigenous nation-based resurgences? It means recognizing that dispossession is our relationship with the state, and like our Ancestors, we simultaneously refuse dispossession as a foundational force in our lives. It means we have to think of dispossession in more complex terms than just land loss. We have to think of *expansive dispossession* as a gendered removal of our bodies and minds from our nation and place-based grounded normativities.

It means resurgence must be concerned with the reattachment of our minds, bodies. and spirits to the network of relationships and ethical practices that generates grounded normativity. It means the reattachment of our bodies to our lands, regardless of whether those lands are rural, reserves, or urban. It means that our resurgent responses to settler colonialism must come from *within* our nation-based grounded normativities. Radical resurgence means nonhierarchical relationships between land and bodies, bodies meaning the recognition of our physicality as political orders, and our intellectual practices, emotions, spirituality, and hubs of networked relationships. A refusal of dispossession that is generative is the process of becoming deeply attached to Nishnaabewin and reembedded and enmeshed in grounded normativity. It means the interdependence of land and bodies in a networked fashion rather than a gendered hierarchy.

The continually generated ethical systems of grounded normativity require us to act in particular ways in the face of oppression even if we cannot name the direct connection to dispossession and even in situations where the oppression is unrelated to Indigenous dispossession. Because settler colonialism is the system that maintains this dispossession in the present, we need to be clear that our attachment to land is not up for negotiation, and that a radical resurgence within grounded normativity necessarily means the dismantling of settler colonialism and the return of Indigenous lands.

Colonialism and Kwe

I understand colonialism as an overwhelmingly dominating force in my daily life that continually attacks my freedom and well-being as kwe. Colonialism tries very hard to keep me off my land. It tries very hard to ensure I cannot speak my language, think as my Ancestors did, find comfort in elders or the river or the lake of rice. It tries very hard to get me to think in a particular way. It tries very hard to get me to resist in a particular way. It tries very hard to get me to move about my territory in a particular way. It controls how I make a living and how I feed my family. It tries to control the relationship I have with my children. It tries to control my sexuality, the ways I express my gender, how I take care of myself, and how I parent with escalating magnitudes of structural and interpersonal discipline and violence if I do not conform. It creates a world where I am never safe. It is a violent system of continual harm forced on my body, mind, emotions, and spirit designed to destroy my ability to attach to my land, to function as kwe, and to be a grounded, influencing agent in the world. I am interested in freedom, not survival, and as kwe, I understand my freedom is dependent upon the destruction of settler colonialism.

I understand settler colonialism's present structure as one that is formed and maintained by a series of *processes* for the purposes of dispossessing, that create a scaffolding within which my relationship to the state is contained. I certainly do not experience it as a historical incident that has unfortunate consequences for the present.[9] I experience it as a gendered structure and a *series of complex and overlapping processes* that work together as a cohort to maintain the structure. The structure is one of perpetual disappearance of Indigenous bodies for perpetual territorial acquisition, to use Patrick Wolfe's phrase.[10] I think the insight that settler colonialism is formed and maintained by a series of processes is important because it recognizes that the state sets up different controlled points of interaction through its practices—consultations, negotiations, high-level meetings, inquiries, royal commissions, policy, and law, for instance, that slightly shift, at least temporarily and on microscales, our *experience* of settler colonialism as a structure. The state uses its asymmetric power to ensure it always controls the processes as a mechanism for managing Indigenous sorrow, anger, and resistance, and this ensures the outcome remains consistent with its goal of maintaining dispossession. It can appear or feel as if the state is operating differently because it is offering a slightly different process to Indigenous peoples. Goodness knows, we'd all like to feel hopeful. We'd like to see a prime minister smudging or acknowledging he is on Indigenous territory and have that signal a significant dismantling of settler colonialism. This is attractive to us because we know we experience colonialism as a series of entrenched processes and practices, particularly in our local place-based realities, and within our own thought systems we know that we can create change by shifting the practices with which we are engaged. If we experience settler colonialism as a *structure made up of processes*, when the practices of settler colonialism appear to shift, it can appear to present an opportunity to do things differently, to change our relationship to the state.

The structure shifts and adapts, however, because it has one job: to maintain dispossession by continually attacking Indigenous bodies and destroying Indigenous families. Neoliberal states manipulate the processes that maintain settler colonialism to give the appearance that the structure is changing. They manipulate Indigenous emotional responses, for instance, to get us to support these slight shifts in process by positioning those who critique the state-controlled processes of reconciliation or the national inquiry into missing and murdered Indigenous women, for instance, as angry radicals who are unwilling to work together for the betterment of Indigenous peoples and Canadians. Colonialism as a structure is not changing. It is shifting to further consolidate its power, to neutralize our resistance, to ultimately fuel extractivism. Our history and our intelligence systems tell us we need to see this in the present.

Indeed, settler colonialism as a structure necessarily has to shift and adapt in order to meet the insatiable need of the state for land and resources. The processes of colonialism don't necessarily look and feel the same every time, but we can't be tricked. Intent matters within Nishnaabeg thought. Over and over again we watch our elders pray and explain intent to the spirits so that they will help and support them. The intention of the structure of colonialism is to dispossess. We cannot allow our processes, our emotions, or our intelligence to be co-opted and *processed* into the structure that is at the root of all of our problems, even if at the outset these processes appear to be kinder and gentler than those we have experienced in the past.

The processes within nation-based grounded normativities destroy the structures of colonialism because they perpetually shift *power* back. In fact, intact, grounded normativity prevents the context and the conditions necessary for colonialism ever taking hold in the first place. I think we need to make a shift from *Indigenizing the processes* that maintain the structures of settler colonialism, and expand, deepen, and reactualize the processes and knowledges of grounded normativity to structuralize Indigenous nationhood and resurgence and mobilizations as a mechanism to dismantle the structure of colonialism in all forms.

Radical Resurgence

When I first began thinking about the Radical Resurgence Project, I struggled in considering whether resurgence was still a relevant and useful lens to frame the interventions I wanted to think and write about. On one hand, resurgent thinkers are a small group of Indigenous scholars and organizers, mainly West Coast based, who continue to write and think about resurgence theory. Few of us have taken up what resurgence looks like within nation-based thought systems. A lot of Indigenous scholarship ends with resurgence as the mechanism to move forward without adding substantively to the conversation of how to do this, and still others have talked about nationhood, nation building, and a recentering of Indigenous political thought without mentioning resurgence to any degree. There are some valid critiques, although rarely written of resurgence, particularly regarding gender violence and queerness. At one point, I considered if it would be relatively easy to write the same book without mentioning resurgence, just grounding my work more deeply in Nishnaabeg thought. The aftermath of Idle No More, and the election of a liberal government changed my thinking. I see a critical need for Indigenous organizing and mobilization more now than I did under Harper because of the subtle, yet powerful forces of neoliberalism demobilizing movements of all sorts and pulling Indigenous peoples into state-controlled processes to a greater degree. I see the natural world, one that I'm entirely dependent upon and in love with, crumbling beneath my feet with the weight of global capitalism. I see a radical transformation that has to occur not just for the Nishnaabeg but for other Indigenous nations as well. I wanted to find a respectful way of talking and thinking about issues that are difficult for us to talk about.

Resurgence has come to me to represent a radical practice in Indigenous theorizing, writing, organizing, and thinking, one that I believe is entirely consistent with and inherently from Indigenous thought.[11] *Radical* means a thorough and comprehensive reform, and I use the term in this book to mean root, to channel the vitality of my Ancestors to create a present that is recognizable to them because it is fundamentally different than the one settler colonialism creates. I am not using the term to mean crazy, violent, or from the fringe, nor do I think a trapper's critique of colonialism by setting their traplines is a *radical* act. It's also normal. It's a valid critique based on direct experience with the system.

I am also not afraid to be radical, because when I hear stories of my Ancestors praying to the water every single day, before they had experience with pollution or with how bad things could get, I see these practices in my current context as a radical act of love. I think the epic nature of settler colonialism requires radical responses. Radical resurgence requires a deeply critical reading of settler colonialism and Indigenous response to the current relationship between Indigenous peoples and the state. Radical requires us to critically and thoroughly look at the roots of the settler colonial present—capitalism, white supremacy, heteropatriarchy, and anti-Blackness. Radical requires us to name dispossession as the meta-dominating force in our relationship to the Canadian state, and settler colonialism as the system that maintains this expansive dispossession.

I'm also not suggesting that we rename resurgence as radical resurgence—to me, this is the movement's collective decision, not mine. Radical resurgence is simply a tool I'm using in this book to communicate more specifically what I mean when I use the term *resurgence*. This is necessary because the word *resurgence* is now used in all kinds of ways, some of which feed nicely into discourses around reconciliation and neoliberalism, and others that remain in critical opposition to both. Radical resurgence means an extensive, rigorous, and profound reorganizing of things. To me, resurgence has always been about this. It has always been a rebellion and a revolution from within. It has always been about bringing forth a new reality.

Resurgence as a lens, critical analysis, a set of theoretical understandings, and an organizing and mobilizing platform has the potential to wonderfully transform Indigenous life on Turtle Island. Nishnaabeg intelligence propels me toward this fundamental transformation because I know that the current man-made global structures of the world are killing the planet and exploiting everything and everyone that is meaningful to me within my own nation. Resurgence is hope for me because of its simultaneous dismantling of settler colonial meta-manifestations and its reinvigoration of Indigenous systemic alternatives—alternatives that have already produced sustainable, beautiful, principled societies. Yet we need more visioning, thinking, acting, and mobilization around these Indigenous systemic alternatives because creating the alternative is the mechanism through which freedom can be achieved. Engagement with Indigenous systems changes Indigenous peoples. It is a highly emergent and generative process. This requires less engagement with the state and more presence within Indigenous realities. This requires struggle and commitment.

So if resurgence was always radical, why use a modifier now? Well, I'm being strategic and deliberate. I am using radical to separate the kind of resurgence I'm talking about from other modifiers. In the context of settler colonialism and neoliberalism, the term *cultural* resurgence, as opposed to *political* resurgence, which refers to a resurgence of story, song, dance, art, language, and culture, is compatible with the reconciliation discourse, the healing industry, or other depoliticized recovery-based narratives. I get worried when I hear the state and its institutions using the term resurgence.[12] Cultural resurgence can take place within the current settler colonial structure of Canada because it is not concerned with dispossession, whereas political resurgence is seen as a direct threat to settler sovereignty. From within Indigenous thought, however, the cultural and the political are joined and inseparable, and they are both generated through place-based practices—practices that require land. Our people have known this for a long time. Our "cultural" practices were hidden from the surveillance of Indian Act authorities because they embodied our political practices, because they were powerful, and regenerating language, ceremony, and land-based practices is always political.[13] Community-based resurgence projects like the language nests are inherently political and cultural because the intent is to facilitate radical transformation rather than just a cultural revitalization. For instance, a giveaway ceremony or part of a ceremony in Nishnaabewin is a mechanism of redistributing wealth in a collective and is at once a political, spiritual, social, and communal practice. We simply cannot achieve a nation-based resurgence within the current hyperextractivist economic and political structure of the Canadian state. Culture as a modifier de-politicizes resurgence into the realm of neoliberalism (this can be a culture practice but not an economic or political one), and my insertion of the word *radical* is a taking back of resurgence from the realm of neoliberalism and reclaiming its revolutionary potential, that is, its potential to offer robust, ethical, and sustainable alternatives to settler colonialism. Cultural resurgence can be read as compatible with settler colonialism because it fits within an inclusive narrative of Canada as a multicultural society. Language, cultural expression, and even spirituality don't (necessarily) pose an unmanageable threat to settler colonialism, because cultural resurgence can rather effortlessly be co-opted by liberal recognition. Indigenous peoples require a land base and therefore require a central and hard critique of the forces that propel dispossession. I'm not interested in a multicultural resurgence or an artistic resurgence as a mechanism for inclusion into the Canadian mosaic. I am not interested in a resurgence that continues to replicate anti-queerness and heteropatriarchy. I am not interested in a resurgence that replicates anti-Blackness. I am not interested in inclusion. I am not interested in reconciling. I'm interested in unapologetic placed-based nationhoods using Indigenous practices and operating in an ethical and principled way from an intact land base. This is the base from which we can develop a "new relationship" with the Canadian state.

Centering Gender in Resurgence

I spend a lot of time in the Radical Resurgence Project writing about gender because dispossession is gendered, settler colonialism is gendered, and our resurgence therefore must critically interrogate the hierarchies of heteropatriarchy in all its forms in order to stop replicating it in our nation and movement building. Gender has been marginalized in resurgence scholarship in particular and in Indigenous scholarship in general and is too often confined to the space of "Indigenous feminisms" or discussed only under the dogma of shallow tradition and rigid protocols.[14] So often when Indigenous women and 2SQ writers and academics write about gender, our work is taken out of the political and theoretical realm and positioned in the margins. We simple must stop practicing heteropatriarchy in our scholarship, organizing, and mobilization. The gendered nature of colonialism and settler colonialism means heteropatriarchy has to be critically considered in every project we're currently collectively and individually engaged in. Otherwise we risk replicating it.

What does it mean then to use the bodies, minds, and experiences of Indigenous children, women, and 2SQ people as the measure of the success of our movements? What does it mean to no longer tolerate heteropatriarchy in communities, in our academic and creative work, and in our movement building and mobilization? How do we set up Indigenous processes to deal with these violences within our movements and in our communities? How do we ensure every Indigenous body, honored and sacred, knows respect in their bones? I see this as the work of radical resurgence.

To be clear, gender and sexual violence has taken place in centuries of overwhelming state violence targeting in different ways all genders and sexualities of Indigenous people, *and* heteropatriarchy is a foundational violence and dispossessing force used by the state, replicated by its citizens, and internalized often unwittingly and unknowingly by Indigenous peoples.

Heteropatriarchy is not a discrimination that has come with white supremacy and colonialism; it is a *foundational disposses-sion force* because it is a direct attack on Indigenous bodies as po-litical orders, thought, agency, self-determination, and freedom.

It is within our reach to stop degrading and devaluing the lives of children, Indigenous women, and 2SQ people right now and to collectively commit to this as a radical resurgence proj-ect. This would be a beautiful expression of radical Indigenous gender politics that we haven't seen before. For some of us, it means conducting ourselves in profoundly different ways in all aspects of our lives. It means processing underlying abuse and trauma in a responsible way. It means a rebellious transforma-tion in how we conduct research, whom we cite as experts, and how our thinking is framed and ultimately takes place. I am not suggesting that we center resurgence around masculinity, even critical masculinity. I'm interested in working with all genders and ages to build nationhoods that refuse to replicate heteropa-triarchy in all forms. This has great potential for building unified movements, and it necessarily involves listening to 2SQ people, children, youth, and women to unlearn the practice of hetero-patriarchy. And while stopping intimate violence without our communities might be within our reach as an everyday act of resurgence, the systemic dismantling of heteropatriarchy is a much larger project.

Gender violence is part of a long history of white men work-ing strategically and persistently to make allies out of straight cisgendered Indigenous men, with clear rewards for those who come into white masculinity imbued with heteropatriarchy and violence, in order to infiltrate our communities and nations with heteropatriarchy and then to replicate it through the genera-tions, with the purpose of destroying our nations and gaining easy access to our land. When we engage in gender violence or are silent in the face of homophobia, transphobia, heterosexism, discrimination, and ongoing gender violence, we are working in collusion with white men and on behalf of the settler colonial state to further destroy Indigenous nationhood. We are traitors to Indigenous nations. For resurgence to work, we have to have each other's backs in our personal and professional lives so we can undo these systems on a macrolevel. We should be each other's greatest allies in this work.

Too often within Indigenous politics, a hierarchy of issues is set up flagging land issues with urgency. Land claims, treaty violations, blockades, and political negotiations are positioned as righteous work, while issues regarding children, families, sexual and gender violence, and bodies are positioned as less important—issues that can wait until we have the land back. There is also a gendered nature to this work and this assumption. Men working on land and political issues are positioned as theorists and leaders. Women working on child welfare issues or gender violence are marginalized and then dismissed and ignored as Indigenous feminists or community organizers. Transgendered and gender-nonconforming people are erased in the binary altogether, as are their substantive bodies of theory, knowledge, labor, and organizing. This serves only to divide us by separating and then positioning sexual and gender violence as *less* important to physical dispossession. It also serves to replicate the heteropatriarchal targeting of women and 2SQ bodies in particular, and in stark contrast to Indigenous knowledge systems. Resurgence must right this. Kwagiulth (Kwakwaka'wakw) scholar Sarah Hunt eloquently explains further that not only must we stop privileging so-called men's work over women's, we must treat body sovereignty with the same urgency and importance as political sovereignty:

> Imagine if we had not lost the capacity to determine and enforce this power over our homelands *and* our bodies. If we started enforcing this now, I can tell you that there would be many chiefs, language speakers, cultural and political advocates who would lose their heads, because the version of resurgence we've been nurturing has allowed for cultural leaders to take up their roles on the "political" front-lines even while violently preying on people at home. And we have left victims of violence at the whim of state actors who regularly demonstrate

indifference or contempt for us, rather than building alternative mechanisms for dealing with interpersonal violence.

This is not true resurgence.[15]

We must continually ask ourselves how we replicate these systems in our own lives and in the lives of the organizations and movements we are a part of, and collectively generate on-the-ground alternatives that center the experiences and analyses of children and youth, women, and 2SQ people. Gender violence and the destruction of Indigenous families are the fundamental dividing and dispossessional issues of our times. Resurgence will not survive, exist, or be useful if it continues to replicate the violence against children, women, and 2SQ people. Dispossession under settler colonialism is gendered, and radical resurgence and nation building must take this into account in a serious and critical manner. There is no choice.

The Radical Resurgence Project simultaneously names an expansive dispossession as our primary relationship with the state, it names colonialism as the meta-system of domination, and it categorically refuses both. It refuses neoliberalism's move to separate cultural resurgence from political resurgence and co-opt it. It faces the root. It demands land. It smashes heteropatriarchy. It centers radical resurgence within our own nation-based intelligence systems of grounded normativities. This does not mean confinement but rather an expansive, emergent, generative theoretical space that engages the best of the world's liberatory thinking within the context of grounded normativity.

FOUR
NISHNAABEG INTERNATIONALISM

WHEN I WAS IN MY THIRD YEAR of biology at the University at Guelph in the early 1990s, I traveled to McMaster University with an antiracism student group for a conference on racism. It was a different time for Indigenous students at Canadian universities. It was rare even to see another Indigenous person on campus at that time. There were two Indigenous speakers at the antiracism conference that day that blew my mind. I didn't know who they were at the time. They were speaking truths to the academy in this brilliant, beautiful way, a truthful way that I hadn't encountered before. They were speaking back to power from a place of strength. I remember talking to both of them after, telling them I was Nishnaabeg. Both said the same thing to me: they told me that everything they had said, all of their knowledge existed in my nation too, although expressed differently, and that it was my responsibility to seek it out. They both sent me to my intellectual home.

The two speakers that day were renowned Haudenosaunee scholars and orators John Mohawk and Trish Monture, and although I didn't realize it at the time, they had just engaged me in what I later think about as Indigenous internationalism.

At this point in the Radical Resurgence Project, it should be clear that I strongly believe that Indigenous thought must propel resurgence. I also think Western liberatory theories can be very useful to Indigenous scholarship and mobilization particularly when they are considered *within* grounded normativity or *within* Indigenous thought systems.[1] This thinking for me comes from within Nishnaabewin itself. Indigenous peoples have always been theoretical people. We've always thought in complex ways about the nature of our worlds. We've always sought out explanations and deeper meanings. In *Dancing on Our Turtle's Back,* I used Edna Manitowabi's retelling of the Seven Fires creation story to illustrate one tiny aspect of Nishnaabeg intelligence to demonstrate this complex thinking, outside of the dream catcher and medicine wheel appropriations of colonial culture. I wanted to emphasize that our theoretical understandings were constructed differently than Western theory: they are woven into doing, they are layered in meaning, they can be communicated through story, action, and embodied presence. There is an incorrect assumption, however, in this narrative that Indigenous scholars and community organizers must therefore engage *only* in what is perceived to be Indigenous theory. My understanding of Nishnaabewin is that our intelligence includes all the thinking that has gone into making the realities we live in and that on a more philosophical scale, internationalism has always been a part of our intellectual practices. With our complex ways of relating to the plant nations, animal nations, and the spiritual realm, our existence has always been inherently international regardless of how rooted in place we are. We have always been networked. We have always thought of the bush as a networked series of international relationships.

While Indigenous thinkers have always been strongly rooted in place, we have also always seen the complicated ways our existence is intrinsically linked to and is influencing global phenomena; indeed, our systems of ethics require us to consider these influences and relationships in all of our decision making. In Nishnaabeg practices, our first intellectual, Nanabush, physically walked the world twice after it was created.[2] Nanabush did not walk the world through a liberal lens to help "those less fortunate." Nanabush did not walk the world to see how natural resources could be harnessed or how people could be exploited into a particular economic or political system. Nanabush walked the world to understand their place in it, our place in it, to create face-to-face relationships with other nations and beings because Nanabush understood that the Nishnaabeg, that we all, are linked to all of creation in a global community. On this epic journey around the world, Nanabush visited with the different human and nonhuman nations that make up our world. They shared and generated story, ceremony, song, and action. They carried with them the political and spiritual practices of the Nishnaabeg as they visited different nations' homes. They created a collective consciousness and set of international relationships with each aspect of creation, which they passed on to the Nishnaabeg. When I teach PhD classes in theory and methodology, I use this story to demonstrate Nishnaabeg methodology or ways of generating knowledge. The idea of Nanabush as the first researcher comes from Edna Manitowabi's teachings as well. On this journey, Nanabush very clearly demonstrates Nishnaabeg research ethics—consent, reciprocity, respect, renewal, relationship. They also demonstrate methodology within this ethical framework—doing or making, relationship, visiting, singing, dancing, storytelling, experimenting, observing, reflecting, mentoring, ceremony, dreaming, and visioning as ways of generating knowledge.

Nanabush's footprints marked all over the Canadian Shield remind us of their internationalism and that the global interconnections of our local place-based existences are intimately intertwined. When Nanabush returned from their journey and visited with Gzhwe Manidoo, Gzhwe Manidoo listened to what they had experienced and then sent them around the world one more time, this time with Ma'iingan, wolf, as a companion. This to me points to the relational nature of our knowledge—the journey changes with a companion, the methodology is relational. The second journey with wolf forged a different, but related, set of relationships. One's experience of the world, of knowledge, or of learning is profoundly contextual, and the body of knowledge generated the second time is different from the first.

The trajectory of Nishnaabeg internationalism, therefore, was formed very early in the creation of our world. Nanabush continues to travel the world and the universe as a teacher, intellectual, and leader. I see Nanabush's journey being repeated over and over again as Nishnaabeg women engage in epic water walks around the Great Lakes, and as young Nishnaabeg walk great distances as a form of protest. But I also see Nanabush's internationalism operating in my own place-based existence. I think a lot about this story as my professional life takes me to the territories of different Indigenous nations. I also remember that one doesn't have to physically travel to be engaged in internationalism. We have many nations that are coexisting within a given land mass already, whether those nations are made up of relationships of human or nonhuman beings. Nanabush's internationalism is layered and multifaceted and is a network of complex interrelationships.

A fundamental difference between Indigenous and non-Indigenous concepts of internationalism is that for Indigenous peoples, internationalism takes place within grounded normativity. Thinking back to this volume's introduction, one remembers that my nation is not just composed of Nishnaabeg. It is a series of radiating relationships with plant nations, animal nations, insects, bodies of water, air, soil, and spiritual beings in addition to the Indigenous nations with whom we share parts of our territory. Indigenous internationalism isn't just between peoples. It is created and maintained with all the living beings in Kina Gchi Nishnaabeg-ogamig. Nanabush didn't just visit with the peoples of the world, they visited with every living being of the world. The following story about the relationship between the Nishnaabeg and the Deer demonstrates internationalism within grounded normativity.

Our Treaty with the Hoof Nation

In a time long ago, all of the deer, moose, and caribou suddenly disappeared from Kina Gchi Nishnaabeg-ogamig.

Well, maybe it wasn't so suddenly. At first, nobody noticed. The relatives of the Hoof Clan had to be very patient. But, after awhile, people starting to notice some changes.

In fall, dagwaagin, the hunters came back with no meat.

When snow blanketed the earth, the people didn't even see a single track in the snow—for the whole bboon!

By ziigwan, the people were getting worried. No one had seen a deer for nearly a year. No one had seen a moose for nearly a year, and no one could even remember the last time they saw a caribou.

The people got worried. Were the Waawaashkeshiwag lost? Were the Moozoog sick and unable to get out of bed? Had Adikwag been kidnapped by aliens? Is this all a game of hide-and-go-seek gone wrong?

The Nishnaabeg wished they had been paying better attention. They wished they had been taking better care of their relatives.

The people started feeling sad and guilty and worried—and hungry. And do you know what happens when you're feeling sad and guilty and worried and hungry? That sad and guilty and worried and hungry mixes altogether and stews and grows and grows and grows.

And then that sad and guilty and worried and hungry turns into something different.

Those Amikwag get a little slappy with their tails.

The Jijaakwag start to get a little bossy.

The Migiziwag start to get nippy.

Those Makwag get even more growly than usual.

Those Zhigaagwag get a little careless with their medicine, spraying it all over.

And then everything starts to go in the wrong direction.

So, those Nishnaabeg decided to do something before everything got all lost. They got up before the sun one morning, lit a sacred fire. They prayed, sang, and offered their semaa.

After a long discussion, where everyone spoke what was in their hearts, the people decided to send out their fastest runners out in the four directions to find those hoofed ones.

Those runners ran for four days. Ziigwan was the first to come back. She hadn't seen so much as a tuft of hair. Then Niibin arrived, exhausted, and reported the same. When Dagwaagin came back, he reported that he'd seen no evidence of deer, moose, or caribou either.

Finally, Bboon returned. He was exhausted, "When I was in the very north part of our land, I saw one young deer. She explained to me that her relatives had left our territory forever because they felt disrespected."

The Nishnaabeg were silent. They felt sad and lost. They thought about how they had been wasting the meat of the Hoof Clan. They thought about how they hadn't been sharing with all their community members. They thought about how they'd killed deer even when they didn't need them.

The people didn't know what to do, so they decided to go and meet with the oldest and wisest people they knew. Those Elders decided to send a delegation of diplomats, spiritual people, and mediators to go and visit the Hoof Clan.

After some negotiation, the people learned that the Hoof Clan had left their territory because the Nishnaabeg were no longer honoring them. They had been wasting their meat and not treating their bodies with the proper reverence. The Hoof Clan had withdrawn from the territory and their relationship with the Nishnaabeg. They had stopped participating.

The diplomats, spiritual people, and mediators just listened. They listened to all the stories and teachings the Hoof Clan had to share. They spent several long days of listening, of acknowledging, of discussing, and of negotiating. All the parties thought about what they could give up to restore the relationship. Finally, the Hoof Clan and the Nishnaabeg agreed to honor and respect the lives and beings of the Hoof Clan, in life and in death. They assured the Hoof Clan that they would use the flesh of the Waawaashkeshiwag, Moozoog, or Adikwag wisely and that they would look after and protect deer, moose, and caribou habitat and homes. They told the Hoof Clan that they would share our meat with all in need, take only what they needed, and use everything they take and that they would rely on other food sources when times were tough for the Hoof Clan. The Nishnaabeg promised to leave semaa to acknowledge the anguish they have brought upon the animals for killing one of their members so that they might live, and they told the Hoof Clan they would perform special ceremonies and rituals whenever they took an animal.

In exchange, the hoofed animals would return to our territory so that Nishnaabeg people could feed themselves and their families. They agreed to give up their lives whenever the Nishnaabeg were in need.

So the Waawaashkeshiwag, Moozoog, and Adikwag returned to the land of the Nishnaabeg. To this day, we still go through the many rituals outlined that day when we kill a member of the Hoof Clan. We remember those original Hoof Clan teachings about how to share land without interfering with other nations. We remember how to take care of the land so we can all bring forth more life. We honor our treaty relationship with Waawaashkeshiwag, Moozoog, and Adikwag—so we can all live good lives.[3]

The idea of having international relations, relationships that are based on consent, reciprocity, respect, and empathy, is repeated over and over again in Nishnaabeg story. The Deer clan, or nation, in this story has power, agency, and influence. They have knowledge that is now shared and encoded in the ethics and practices of hunting deer for the Nishnaabeg. There is an assumption on the part of the Nishnaabeg that the deer have language, thought, and spirit—intellect, and that intellect is different than the intellect of the Nishnaabeg because they live in the world in a different manner than the Nishnaabeg, and they therefore generate different meaning. Our shared diplomacy has created a relationship that enables our two nations to coexist among many other nations in a single region. From within Nishnaabeg thought, our political relationship with the deer nation isn't fundamentally different from our political relationship with the Kanien'kehá:ka.

Nishnaabeg internationalism is a consistent force in Nishnaabeg thought. The mutual influence of our relationship with Rotinonhseshá:ka can be seen in our ceremonies, political practices, and intellectual endeavors. There are both Rotinonhseshá:ka and Michi Saagiig Nishnaabeg thought and practices in our treaties and associated ceremonies. The eagle and the white pine tree, for instance, carry symbolic meaning in our nation and in the confederacy. Michi Saagiig Nishnaabeg carries stories of Kanien'kehá:ka influence, and Kanien'kehá:ka stories carry our influence. We both have creation stories from floods and Skywoman. In my territory, babies are carried in carriers called Tikinagan. Our story is that a young Nishnaabeg parent had a baby that needed to be carried to feel calm and content. The parent was struggling to get work done in addition to baby care and was becoming increasingly tired and overwhelmed. One day, in the bush, the parent saw a Kanien'kehá:ka mother using a cradle board as a carrier. The Nishnaabeg parent made an Nishnaabeg version and was able to carry the baby close to her while getting other tasks accomplished. This made life easier, and the baby's life easier. In this story, the concept and technology of the Tikinagan are attributed to the Kanien'kehá:ka people, and this is acknowledged in the story, although in the process of making and using the Tikinagan, we embed Nishnaabeg parenting practices and styles. The Tikinagan is created and used within Nishnaabeg grounded normativity.[4]

Internationalism between the Kanien'kehá:ka and the Michi Saagiig Nishnaabeg extends beyond story and theory. We share a very powerful body of water, Lake Ontario. We are very distinctive, separate nations, and we continue to practice an intellectual and conceptual internationalism that has been a core practice of our Ancestors. This is embedded into our treaties and political diplomacy and the ceremonies that accompany these practices. It is also in the space of community. The Michi Saagiig Nishnaabeg reserve community of Alderville has a strong relationship with the Mohawk reserve community of Tyendinaga, and Tyendinaga recognizes this in a yearly ceremony commemorating their flight from the United States after the American Revolution to the north shore of Lake Ontario and being welcomed by Michi Saagiig Nishnaabeg.[5] Internationalism is also expressed between individuals. In my own case, my theoretical thinking been has been influenced during my career by several Rotinonhseshá:ka/Haudenosaunee scholars, and whether I know them personally or through their work, scholars, writers, and thinkers from these nations continue to influence and inspire me. These relationships provide the basis for engaging with different nations and different theoretical positions. Perhaps consistent with "theoretical promiscuity" as a frame, which may be useful for many, Nishnaabeg grounded normativity provides the instigation for wide intellectual engagement but centers it within place-based practices and knowledges.[6] This means we have to continually be knowing and expressing who we are as Indigenous peoples within grounded normativity and assessing the usefulness of theories from other nations from the inside. I think grounded normativity in its Nishnaabewin formation compels us to ask particular questions when we're engaging with theories from outside our own practices. Before I use work by writers, scholars, and artists outside of the Nishnaabeg nation in my own writing and thinking, I ask myself the same series of questions. Where does this theory come from? What is the context? How was it generated? Who generated it? What was their relationship to community and the dominant power structures? What is my relationship to the theorist or their community or the context the theory was generated within? How is it useful within the context of my own people? Do we have a similar concept or theory? Can I use it in an ethical and appropriate way (my ethics and theirs) given the colonial context within which scholarship and publishing take place? What are the implications of citation, and do I have consent to take this intellectual thought and labor from a community I am not a part of? Does this engagement replicate anti-Blackness? Colonialism? Heteropatriarchy? Transphobia? This critical process, I think, is a process that many Indigenous academics already do naturally, and the answers are not easy, nor will they be the same for everyone.

Over the past few years, I have spent time in Denendeh, working with Dene people at the Dechinta Centre for Research and Learning. When I was first invited to this territory, I was very reluctant to teach in the program because I could not understand what I could possibly contribute, as a non-Dene from the south. I was encouraged by both Dene and Nishnaabeg to go and figure out a way of contributing that honored the ethics, politics, and histories of both nations. This began with remembering Michi Saagiig Nishnaabeg political practices for visiting other territories, practices that include a particular way of introducing oneself and an acknowledgment of territory. This territorial acknowledgment is also an agreement to act in a peaceful manner and with respect for Dene sovereignty, self-determination, and governance. It is a commitment to follow the practices of the Dene and to conduct myself according to those laws and practices. This is no way impacts my identity as an Nishnaabeg person. I am not becoming Dene; I am operating as an Nishnaabeg person in Dene territory in a careful manner so as to continually demonstrate respect and peaceful intent between our two nations.

There is a flip side to my time in Denendeh, and that is seeing Dene scholar Glen Coulthard explain his academic work in the context of his own community and nation. *Red Skin, White Masks* clearly speaks to an international audience, and the scholarly community has embraced and celebrated the work in this context. I have been fortunate to witness Glen sharing *Red Skin, White Masks* with his people in his homeland, Chief Drygeese Territory of the Akaicho region of Denendeh, and I have seen a glimpse of what I've come to know as a long practice of Dene internationalism. I've seen Glen explain this work, a rather difficult and challenging work at that, in a language and a manner that are fundamentally Dene—gentle and tough, careful and expansive, and riding a current of profound love—to uncles and cousins, elders, hunters, Dene theorists, political leaders from the 1970s, and current chiefs and councils, and to my favorite, a group of young Dene feminists. I've watched his people connect with the concepts of recognition and resentment and the pitfalls of reconciliation, and even Marx and Fanon, as they live out as best they can the grounded normativity he articulates in *Red Skin, White Masks* in a deeply meaningful way. I've watched these non-Indigenous theories resonant within their grounded normativity.

At its core, *Red Skin, White Masks* is in part reflective of their history, their resistance, their mobilizations, their reality, and their way of life. In essence, they first *recognize* themselves and their experiences in this book. *Red Skin, White Masks* brings international theories to Dene people on their terms. Recognition is discussed at length in chapter 1, but here it is important to recognize the importance of a Dene scholar reflecting and recognizing his community and nation while naming very clearly the processes of domination and extermination that they have so fiercely resisted in the past century. There are parts of this book that are a moving honor song to the strategic political organizing and rebellion of the Dene nation. This kind of recognition is far too rare within our own communities, yet it is critical in terms of breaking out of the bonds of negative interpellation. I understand Indigenous collective self-recognition as resurgence because *Red Skin, White Masks* strengthens us. I see that reflected in the Dene nation when I hear Dene responses to *Red Skin, White Masks* that range from:

"You're right. You got it right. That's what happened."

"Mahsi Cho for saying that women are equal to men and that feminism is important."

"You're right! It wasn't communist white people from Toronto, it was us, and a flip chart."

Having spent time in Glen's homeland, I find none of this is surprising, because to me the impetus for writing this book is very clear. The fire in these pages is founded upon and propelled by a tremendous love of land, love of people, and love of Dene intelligence, whether that is hunting, making dry fish, scraping moose hides, storytelling, or visiting with aunties in Dettah. *Red Skin, White Masks* holds Dene people up, and watching how this work has been greeted in Denendeh, I've learned how important it is that our work as Indigenous scholars leaves our communities and nations in better shape than when we started, and how important it is to hold our peoples up as the brilliant, tough, loving, revolutionaries we are, even when we are telling our most brutal and horrible truths, even when we are using big ten-dollar words. The most critical test of our work is whether it validates, clarifies, challenges, inspires, and confounds our own communities. We don't always need to rely on the theories generated within grounded normativity, but we do need to interpret and apply those within the context of nation-based internationalism and from within the ethical frameworks of grounded normativities.

What about the theories and practices of Black Radical Tradition, of revolutionary movements in the Global South, the work of Black womanists and feminists, anticapitalism, anti-white supremacists, antiheteropatriarchy, abolition?[7] Can we ethically engage these bodies of work and struggle? Do our ethical practices within grounded normativities require us to engage not just with their theories but with the people and peoples that embody these theories? Do our ethical frameworks teach us that we must develop relationships of reciprocity and coresistance with these communities that embody both our ethical practices? How can our intellectual processes of ethical engagement be used to decenter our intellectual study from whiteness and produce productive ethical engagement with our global provocateurs?

For me, engagement with the theories and practices of coresistors is powerful because it often illuminates colonial thinking in myself, and it demonstrates different possibilities in analysis and action in response to similar systems of oppression and dispossession. The ethical practices within Nishnaabeg grounded normativity, though, require me to engage not just with their theories but with the people and peoples that embody and enact these theories. I think my Nishnaabeg ethical practices demonstrate that I must develop relationships of reciprocity and coresistance with these communities that embody our ethical practices of solidarity. I cannot not just *take* their theories. This process of ethical engagement has the potential to decenter our intellectual study from whiteness and produce productive ethical engagement with our global provocateurs. Building alternatives with communities of coresistors is powerful because our struggle for liberation is profoundly related to theirs. But to engage in a truthful way, we have to first know who we are, and I worry we are not committing the time and energy to Indigenous intelligence and theory, because it is a struggle. Indigenous intellect and grounded normativity is under attack. It is easier to rely on Western liberatory theory already well established in the academy. It is easier than concerning ourselves with land. But if we don't do the hard work of revitalizing our intellectual practices and our relationship to land, we will lose it within this generation. This is our struggle. It is hard work. It is responsibility and accountability and real, and you cannot get a degree in it. It's not a hashtag or a sticker or a T-shirt or a selfie or anything white liberals think is important. It isn't recognition. It is struggle.

We live in a time of global rebellion, where struggles against U.S. imperialism, for instance, have led to uprisings against neoliberalism across the world and within Canada and the United States. Increasingly, we're experiencing organizing against climate change as the epochal struggle of our times, with revolutionary movements taking on the fight as a fight against global capitalism. This interests me because I see the dismantling of global capitalism as inseparable from the struggle for Indigenous sovereignty, self-determination, and nationhood because capitalism at its core is not just incompatible with core Indigenous values but has to violently shred the bodies who house those values in order to sustain itself. Capitalism cannot create Indigenous worlds, because, as Vijay Prashad says, "capitalism has never been able to produce decency."[8]

Indigenous thinkers have always engaged in internationalism, but we knew ourselves first, or rather not at the expense of knowing within our own nations. Imagine if twenty years ago we had collectively decided to sink our energies not into establishing ourselves as a discipline in the Western academy but into invigorating nation-based Indigenous intelligence systems on our own terms. Some of us did, many of us always have, and thus sites of Indigenous intelligence remain where they've always been: in the bodies and practices of Indigenous peoples who are engaged in these processes in a deep and meaningful way.

When I first started thinking through Nishnaabeg internationalism, I thought of Michi Saagiig Nishnaabekwe, Nahnebahnwequay, who had lost her Indian status and rights to her
home and land because of her twenty-year marriage to a white
man.[9] In 1860, she left her home and traveled alone and preg-
nant to New York to meet with Quakers, and then on to England
to petition Queen Victoria, reenacting the journey of Nanabush.
Nahnebahnwequay gave many important speeches in England
about the situation our people were facing. She addressed the
Aborigines Protection Society, an English organization concerned for the rights of those dispossessed by British colonialism. She also met with the British press and, on June 19, with the
queen. Three weeks later, she gave birth.[10] There were other Michi Saagiig writers, activists, and artists actively engaged in this
sort of internationalism, but Nahnebahnwequay is significant to
me because she was a women engaged in politics at a time when
colonialism had already ravaged Nishnaabeg women's political
influence.[11] She was also, as an Nishnaabeg woman, a political
order, fostering solidarity on the terms of Nishnaabeg grounded
normativity.[12] The Quakers became part of a network of allies
who existed outside of the dominant political landscape and
forged a solidarity with these allies that gave her support and
access to power she would not have had otherwise, particularly
had she stayed in southern Ontario. Similarly, in the mid-1800s,
Michi Saagiig Nishnaabeg artists Maungwudaus, Uh wus sig gee
zhig goo kway, and their children traveled and performed with
other family members extensively in Canada, the United States,
Great Britain, France, and Belgium. I include Maungwudaus's
wife, who traveled and performed with him, when I talk about
Maungwudaus because to do otherwise would replicate heteropatriarchy and once again erase the agency and contributions of
Nishnaabeg women. There is very little written about her, and
what we do know comes through Maungwudaus himself. There
is no information regarding their artistic relationship. I feel confident in assuming it was significant and that she deserves as
much credit as Maungwudaus himself because she traveled with
him and performed with him, and I'm assuming she did all this

while being the primary caregiver to their children in hostile European countries and during extraordinary circumstances, including the death of her children. Maungwudaus recorded his critical observations of his European journey in a journal he published in 1848 in a clear and articulate expression of Michi Saagiig thought and internationalism.[13] Maungwudaus's journey and his journal are discussed in more detail in chapter 11, as is Nishnaabeg artist Robert Houle's installation of Nishnaabeg internationalism *Paris/Ojibwa*.

Similarly, in my own lifetime, Nishnaabeg women have consistently engaged in these same practices. Judy DaSilva and several other Nishnaabeg leaders from Grassy Narrows First Nation have replicated the journey of Nanabush, traveling to Japan to learn from doctors, researchers, and survivors about mercury poisoning. The industrial dumping of mercury into the English-Wabigoon River system in the late 1960s and early 1970s has caused severe long-term health and social impacts in the surrounding First Nations communities for decades. The long-term relationship between Dr. Masazumi Harada, a Japanese medical doctor working on Minamata disease, and the community of Grassy Narrows is but one example of place-based Nishnaabeg internationalism, and this strikes me as highly relevant to our current situation. It is different from Nahnebahnwequay's journey in that DaSilva is connecting with people who are engaged in resistance, research, and activism related to mercury poisoning as a mechanism for improving the health of her own people.[14]

This book in many ways is the continuation of the journey that the elders of Long Lake #58 inspired in me so many years ago. I wanted to be able to think like them, from within Nishnaabewin. I wanted to know our philosophies and concepts well enough to break out of the bounds of tradition and culture. I wanted to be like them—to live in a different world. I wanted to be part of a community, a real-world community of Indigenous peoples actively creating the alternative. This Nishnaabeg future, though, at this point in time is so very threatened. I've just lived through a year where the fall was too warm, and this affected the migration of geese through our territory and the movement of deer. The winter was also too warm, which impaired our ability to ice fish. The spring is now too warm, and our production of maple sugar is devastated. It is crucial then that the Radical Resurgence Project take on global capitalism and its link to global warming, which is a direct threat to Indigenous presence and our visions for the future. And so the next chapter explores Nishnaabeg practices of anticapitalism.

FIVE
NISHNAABEG ANTICAPITALISM

IN EARLY 2013, author, social activist, and filmmaker Naomi Klein, known for her political criticism of corporate globalization and capitalism through her activism and her international best sellers *No Logo* and *The Shock Doctrine*, e-mailed me and asked if she could interview me for what would become a *New York Times* best seller, *This Changes Everything: Capitalism vs. the Climate*. And so, on an icy February morning, I drove the same section of the 401 that inspired "I Am Not a Nation-State" in the introduction to meet her in the Toronto neighborhood of Roncesvalles.

I was nervous. Naomi Klein was a big deal, and I wasn't sure why she wanted to interview me. I knew she had close ties to other Indigenous activists and writers, including the late long-time Secwepemc activist, leader, and writer Art Manual and Lubicon Cree activist and organizer Melina Laboucan-Massimo; I was unsure what I could possible add to her research. I went because she lives in my territory, because her work is smart and widely read—more widely read and considered than any works by Indigenous peoples, particularly Indigenous women. I went because not very many people reach out to me in the way that she did.

We met in a coffee shop. I remember both of us being nervous. She was a little bit late because she had slipped on an icy sidewalk. I remember wishing that I had dressed better. She brought her copy of *Dancing on Our Turtle's Back,* which was covered in colored sticky tabs. She had read the book, *really* read the book. I wished I had reread it, so I could remember what I had written. I was afraid she thought that I might be smarter than I was in real life.

Naomi and I talked for a few hours in a conversation guided by her questions. She recorded the interview on her iPhone and had offered to transcribe it and publish it in a manner that suited us both, and then to use snippets in her book. The interview has now been blogged and reblogged in a variety of places.[1] The significance of this in my own thinking is that this is when I began to understand the importance of critiquing and analyzing capitalism from within Indigenous thought, from within grounded normativity or Nishnaabewin, from within Nishnaabeg intelligence. I've always shied away from taking capitalism on in my work because I have always felt that I haven't spent enough time reading, thinking, and analyzing Marx—that I should leave the analysis of capitalism, its role in dispossession, and its impact on me as an Indigenous woman to others more qualified to do so. I didn't feel qualified to speak back to capitalism as an Indigenous woman. Once I recognized that bit of cognitive imperialism in myself, it became just the thing I knew I had to speak back to. And so I've changed my mind. I think it is way too important a conversation not to have within the Nishnaabeg nation in particular and within the broader Indigenous nation-building movement, even if it is difficult. Indigenous peoples have extremely rich anticapitalist practices in our own histories and current realities. I think it is important that we continue the work of our Ancestors and our elders in critiquing and analyzing capitalism, how it drives dispossession, and its impacts on us from our own perspectives. Indigenous peoples in my mind have more expertise in anticapitalism and how that system works than any other group of people on the planet. We have thousands and thousands of years of experience building and living in societies outside of global capitalism. We have hundreds of years of direct experience with the absolute destruction of capitalism. We have seen its apocalyptic devastation on our lands and plant and animal relations. This in no way diminishes the contributions of other anticapitalism theorists, thinkers, and writers; rather, I think it adds the beginnings of a critical reframing of the critique, one that is centered within grounded normativity.[2]

Naomi wanted to talk about extractivism, what she describes in her book as a "nonreciprocal, dominance-based relationship with the earth, one of profound taking. It is the opposite of stewardship, which involves taking but also taking care that regeneration and future life continue."[3] Extractivism wasn't something I had thought a lot about, but the conversation unfolded as follows.[4]

> **NAOMI KLEIN:** Let's start with what has brought so much Indigenous resistance to a head in recent months. With the tar sands expansion, and all the pipelines, and the Harper government's race to dig up huge tracts of the north, does it feel like we're in some kind of final colonial pillage? Or is this more of a continuation of what Canada has always been about?

> **LEANNE SIMPSON:** Over the past four hundred years, there has never been a time when indigenous peoples were not resisting colonialism. Idle No More is the latest—visible to the mainstream—resistance and it is part of an ongoing historical and contemporary push to protect our lands, our cultures, our nationhoods, and our languages. To me, it feels like there has been an intensification of colonial pillage, or that's what the Harper government is preparing for—the hyper-extraction of natural resources on indigenous lands. But really, every single Canadian government has placed that kind of thinking at its core when it comes to indigenous peoples.

> Indigenous peoples have lived through environmental

collapse on local and regional levels since the beginning of colonialism—the construction of the St. Lawrence Seaway, the extermination of the buffalo in Cree and Blackfoot territories and the extinction of salmon in Lake Ontario—these were unnecessary and devastating. At the same time, I know there are a lot of people within the indigenous community that are giving the economy, this system, ten more years, twenty more years, that are saying "Yeah, we're going to see the collapse of this in our lifetimes."

Our elders have been warning us about this for generations now—they saw the unsustainability of settler society immediately. Societies based on conquest cannot be sustained, so yes, I do think we're getting closer to that breaking point for sure. We're running out of time. We're losing the opportunity to turn this thing around. We don't have time for this massive slow transformation into something that's sustainable and alternative. I do feel like I'm getting pushed up against the wall. Maybe my ancestors felt that two hundred years ago or four hundred years ago. But I don't think it matters. I think that the impetus to act and to change and to transform, for me, exists whether or not this is the end of the world. If a river is threatened, it's the end of the world for those fish. It's been the end of the world for somebody all along. And I think the sadness and the trauma of that is reason enough for me to act.

NAOMI: Let's talk about extraction because it strikes me that if there is one word that encapsulates the dominant economic vision, that is it. The Harper government sees its role as facilitating the extraction of natural wealth from the ground and into the market. They are not interested in added value. They've decimated the manufacturing sector because of the high dollar. They don't care, because they look north and they see lots more pristine territory that they can rip up.

And of course that's why they're so frantic about both the environmental movement and First Nations rights because those are the barriers to their economic vision. But extraction isn't just about mining and drilling, it's a mindset—it's an approach to nature, to ideas, to people. What does it mean to you?

LEANNE: Extraction and assimilation go together. Colonialism and capitalism are based on extracting and assimilating. My land is seen as a resource. My relatives in the plant and animal worlds are seen as resources. My culture and knowledge is a resource. My body is a resource and my children are a resource because they are the potential to grow, maintain, and uphold the extraction-assimilation system. The act of extraction removes all of the relationships that give whatever is being extracted meaning. Extracting is taking. Actually, extracting is stealing—it is taking without consent, without thought, care or even knowledge of the impacts that extraction has on the other living things in that environment. That's always been a part of colonialism and conquest. Colonialism has always extracted the indigenous—extraction of indigenous knowledge, indigenous women, indigenous peoples.

NAOMI: Children from parents.

LEANNE: Children from parents. Children from families. Children from the land. Children from our political system and our system of governance. Children—our most precious gift. In this kind of thinking, every part of our culture that is seemingly useful to the extractivist mindset gets extracted. The canoe, the kayak, any technology that we had that was useful was extracted and assimilated into the culture of the settlers without regard for the people and the knowledge that created it. . . .

The alternative to extractivism is deep reciprocity. It's respect, it's relationship, it's responsibility, and it's local.[5]

As I drove home after the interview, and in the editing process that followed, I could see why Naomi was focusing on extractivism as a narrative that could open up a conversation with Canadians and spark mass movement on climate change without bringing up capitalism and the backlash that entails, but the more I thought about extractivism as a concept, it didn't explain what had happened to my people and to me. Stewardship as an alternative was too simplistic a concept to describe the relationship of Nishnaabeg with land. The more I thought about extractivism, the more important it became to name capitalism, particularly in the context of radical resurgence. I was recently reminded of this by Nipissing elder Glenna Beaucage in Ryan McMahon's Redman Laughing podcast season on reconciliation, because she names it, and she remembers an old man, or an elder, naming it. She says:

> When the treaty came, it turned the word creation into resources, and resources are to be exploited. To me creation is to be respected, but when we say resources, now we can exploit them. We got mixed up. I heard an old man tell me we've become capitalists. Even with our fishing and hunting we've become capitalist. We see money.[6]

Later on in that same conversation, another Nipissing elder talks about how the education system in Ontario is designed to move our people into the middle class, away from Nishnaabewin. Like these elders, I can't see or think of a system that is more counter to Nishnaabeg thought than capitalism, and over the past two decades I have heard elders and land users from many different Indigenous nations reiterate this, and it is part of the elder's analysis and thinking we ignore. We hold a collective apathy around critiquing, organizing, and creating alternatives, despite the fact that Nishnaabeg people and our society are the alternative—we lived without capitalism for centuries. There is an assumption that socialism and communism are white and that Indigenous peoples don't have this kind of thinking. To me, the opposite is true. Watching hunters and ricers harvest and live is the epitome of not just anticapitalism but societies where consent, empathy, caring, sharing, and individual self-determination are centered.

My Ancestors didn't accumulate capital, they accumulated networks of meaningful, deep, fluid, intimate collective and individual relationships of trust. In times of hardship, we did not rely to any great degree on accumulated capital or individualism but on the strength of our relationships with others. The Michi Saagiig oral tradition has within it stories of Wendat and Rotinonhseshá:ka /Haudenosaunee coming to us and asking to hunt or farm in our territory during times of famine. Our grounded normativity compelled us to assist our neighbors if we were able. We also have a series of embedded practices that redistribute wealth within the community. Harvests are distributed in community to our most vulnerable members—those who cannot harvest for themselves. Many of our ceremonial practices include a giveaway component where goods are distributed among participants. Gift giving is part of our diplomacy and designed to reinforce and nurture relationships. In daily life, greed, or the accumulation of capital, was seen as an assault against the collective because it offended the spirits of the plant and animal nations that made up our peopled cosmos, and therefore put Nishnaabeg at risk. "Capital" in our reality isn't capital. We have no such thing as capital. We have relatives. We have clans. We have treaty partners. We do not have resources or capital. Resources and capital, in fact, are fundamental mistakes within Nishnaabeg thought, as Glenna Beaucage points out, and ones that come with serious consequences—not in a colonial superstitious way but in the way we have already seen: the collapse of local ecosystems, the loss of prairies and wild rice, the loss of salmon, eels, caribou, the loss of our weather.

Another mistake is the idea of excess. There are lots of Nishnaabeg stories about the problems with excess. Recall the Deer clan story in chapter 4. When the Nishnaabeg killed an excess of deer, the deer left the territory, to the point where today we have an abundance of deer in my territory but very few Deer clan people, and this reminds us of that imbalance. Medicine people often look for excess and imbalance in a person's life when they look for and treat root causes of illness and disease. Going back, even one generation in my family, I see a way of life that was careful, frugal, full of making and self-sufficiency, and one that frowned upon waste, surplus, and overindulgence. Older members of our communities will often comment on this, particularly with regards to my generation and our children and the sea of things they are growing up in. It concerns them. It worries them. They see it as a problem with the way we are living.

On one hand, for Michi Saagiig Nishnaabeg living Nishnaabewin, material wealth simply didn't make sense, because we never settled in one place. We were constantly moving throughout our territory in a deliberate way, carrying and making our belongings as we went. Having a lot of stuff made life more difficult on a practical level. On an ethical level, it was an indication of imbalance within the larger system of life. When Nishnaabeg are historicized by settler colonial thought as "less technologically developed," there is an assumption that we weren't capitalists because we couldn't be—we didn't have the wisdom or the technology to accumulate capital, until the Europeans arrived and the fur trade happened. This is incorrect. We certainly had the technology and the wisdom to develop this kind of economy, or rather we had the ethics and knowledge within grounded normativity to *not develop* this system, because to do so would have violated our fundamental values and ethics regarding how we relate to each other and the natural world. We chose not to, repeatedly, over our history.

Similarly, we don't have this idea of private property or "the commons." We practice life over a territory with boundaries that were overlapping areas of increased international Indigenous presence, maintained by more intense ceremonial and diplomatic relationship, not necessarily by police, armies, and violence, although under great threat we mobilized to protect what was meaningful to us. Our authority was grounded and confined to our own body and the relationships that make up our body, not as a mechanism for controlling other bodies or mechanisms of production but as structures and practices that are the very practices of Nishnaabeg life. We have stories warning us of the perils of profit—gain achieved not through hard work within grounded normativity but gain, benefit, and advantage achieved in disproportion to effort and skill or exploitation. Nanabush is the most obvious example of all of this. He experiments with capitalist modes of production when he tries to get various beings—skunks, ducks, geese, for example—to do the hard work of life for his own personal gain and accumulation. He tries in various stories to outsource the work of feeding himself, and disaster ensues. There are stories where he is greedy; he experiments with capital accumulation, and disaster ensues. There are stories of Nanabush manipulating animals to create competitive markets for his goods and services, and again disaster ensues. There are stories where Nanabush engages in a host of exploitive and extractivist practices at the expense of plants, animals, or the Nishnaabeg, and this results in his demise. His preference in these stories is to employ various beings of creation in service to him, while he lounges around and enjoys the profit of this unequal labor. He is categorically met with his demise every time, and eventually he learns his lesson.[7] One of his brothers, however, does not. He insists that the community feed him by hunting, fishing, and gathering on his behalf. We do, because we are kind, empathic, and decent people. We give him time to work his shit out. We try to bring him back into the fold by encouraging him to be a self-determining part of the collective by engaging in some practice, *any* practice really. Nanabush's other brother, in a similar circumstance, becomes an artist as a way of contributing and living in our nation and is celebrated for his contribution. But this brother, the lazy one, doesn't. Eventually, the nation can no longer carry him, and he withers away and dies. His death is a transformation, and he becomes the moss on the rocks that you see in our territory.[8] Moss reminds us. Moss, like pine trees, or maple trees, or geese, is an algorithm, a practice for solving a problem, and all of these Nishnaabeg algorithms are profoundly anticapitalist at their core. To me, Nanabush embodies anticapitalism because the system of grounded normativity within which he exists demands nothing less. Capitalism cannot exist within grounded normativity.

I wrote in *Dancing on Our Turtle's Back* that Nishnaabeg society is a society of makers, rather than a society of consumers. This is the foundation of our self-determination and freedom —producing everything we need in our families within grounded normativity within a network of caring and sharing. We made our food, our clothes, our homes. We made our education system, our health care system, our political system. We made technology and infrastructure and the systems of ethics that governed its use. We made our social services, our communication system, our histories, literatures, and art. We didn't just control our means of production, we lived embedded in a network of humans and nonhumans that were made up of only producers. In terms of resurgence, this holds a lot of hope for me in creating alternative economies and ways of living. Education cannot just be about shifting our children into the urban middle class. Resurgent education must be about turning our children inwards toward Nishnaabewin making.

Too often, in my experience, Indigenous peoples in Canada start from the place that global capitalism is permanent and our survival depends upon our ability to work within it. The poverty facing Indigenous communities is an imposed poverty, the result of being a target of extractivism for generations now. Solutions to social issues like housing, health care, and clean drinking water that divorce the cause (dispossessive capitalist exploitation under settler colonialism) from the effect (poverty) serve settler colonial interests, not Indigenous ones, by placing Indigenous peoples in a never-ending cycle of victimhood, and Canadians in a never-ending cycle of self-congratulatory saviorhood, while we both reinforce the structure of settler colonialism that set the terms for exploitation in the first place. Organizing around issues of poverty and social conditions in urban and reserve communities as a critical core of the project of resurgence, as a political issue, breaks this cycle. It also has the potential to build collectives of individuals taking on the responsibilities of the nation, while aligning themselves with those who face the greatest struggle and carry the greatest burden of settler colonialism. The division between reserve and city is an artificial colonial division. We are all related, and this is all Indigenous land. Strengthening reserve-urban relationships strengthens nations, and it has the potential to build movement.

Throughout my adult life, I've spent time on traplines and hunting territories in northern Ontario and in Manitoba. These trappers were inevitably dealing with the logging industry clear-cutting their traplines. Canada and the provinces have from their legal perspective successfully dispossessed Nishnaabeg people of our territories through a series of settler colonial processes. These settler colonial processes—treaty making, policy making, consultation, impact assessments, and the court system—provide them with the ethical justification to clear-cut a particular trapline, removing another Nishnaabeg family from the land and effectively destroying their grounded normativity, destroying remnants of an Nishnaabeg economy, plant and animal habitat, medicines, ceremonial grounds, burial grounds, hunting places, libraries of knowledge, and networks of relationships, because it is in the best interest of Canadians to do so. Often Nishnaabeg people will participate in all the processes settler colonialism sets up for us to have a voice in this, except the processes are set up to reinforce settler colonialism, not disrupt it. Oftentimes this results in blockades, as it has in Grassy Narrows, with people now having blocked a logging road for over a decade. To me, this is a clear indication that land users do not see this situation as inevitable. On a local level, individual families are living this way of life, in some cases choosing a lower standard of living and to not move to the city, to live Nishnaabewin. Resistance to capitalism isn't futile, it's the way out.

It is critical that this generation inspires and creates the next generation of Indigenous peoples that can think and live inside of their own intelligence systems more deeply than my generation. I worry we're not doing that. I think resurgence must be centered on nation-based, diverse, and unique Indigenous thought systems that house Indigenous intelligence. This is our source and our seed. We cannot be Indigenous without it, and these systems have been under assault for over four centuries. This is a political issue, an education issue, and a mobilization issue. Just as the Nipissing elder reminded us, the goal of radical resurgent education and mobilization cannot be the proletarianization of our people. This is not the new buffalo. The massive shift of Indigenous peoples into the urban wage economy and the middle class cannot be the solution to dispossession, because this consolidates dispossession. We cannot build nations without people, and we cannot build Indigenous nations without people who house and practice Indigenous thought and process, and we also cannot build sustainable Indigenous nations while replicating gender violence. In the next three chapters, I make the case for the dismantling of heteropatriarchy as a core project of the Radical Resurgence Project.

SIX
ENDLESSLY CREATING
OUR INDIGENOUS SELVES

FOR THE PAST FEW YEARS, when I talk about gender in Indigenous postsecondary classrooms, primarily classes on self-determination, resurgence, and governance, I lead the students through a simple exercise to begin. As a group, I ask them to list all the stereotypes they have been the target of or have heard about Indigenous women. There is a moment of pause after I outline the exercise, and I always make sure I look into the eyes of Indigenous women, because I know they are wondering if this is a safe thing for them to participate in, and they are wondering why I'm asking them to go to such a horribly painful place inside themselves. Often, I will start by writing the word *slut* on the flip chart or chalkboard and explain that for as long as I remember, going way back into my history as a girl of five or six, people have associated me and my body with this word. I explain that this term is used by colonialism to regulate and control my body and sexual behavior, and I explain that I have sovereignty over my body, my sexuality, and my relationships.[1] I explain that many women and 2SQ people have reclaimed this word as a mechanism for enacting their own self-determination, values, and ethics over their bodies. There are always nods, and eyes drop to the ground. The class adds to the list: dirty, squaw, bad mothers, lazy, promiscuous, irresponsible, addicts, criminals, prostitutes, easy, bad with money, bad wives, dumb, stupid, hysterical, angry, wild in bed, useless, drunks, worthless, without feeling, violent, weak, partiers, alcoholics. After the first three or four stereotypes are on the list, they come faster, and the energy starts to shift from shame and hurt to an expulsion of those same things. Heads are held up high, as we name and then cast off and cast out the internalized racism and patriarchy of the colonizer.

Then I ask the group to list all of their truths about Indigenous women: intelligent, strong, brave, courageous, sexy, committed, hard-working, good mothers, partners, wives, loving, caring, honest, brilliant, spectacular, empathetic, compassionate, beautiful, smart, kind, gentle, good lovers, organized. We do the same for Indigenous men and for the queer community. Groups come up with between thirty to fifty gendered stereotypes specific to each gender and gender/sexual orientation. They come up with beautiful lists of truths, and in essence all three lists are the same. In one class, at the land-based Dechinta Centre for Research and Learning, the women of the group came up with the list of racist stereotypes for Indigenous women.[2] As the instructor, I often have to start the process because it is too painful for young Indigenous women to even speak. With this group, when it came time to list the truths, they were silent, and then something really profound and transformative happened. The Dene men in the group made a beautiful list that left nearly everyone in the room in tears (smart, intelligent, beautiful, sexy, good mothers, good partners, strong, connected, spiritual, good hunters, good fishers, good providers, excellent sisters, aunties, and grandmothers, powerful). When we got to the part of the exercise where we listed the positive things about men, the women did the same, and then the group came together and generated a similar list for 2SQ people.

During our discussion of 2SQ people, we talk about sex,

gender, sexual orientation, and relationship orientation. We talk about terminology and pronouns. We talk about transphobia and how all bodies are real bodies. We talk about how groups with the highest rates of suicide in our communities are 2SQ people and trans youth. We talk about how learning on the land can be a safe space, or it can be a nightmare for trans youth.

This particular time I did the exercise was special. It was moving for everyone involved. As the men listed off positive attribute after positive attribute, the women, myself included, were emotional because we have been told over and over again, through pop culture, the mainstream media, our experiences with the church and Indian Affairs, by teachers and parents that we are all of the things on the negative list. This was perhaps the first time in our lives we had been told directly that we are not any of those things, and to have it come from our Dene male colleagues was extremely meaningful. It felt like they had our backs.

This is one of the most powerful learning experiences that I've had in a classroom in my teaching career. The exercise is simple enough in itself. The act of naming stereotypes is a commanding space because it brings my attention to the very personalized violence of colonialism on my internal thoughts and beliefs about myself. When I write the word *slut* on the chart, I am thinking and feeling every time that word has been used to push me down, control me, and limit my potential. When I write *dumb* on the chart, I can't help but to reflect on how that internalized belief is so implanted in me by settler colonialism that I have to remind myself every time I speak or sit down to write or walk into the classroom that I'm not actually dumb. Each time I participate in this exercise, it reveals to me the degree to which I have unconsciously internalized these lies, and that we as communities of people have unconsciously internalized these lies, and it provides a chance to speak back.

The next layer is a collective realization that we all to varying degrees carry around these unconscious colonial beliefs about ourselves, despite the fact that some of us have obtained measures of success in Indigenous worlds, settler colonial society, or both. This begins to shift the power dynamics between the students and me and how the class sees me as an Indigenous women instructor. I am no longer "better" than them because I have a PhD or because of these false successes. I have not been removed from the violences of settler colonial life. I carry the same damage as they do, and I am not ashamed of that damage, because the shame does not rest within Indigenous peoples but with settler colonial Canada.

As the group moves through the exercise, the energy of the class moves from shame and humiliation, to celebration and joy, to happiness. We talk about how *good it feels* to recognize when our own people recognize our positive attributes and see us through Dene or Nishnaabeg eyes rather than through the eyes of settler colonialism. We talk about how good that feels in ourselves, and we pause and feel it. We link our personal feelings and experiences with the other subjects of the course—the Indian Act, residential schools, the public education system, self-government policy, the criminalization of Indigeneity, environmental destruction, gender violence—and students begin to realize that the negative beliefs they carry within themselves were planted in them and the generations that came before them for a very specific reason: dispossession of their lands. We talk about how shame prevents us from connecting to our loved ones, learning our languages, and being on the land. We are honest about the stereotypes of other genders and sexual orientations that we carry and amplify in our own lives.

People bring up stories of grandmothers chopping wood, hunting, trapping, and fishing, and of grandfathers cooking, sewing, and doing childcare. We talk about binaries and fluidity around gender and how in Indigenous contexts it is often important that we all have a baseline of skill and knowledge about how to live. Oftentimes someone will bring up a relative who didn't fit so easily into the colonial gender binary, and we talk about how the community, the church, and the state responded and responds to this. We talk about how we gender the land in English and if this is the same in their languages.

We talk about Indigenous men and how all genders have

experienced and do experience gender violence, although it affects individuals in asymmetric ways because of the hierarchy it instills. We talk about how Indigenous peoples are in a difficult position: simultaneously being targeted by gender violence and therefore carrying trauma, benefiting to varying degrees from hierarchy, and oftentimes knowingly or unknowingly perpetuating gender discrimination, violence, and anti-queerness. We talk about how difficult it can be to hear that an action or a phrase is hurting Indigenous women or 2SQ people. We talk more about shame.

Inevitably someone will ask if some of the stereotypes are true, often referring to the epidemic of gender violence in our communities, and if the students themselves don't bring that up, I do, because I know someone is thinking about that. We talk about the nature of stereotypes. We talk about how we are not the sum of the list of stereotypes. We talk about how stereotypes are not just "backwards thinking" but a system of social control. We talk about consent, accountability, self-determination, responsibility. We acknowledge how all genders, including Indigenous men, have been the target for sexualized and gender violence. We talk about how that is not an excuse for perpetuating it. We account for things. I ask them to pick one of the stereotypes from the negative list. I use my own nation as an example and draw a rough trajectory that cuts through four centuries of heteropatriarchy as a tool of dispossession:

- Nishnaabeg people have self-determination over their bodies and sexuality. Sex is not shameful within Nishnaabewin. All genders and ages hold political power and influence. There is a diversity of genders, sexual orientations, and relationship orientations and respect for body sovereignty.[3]

- Colonizers want land, but Indigenous bodies forming nations are in the way because they have a strong attachment to land and because they replicate Indigeneity. All Indigenous genders as political orders also replicate Indigenous nationhood, but the colonizers are looking through the eyes of heteropatriarchy, so they see Indigenous women's and girl's bodies as the bodies that reproduce nations, and they see 2SQ bodies as the biggest threat to their assimilation and dispossession project.[4]

- Colonizers notice that women, children, and 2SQ people hold power and influence in Indigenous governance. They notice this is not the same in European nations. Hierarchy is key to their system of control.[5]

- During times of violent conflict, sexual and gender-based violence is widely recognized as a tactic of both war and genocide because it is frequently used as "a military tactic to harm, humiliate and shame" and because violence and war weaken systems of "protection, security and justice."[6] Sexual violence is an effective colonial tool in genocide and dispossession because the damage it causes to families is so overwhelming that it makes it very difficult to have the emotional capital to continue to resist.

- Indigenous nations are attacked physically and symbolically through things like the Indian Act, policy, colonial laws, and fraudulent and unfair treaty negotiations at the same time as they are coping with violence, land loss, loss of an economic base, and disease.

- Indigenous nations lose political power and can no longer hold settlers accountable in their lands. There are fewer Indigenous bodies on Indigenous lands. We are confined to reserves. We are "governed" by the heteropatriarchy and settler colonialism of the Indian Act. Our children are in residential or day schools. We are rewarded with recognition when we assimilate.

- The gender binary is introduced and reinforced through residential schools, the church, and the Indian

Act. 2SQ people are disappeared. Indigenous women
are domesticated into the role of Victorian housewives.
Native men are domesticated into the wage economy
and taught their only power is to ally with white men in
the oppression of Indigenous women through church,
school, law, and policy.[7]

- Christian beliefs about heterosexual, monogamous,
  churched relationships and sexuality are infused into
  the community through missions and residential
  schools and reinforced by Indian agents.[8]

- Propagation of negative stereotypes of Indigenous
  women, men, and 2SQ people is widespread in popular
  culture, as evidenced in the first newspaper reporting
  on Indigenous peoples in Canada.[9]

- Canadian society through the media, books, and oral
  culture continues to justify the strangulation of Indigenous women's body sovereignty and to justify the
  violence against Indigenous women, which has led
  to the epidemic of murdered and missing Indigenous
  women and girls.[10]

- Indigenous women are blamed by the state for causing the violence by making poor lifestyle choices, and
  Indigenous men are named as the perpetrators of this
  violence.[11]

- Canadian citizens born into heteropatriarchy and normalized gender and sexualized violence against Indigenous peoples replicate this violence in their personal
  lives with structural support of the state's legal, education, and political systems.

- Disconnected from land and our knowledge systems,
  and the targets of four centuries of state violence,
  we replicate the violence we've experienced in our
  communities.

- We as a class can list in less than thirty minutes nearly a hundred stereotypes of Indigenous peoples, and many of us hold particular ones inside us that make us feel not good enough.

At first, they are surprised the Nishnaabeg prof from the south with degrees and the privilege credentials gives me still sometimes believes the worst about myself because colonialism has conditioned me to do so. This reframing, though, illuminates the deliberate nature of this on the part of the colonizer to get land, and that when we repeat it and live it, we are helping the colonizers.[12] This critical reframing, drawing on issues already discussed in class, then offers students a new orientation to themselves and their communities, one in which the interrogation of colonialism, the historical context, and the resistance of Indigenous peoples figure prominently. It is the approach Mohawk scholar Audra Simpson takes in her fantastic book *Mohawk Interruptus*: that there are signposts in our nations, communities, and bodies of colonialism's ongoing existence and simultaneous failure. She writes,

> Colonialism survives in a settler form. In this form, it fails at what it is supposed to do: eliminate Indigenous people; take all their land; absorb them into a white, property-owning body politic. Kahnawa:ke's *debates over membership* index colonialism's life as well its failure and their own life through their grip on this failure.[13]

This is a subtle and elegant shift in our analysis of Indigenous politics because it provides the proper and truthful context within which our analysis can take place. This approach also nests and confounds polarity: colonialism is violent and evil, and Indigenous peoples agree on that, and we have a range of *responses* to that horrific and ongoing violence that is ultimately rooted in a fog of love, anger, fear, shame, pride, and humiliation. For Simpson, the issue of membership is not about whether we should kick white people off the reserve; the fundamental question her people are grappling with is how do we continue to exist as *Kanien'kehá:ka* people in the face of settler colonialism elimination?

Simpson emphasizes "debates over membership" because this could be any issue in Indigenous political life. You can replace that phrase with "debates over land protection," "debates over governance," "debates over gender violence" because her intervention is that we need to shift our lens of analysis from one that plays into the limits of Western thought to one that is holy and diversely Indigenous at its core, both in experience and in intellectual thought, but that brings with it the most robust critical analysis of our times.

Following Simpson's intervention on framing, I want to use the pain and anger that heteropatriarchy strikes to reject the replication of settler colonial gender violence within our bodies, communities, and nations. We need all genders to do this, and we all need to think critically about how we replicate this in our communities and in our daily lives. Placing the interrogation of heteropatriarchy at the center of our nation-building movements ensures that our nation building counters the impact the settler colonial political economy has on Indigenous bodies, intimacies, sexualities, and gender. It counters the continual violent attack on bodies, intimacies, sexualities, and gender as a dispossessing force. We have a choice. We can choose to uphold white, heterosexual, masculine control over Indigenous bodies, or we can choose to collectively engage in the dismantling of heteropatriarchy as a nation-building project. Nation building in Indigenous contexts is a collective effort, and in critically undoing the gender hierarchy, what happens to Indigenous women, children, and 2SQ bodies is the measure of our success as nations.

Stereotypes are not attitudes that can be changed by using a different terminology. They are windows into the pervasive logics of white supremacy and heteropatriarchy and how they operate through time and space in Canada on my body and mind as an Indigenous woman. These terms are part of a much more omnipresent and ubiquitous system of control that has stolen not only my land from me but also my body and the way I think about my body. I am not murdered, and I am not missing, but parts of me have been disappeared, and I remain a target because I was born a Native women, and I live as kwe.

Students at Dechinta have already heard me talk about consent and individual self-determination within the context of Indigenous politics, and so we then talk about creating these alternative systems of accountability. I use the example of the Community Holistic Circle Healing project in Hollow Water First Nation, an Nishnaabeg community on the east side of Lake Winnipeg, in Manitoba. We talk about how this group found that 80 percent of their residents had experience with sexual abuse, and how they used Nishnaabeg processes of accountability to create a community-based alternative to the Canadian criminal justice systems for cases of sexual violence.[14] We talk about how this system requires the admission of guilt on the part of the perpetrator to proceed. There is a truth telling as the first step. The circle of healing involves support for all of the individuals and families involved. It involves the perpetrator witnessing the full impacts of his actions. It involves the larger community witnessing the full impacts of sexualized violence and an accounting for how we contribute to the epidemic levels of violence in our communities. It involves ceremony and Nishnaabeg practices of regeneration. It involves regenerating relationships.

Students often share their frustrations with the criminal justice system and with our communities in terms of how we handle these issues. They often have a wealth of ideas for visioning systems of accountability in their own lives.

Thinking back to the bush classroom at Dechinta and Denendeh, I learned something else important that day. I learned that I *want,* but don't necessarily need, Indigenous men to have my back. I don't want to be continually seeking out the solidarity, the recognition of white women because I want the solidarity of straight cisgendered Indigenous men. I want them to stop exploiting, abusing, and degrading women and children. I want them to stop engaging in systemic, structural and casual sexism and patriarchy. I want them to hold each other accountable when there are no women around, and casual and not-so-casual sexism in the form of the objectification, ongoing criticism, and other forms of white patriarchy enter their social, personal, and professional lives. I want them to hold each other accountable when casual and not-so-casual homophobia, transphobia, heterosexism and all forms of anti-queerness appear. I want them to support and assist and to be critically engaged in, but not lead, the dismantling of heteropatriarchy as the crucial nation-building exercise of our time. I want them to see that they have been targeted by white men working strategically and persistently to make allies out of Indigenous men, with clear rewards for those who come into white masculinity imbued with heteropatriarchy and violence, in order to infiltrate our communities and nations with heteropatriarchy and then to replicate it through the generations, with the purpose of destroying our nations and gaining easy access to our land.

White supremacy, rape culture (although Sarah Hunt recently reminded me that when rape happens to us, it is rarely named as "rape"), and the attack on gender, sexual identity, agency, and consent are very powerful tools of colonialism, settler colonialism, and capitalism primarily because they work very efficiently to remove Indigenous peoples from our territories and to prevent reclamation of those territories through mobilization.

These forces have the intergenerational staying power to destroy generations of families, as they work to prevent us from intimately connecting to each other. They work to prevent mobilization because communities coping with epidemics of gender violence don't have the physical or emotional capital to organize. They destroy the base of our nations and our political systems because they destroy our relationships to the land and to each other by fostering epidemic levels of anxiety, hopelessness, apathy, distrust, and suicide. They work to destroy the fabric of Indigenous nationhoods by attempting to destroy our relationality by making it difficult to form sustainable, strong relationships with each other.

Dismantling heteropatriarchy and generating modes of scholarship, organizing, mobilizing, and living that no longer replicate it must be a core project of radical resurgence. Centering the voices of children, women, and 2SQ people within the Radical Resurgence Project is a mechanism through which to counter the gendered nature of heteropatriarchy and build systems of consent, accountability, and agency so that all Indigenous political orders are valued, cherished, and celebrated as a crucial part of our communities and nations, and fully engaged in the regeneration of alternative Indigenous worlds. Indigenous freedom means that my sovereignty over my body, mind, spirit, and land is affirmed and respected in all of my relationships.

SEVEN
THE SOVEREIGNTY OF INDIGENOUS PEOPLES' BODIES

MY MATERNAL FAMILY can trace our ancestry to the original families in the Grape Island Mission and the Bay of Quinte Michi Saagiig Nishnaabeg. The attempts to assimilate us were the responsibility of Indian agents, the Methodist missionaries, and the education system because settlers wanted our lands. In the four generations of living Nishnaabekwewag in my family, I can so clearly see the devastating impacts of policies and regulation of Nishnaabeg gender, sexuality, and relationships and of the assimilatory nature of domesticity in myself, my mother, and my grandmother. We grew up believing the stereotypes and believing that if we existed outside of the domestic sphere, outside of heteropatriarchal, monogamous Christian marriage, we embodied the dirty, stupid, useless, promiscuous, and irresponsible assumptions built into the word *squaw*. I grew up believing the worst of the stereotypes. It is not something I was able to dig myself out of until the 1990s when my sisters and I began to critically question these assumptions and our experiences in activist communities and in women's studies programs at universities. I can trace, then, through the historical record and the oral tradition in my family over two hundred years of intense targeting of Indigenous bodies, self-determination, sexuality, and relationships, and this targeting continues to happen to my children.

The Michi Saagiig Nishnaabeg had been dealing with evangelization and assimilation by the Methodists at least since the end of the War of 1812, which signified a massive influx of United Empire Loyalists (American loyalists who resettled in British North America during the American Revolution) into Michi Saagiig Nishnaabeg territory.[1] These English-speaking white people were offered land grants in Ontario—land that required the dispossession and control of the Nishnaabeg. This resulted in an increase in activity of the Methodist missionaries as a form of assimilation and marked the beginning of a non-Native majority in our territory. This was also accompanied by a shift in Indian policy in Upper Canada that resulted in increased pressure on officials to promote "Christian civilization" among Native peoples and the recognition that the "financial burden" and political burden of honoring treaties could be eliminated if Native peoples were assimilated into Canadian society. This in turn led to the establishment of Methodist missions in the 1820s at the Credit River near Toronto, Mud Lake (now Curve Lake First Nation), and Grape Island (an island in Lake Ontario off the coast of Kingston). These missions were intense sites of assimilative education designed to make Michi Saagiig Nishnaabeg devout Methodists, the men and boys farmers and carpenters, the women and girls managers of effective British households and patriarchal nuclear families in village-like settings, thus removing Indigenous peoples from the land completely and erasing those who did not conform to the colonial gender binary completely.

Much of the teaching at the Methodist missions was done by white women, which means in this context that much of the policing of Michi Saagiig Nishnaabeg bodies, intimate relationships, and parenting was done by and through white women.[2] White women were the ideal, and missions were out to quietly destroy Nishnaabeg nationhood by erasing strong, powerful Nishnaabeg women who were skilled at fishing, hunting, trapping, sugaring, ricing, and medicine. White women were out to destroy our political system, health care system, economy, and system governance. White women were out to destroy gender variance and fluidity, our knowledge of families, kinship, birth, birth control, sexuality, breastfeeding and attachment, and community parenting. They were out to destroy our education system and spirituality. White women were out to remove us from political influence in our communities and our nations and to position us as "less than" our male counterparts. They were out to destroy our agency, self-determination, body sovereignty, and freedom and to contain us under the colonial heteropatriarchy within which they lived and used to have power over us. White women were out to destroy our intelligence and political systems.

This is genocide.

This is sexual and gendered violence as a tool of genocide and as a tool of dispossession. It is deliberate.

Two celebrated white women writers figure prominently in the local settler historical record in Peterborough, Ontario. The two sisters, Catherine Parr Traill and Susanna Moodie, moved uninvited into the heart of Michi Saagiig Nishnaabeg territory in disregard of and seemingly oblivious to the international agreements my nation had made with theirs in the 1830s. Susanna Moodie subsequently, at the direction of her publisher in Britain, wrote *Roughing It in the Bush* as a guide for settler life for those British subjects considering moving to occupied Nishnaabeg territory. Moodie's work remains a canonical work in Canadian literature for both its literary and Canadian cultural contributions, with Margaret Atwood's 1972 book of poetry *The Journals of Susanna Moodie* further cementing Moodie into Canadian prominence.

I've read *Roughing It in the Bush* a number of times, and it is never an enjoyable experience. At one point, Moodie writes about the lynching of a Black man in Michi Saagiig territory, with all the anti-Blackness that is Canadian and that Canada would not exist without. Passages such as "[the] Mississauga Indians, perhaps the least attractive of all these wild people, both with regard to their physical and mental endowments" grate on my being, not because of their historic inaccuracies or their reflection of the normalcy of white supremacy at the time but because so much Indigenous effort has gone into disproving her lies, and because this pillar of white supremacy and colonialism—the idea that we are naturally *less* than our white counterparts—continues to produce generations of Native youth that believe they are, or, perhaps more dangerously, believe that achieving what matters in settler colonial Canadian society—degrees, economic prosperity, home ownership, or whatever—makes them a more valuable Indigenous person. It does, but only through the lens of white supremacy.[3]

Moodie's detailed descriptions of Mississauga men with their "coarse and repulsive features" and "intellectual faculties scarcely developed," and of Mississauga women as "a merry, light-hearted set . . . in strange contrast to the iron taciturnity of their grim lords" set the tone for an overwhelmingly anti-Indigenous and anti-Black characterization of life in occupied Upper Canada.[4] She goes on to repeatedly position Michi Saagiig Nishnaabeg as stupid and ugly throughout the chapter titled "The Wilderness and Our Indian Friends," freely commenting on physical attributes and sexuality of Mississauga men. She writes, "The vanity of these grave men is highly amusing. They seem perfectly unconscious of it themselves; and it is exhibited in the most child-like manner," and "I'm inclined to think that their ideas of personal beauty differ very widely from ours."[5] She also freely comments on the bodies and sexuality of Mississauga women: "Tom Nogan, the chief's brother had a very large, fat, ugly squaw for his wife. She was a mountain of tawny flesh, and, but for the innocent, good-natured expression which, like a bright sunbeam penetrating a swarthy cloud, spread all around a kindly glow, she might have been termed hideous"; "she appeared very dirty, and appeared quite indifferent to the claims of common decency."[6]

I could go on, but I won't. Much of this overt racism is dismissed or absent in the analysis of *Roughing It in the Bush,* or at least neutralized by placing it in "the context of the historical record," even in specific analysis of the representations of Native women.[7] The historical record in this context is meant to be the "original literary context" in which they were writing and the prevailing and normalized attitudes and beliefs about Indians at the time.[8] It is a prevailing racist Canadian attitude that we cannot judge writers from the past by today's standards.

Which leads me to ask whose historical context and whose standards?

We know the answer, and it certainly is not the historical context of the Michi Saagiig Nishnaabeg or Black people in Canada. The Michi Saagiig Nishnaabeg nation was under the violent attack of colonialism from every angle. The end of the War of 1812 for the Michi Saagiig Nishnaabeg was devastating. We witnessed the extirpation of salmon and eels from our territory, and the construction of the Trent-Severn Waterway, which destroyed the water in most of our lakes and our food security as the flooding destroyed the wild rice beds, an unprecedented (at the time) level of environmental destruction. We were in negotiations that resulted in the 1818 treaty, the residential schools system was being set up, with the first school opening in Alderville First Nation in 1828, and we were under the height of the efforts of the Methodist missions designed to carry out cultural genocide and assimilation. All of these processes were designed to clear Michi Saagiig Nishnaabeg bodies from the land to the extreme benefit of settlers.

Moodie is writing about my relations while living on stolen land in an enclave of white supremacy. She is both witness to and beneficiary of the violent dispossession of Michi Saagiig Nishnaabeg from our homeland. Her entire existence and that of her family are predicated on that crime, and she is willfully oblivious as she constructs Michi Saagiig Nishnaabeg people as also willfully oblivious. This trumps any possible shared sisterhood Michi Saagiig Nishnaabeg women might have with her as female. Carole Gerson writes, "powerful as white but disempowered as female, Moodie and Traill share with Native women some marginal space on the outskirts of frontier culture."[9] Genocide sets up a clear dichotomy in which, unless white women are willing to divest themselves of the power of being white, there is no shared marginal space with Michi Saagiig Nishnaabeg women. Describing interactions between white women and Mississauga women as "experimental and not oppositional" is a fiction that exists in white women's theorizing themselves out of responsibility for benefiting from and replication of the gendered violence of colonialism through assumed allied spaces of women-to-women contact zones. Think about how Moodie so completely steals the self-determination of Indigenous women and recasts us as dirty and stupid, a recasting that I still live with nearly two hundred years later. She comprehensively steals and erases the bodies of Indigenous peoples and exerts an absolute power over Indigenous life as if this is her birthright. Think this is just in the past? Think again. Think about how those very same ideas are still the top four in 2015 when Indigenous youth, fresh out of high school, list the stereotypes they have heard in their own lives.

The ways in which Moodie negates Indigenous nationhood, obfuscates colonialism, and replicates the gendered nature of colonial violence that both informs and influences Indian policy cannot be dismissed and excused as the "racism of the times," because it is these unexamined foundational beliefs about Indigenous peoples that were used and are used as justification for dispossession, residential schools, the Indian Act, and the violence against Indigenous women that is normalized in settler Canadian society, and for the continued paternalism of *helping* Indigenous peoples and dealing with the "Indian problem." It seems to me that the point of the words "original literary context" is to provide a broad exoneration that fits seamlessly into the Canadian narrative of the past: Mistakes were made. Land was lost. Children were stolen. Cultures were adapted. Treaties didn't work out. We meant well. We tried our best. Progress is inevitable, and while it is regretful you didn't have the intelligence or fortitude to be successful, that's life. Maybe we'll try and be nicer and help more.

Very few Canadians will directly proclaim they are in favor of the position of Indigenous peoples in Canada, but a very large number of Canadians will do everything they can to preserve the social, cultural, and economic systems of the country, even though this system is predicated on violence and dispossession of Indigenous lands and bodies. Therefore, we do not need the help of Canadians. We need Canadians to help themselves, to learn to struggle and to understand that their great country of Canada has been and is a death dance for Indigenous peoples. They must learn to stop themselves from plundering the land and the climate and using Indigenous peoples' bodies to fuel their economy, and to find a way of living in the world that is not based on violence and exploitation.

The Indian Act

I've taught the Indian Act and its devastating impact on Indigenous nations for over fifteen years in various Indigenous Studies courses. I talk about the consolidation of legislation that led to the first act in 1876. I discuss the most oppressive forms of the act: the banning of the Sundance and Potlatch ceremonies, the pass system, the imposition of chief and council administration, the restrictions on organizing and hiring legal counsel, and so on. I make a point of how this undermined the political influence of Indigenous women through the patriarchal rules related to leadership and elections. We discuss the patriarchal nature of status and membership clauses, and I highlight the resistance of Indigenous women and our organizing related to Bill C31, and Bill C3. I present all of this as the historical fact that it is, and in doing so, I present a fairly straight, masculinist view of the Indian Act; that is, I don't fully interrogate the targeting of Indigenous women and the 2SQ community, and therefore I obfuscate the gendered nature of colonialism and the Indian Act. I underreport the targeting of Indigenous women and the 2SQ community in Indian policy, targeting that has directly and indirectly impacted me and the women in my family in violent ways.

I was not conscious of this underreporting until I sat through a lecture on the Indian Act by a male colleague and friend of mine, and I felt a swell of emotion in me—strong feelings of anger, injustice, and erasure. At first, I thought it was me, that I couldn't somehow support my friend and colleague doing what was by all standards in Indigenous Studies a very thorough and complete discussion of the Indian Act that highlighted gender in the same way that I did. But my experience of his lecture, as essentially a student or as someone who wasn't directing the content or the discussion, was one of profound disempowerment. My first reaction was to blame myself. Why couldn't I cope with not being in charge? Why was I angry with someone who has always had my back? What was untrue about what my colleague was saying? Was this just a trigger for my own unprocessed shit? Was I being hysterical?

I sat with this. I hiked around the bush with this. Eventually I uncovered a tiny part of me that was saying that there was a strong disconnect between my lived experience as kwe and how the Indian Act and its implications had been discussed in class. That the women in my family experienced the loss of status, and then some of us gained it back, was only part of the deep pain inside of me. The rest of the pain stemmed from the racist stereotyping of Indigenous women as promiscuous, sluts, dirty, unfit mothers, stupid, angry, apolitical, useless, skill-less, bad, crazy, unstable, disposable beings, which then became codified in the Indian Act and to some degree remains encoded in the Indian Act. And not just the stereotypes. My family, like all Indigenous families, has directly suffered under the colonial systems that white supremacist hatred has justified, including the child welfare system, disease, imposed poverty, addictions, mental health issues, and even death.

I sat with the trees and this pain, trying to make sense of things, like I am now, trying to figure out why the words *squaw, slut, dirty Indian,* and *stupid* have so much power over me. I considered that I don't necessarily want to "heal," because I am not damaged, or diseased, or unhealthy. My response to the intergenerational trauma of settler colonial violence is correct and strong and vital. I don't believe that one can be Indigenous in Canada in 2016 and live a normal and fulfilling existence unless one is completely delusional and is living as a full Canadian; that is, with an unexamined, uncritical view of Indigenous-settler relations, or having adopted the measures of success of Canadian society to the point where one views the scars of oppression as cancers. I don't want to be "healed." I want to have processed hurt and pain to the point where I can speak back to those words and harness the power of fear, hatred, and love into sustained mobilization—to the point where they don't control me, but they are experiences I can draw on when it is useful to do so.

I need to place my emotional experience, my life, in a position of honor. I need to respect and listen to my intelligence as a cisgendered Indigenous woman and as an Indigenous person. As kwe.

From this standpoint, my reaction to my colleague's Indian Act lecture makes sense because "promiscuous, sluts, dirty, unfit mothers, stupid, angry, apolitical, useless, skill-less, bad, disposable, crazy, unstable beings" are not just words, and they are not just racist, sexist stereotypes or significrs. They are four centuries–old weapons used to take power and influence away from Indigenous women in a habitual and strategic fashion, to promote the state's goals of assimilation and dispossession. They are attacks on my sovereignty. Without analyzing how these beliefs were perpetuated by settlers in settler society and used to justify violence against Indigenous peoples, we erase how they became encoded in policy, legislation, and all of the institutions of colonial society. And not only do we erase this history and this present, we erase how we replicate this in our scholarship and in our personal lives. Our societies, then, force Indigenous women, 2SQ, and trans people to ignore what *feels* wrong, so we police and silence ourselves, or maybe I should just speak for myself and say, I'm paying much more attention to figuring out what feels wrong and why and then sitting with, analyzing, and voicing those feeling-inspired interventions.

So how did the practice of the Indian Act specifically target Indigenous women and queer Indigenous peoples (and by practice I mean not just the policies on paper but how they played out on the ground in the lives of Indigenous peoples) from the perspective of Indigenous peoples and of Indigenous women and 2SQ peoples in particular?

To begin to understand this, we must understand that colonizers saw Indigenous bodies—our physical bodies and our constructions of gender, sexuality, and intimate relationships—as Audra Simpson says, as a symbol of Indigenous orders of government and a direct threat to their sovereignty and governmentality. The church, the state, and broader Canadian society worked in concert to surveil and confine Indigenous bodies and intimacies to Euro-Canadian heteropatriarchal marriages, that is, singular, lifelong monogamous relationships designed to reproduce the building blocks of Canadian nationalism instead of the replication of Nishnaabewin and Nishnaabeg nationhood, while also placing Indigenous conceptualizations and forms of intimacy and relationship as transgressive, immoral, uncivilized, and criminal.[10] The "bedrock" of the Canadian nation-building project rested on the creation of "moral and responsible citizens" born out of "moral families, based on Western (largely Anglo) middle-class notions of sexual purity, marital monogamy, and distinct gender roles" in which women were domesticated and men were breadwinners.[11] Gender and sexuality were crucial areas in which officials evaluated Indigenous nations and intervened when Indigenous practices contravened assimilatory policies.[12]

The Indian Act is long-standing legislation in Canada and is the primary document that outlines how the state interacts with the individuals and communities the state recognizes as Status Indians and Bands. The Indian Act in 1876 and its subsequent revisions had lots to say about gender. It is widely known and documented that the earliest versions of the Indian Act were imbued with heteropatriarchy by which queer Indigenous peoples and relationships were disappeared, and there is no doubt in my mind that queer Indigenous peoples would have experienced extreme pressure and often violence to conform to colonial heteronormativity. In the 1876 version of the act, Indian women were not allowed to possess land and marital property unless they were widows, but a widow could not inherit her husband's property upon death—everything went to his children. This was revised some in 1884, when Indian men could will their property to their wives if the Indian agent deemed the wife to be in good moral character. This remained intact until 1951, although men still often hold exclusive rights to property even if a relationship ends.[13] The gender discrimination in rules for who are deemed Status Indians is widely documented and has been partially addressed with Bill C31 and Bill C3, but the gender discrimination still exists in the act, albeit pushed back one generation. The political influence of Indigenous women was also attacked in versions of the act from 1876 to 1951, when we were removed from Indian Act administrations completely. The acts did not allow women to run for chief or council positions, nor did they allow for Indigenous women to vote in band elections. This combined with provisions that made it illegal for Status Indians to hire legal counsel and to organize politically made it more difficult for Indigenous women to have influence.

Indian agents perhaps caused severe damage in intimate Indigenous spaces because they were provided the authority to punish Indigenous peoples for not adhering to heterosexuality, monogamy, and colonial gender expressions. Indian agents could punish disobedience by taking away children, by refusing economic relief in times of need, by taking away treaty and interest payments, and by formally charging Indigenous peoples and subjecting them to court and criminalization.[14] Indian agents had considerable authority on reserves and actively policed gender, sexuality, and marriage, as evidenced by the "Immorality on Reserves" filing system at Indian Affairs.[15] Robin Jarvis Brownlie, a non-Indigenous historian, has produced focused work on the surveillance of Nishnaabeg intimacies by Indian Affairs in the 1920s and 1930s by examining the records of Indian agents working at the time in Georgian Bay. Indian agents held a lot of power over Indigenous peoples, and Brownlie's examination of these records reveals the regulation of Indigenous women's gender and sexuality and the "considerable interest DIA officials took in the marital and sexual habits of both men and women."[16] Brownlie opens with a discussion of a letter sent by Duncan Campbell Scott, deputy superintendent of Indian Affairs from 1913 to 1932, to an Nishnaabeg woman living as a member of the Chippewas of Nawash First Nation at Neyaashiinigmiing (Cape Croker). The letter was sent at the request of her local Indian agent because her husband was "paying attentions to other women." Scott's letter threatened that his department would cancel the loan on her husband's farm if the woman failed to mend her ways in her marriage. Scott encouraged her to properly perform "her duties as a wife and a mother" and spend more time in the home and less time "running around to the neighbours," thus making the place more attractive so that her husband would be interested in staying there.[17] Brownlie goes on to note that the Indian agent had requested a letter to also be sent to the husband, but that letter appears to never have been written.[18] Threats of economic sanctions were common and particularly targeted women during this time period because they were often poor.

The threat of economic sanctions is particularly relevant in the Williams Treaty area because these communities had lost their hunting and fishing rights through the fraudulent process of signing the treaty (which wasn't negotiated), in the midst of a century of environmental destruction (of wild rice beds and fish populations through the construction of the Trent-Severn Waterway), settler encroachment, and dispossession, which destroyed the foundation of our economy.[19]

There is a strong parallel between the dispossession of Michi Saagiig Nishnaabeg from our homelands and the dispossession of Indigenous bodies from our grounded normativity. Within Nishnaabeg political practices, governance begins with how our minds (emotional and intellectual), bodies, and spirits interact and relate to one another. Illness often arises out of an imbalance of these four aspects of being. The interaction and interdependence of these aspects of being enable us to make decisions about our bodies, and thus individual self-determination becomes a driving force in Nishnaabeg practice. Individuals within Nishnaabeg society are afforded a large amount of freedom within our philosophical and ethical understandings of the world to conduct themselves in a way that is beneficial and contributing to their families but also honors and respects their gifts, talents, and desires.

Everywhere in the world Indigenous women and our sexual agency provided a dilemma for the colonizers.[20] Initially, in the absence of white women, colonizers positioned and used Indigenous women for sexual gratification. By the mid-nineteenth century, the colonizers positioned all the sexual autonomy (and the autonomy in general) of Indigenous women to be illicit— especially if it occurred "in public," the domain of white men.[21] The more Indigenous women exercised their body sovereignty, the more we were targeted as "squaws" and "savages," subjected to violence and criminalized. A large part of the colonial project has been to control the political power of Indigenous women and queer people through the control of our sexual agency because this agency is a threat to heteropatriarchy, the heteronormative nuclear family, the replication and reproduction of (queer) Indigeneity and Indigenous political orders, the hierarchy colonialism needs to operate, and ultimately Indigenous freedom. Indigenous body sovereignty and sexuality sovereignty threaten colonial power.

By the mid-1800s, federal, provincial, and white governments had set up various legal and regulatory mechanisms to manage the agency of Indigenous women and Indigenous political orders through the management of prostitution as any "illicit" sexual agency taking place in the public sphere, often meaning any expression of relationship outside of churched, monogamous marriages between men and women of the same "race."[22] Public expressions of Indigenous sexuality outside of the norms of the colonizers were contained in the charge of prostitution in order for the state to destroy Indigenous self-determination by attacking Indigenous bodies through regulatory mechanisms.[23]

The first Canadian statute dealing with prostitution was in the mid-1800s in Lower Canada. In 1879, provisions regarding prostitution were included in the Indian Act—shortly after the Royal Canadian Mounted Police (RCMP) was created, in 1873. These provisions were amended in 1884 and eventually moved to the criminal code in 1892, resulting in the first expulsion of Indigenous women from urban spaces back to reserves, although the coded term *profligacy,* meaning "promiscuity," remained in the act to continue the regulation of sexuality.[24] Nishnaabekwe writer Naomi Sayers recently addressed the link between Canada's current prostitution laws and colonialism, writing that these laws "were really there to protect society's whiteness/maleness. As such these laws were disproportionately applied to racialized and Indigenous bodies." Sayers continues:

> Specifically, the first sections [of the Indian Act] relating to prostitution, written in 1879, included sections banning "houses of prostitution" (or in a contemporary context, "bawdy houses"). Initially, "houses of prostitution" were defined as being disorderly, a definition which had almost nothing to do with sexual behaviors. These sections also explicitly included wigwams—that is, Indigenous peoples' houses—meaning that Indigenous houses were assumed to be disorderly by nature. This gave government and policing agencies the permission to enter Indigenous people's houses on spurious grounds unrelated to the actual offense in question. These same claims that Indigenous houses were disorderly also led to the removal of Indigenous children from their homes, forcing them to attend residential schools designed to erase Indigenous identities from society. Following this, several other sections were included, but were later repealed and replaced in 1880 and 1884. Even though these sections were repeatedly repealed and replaced, changes to prostitution laws always increased the force and effect of these laws on Indigenous women's bodies. Because these laws originated under the Indian Act, there were no attempts to criminalize non-Indigenous men for similar offenses.[25]

In the 1930s a young Nishnaabeg woman living on a reserve in northwestern Ontario was sentenced to two years in provincial reformatory for vagrancy. The evidence centered on her supposed sexual promiscuity, including graphic evidence of her most recent sexual encounter, and that she had two "illegitimate" children. A petition was presented to the court signed by the Indian agent and her family that in the interests of morality on the reserve she be sent to a reformatory.[26] Her name was Emma. She was convicted under section 101 of the Indian Act in 1933 for profligacy (promiscuity).[27]

Because these measures were continually and violently introduced and reinforced by the church, the education system, and the state and through settler culture, the degree to which these colonial values were infiltrated into the practices of Indigenous peoples and communities means very little to me because it occurred without informed consent or critical thought and under extreme oppression and duress. To say that Indigenous cultures, values, and morals "shifted" or "changed" under these conditions is absurd. This was a strategic and habitual all-out attack on Indigenous intelligence that is tantamount to culture genocide and part of genocide in general.

Hierarchy had to be infiltrated into Indigenous constructions of family so that men were agents of heteropatriarchy and could therefore exert colonial control from within. This was accomplished by placing Indigenous men in more powerful positions within Indigenous communities than Indigenous women, and by teaching through example, the church, and various Indian agent interventions that the role of a good wife was to serve her husband in every conceivable way. One example of this is the Indian Act elections. Until 1951, Indigenous women could not run for chief and council, nor could they vote in these elections. Missions, such as the Methodist one at Grape Island and later in Alderville First Nation, made Michi Saagiig Nishnaabeg men into farmers and carpenters, and Michi Saagiig Nishnaabeg women into wives, in the traditions of England, meaning they engaged in unpaid labor contained inside a British-like household, ruled by their husbands. Michi Saagiig Nishnaabeg women were transformed from being autonomous, influential, and economically and politically powerful within our nation to being dependent, subservient, second-class citizens confined to the domestic sphere in colonial society.

Since Michi Saagiig Nishnaabeg nationhood is at its core relational, and all of our political practices stem from the establishment and maintenance of good relations, Indigenous forms of social kinship had to be destroyed and replaced with the heteronormative nuclear families. Indigenous intimate partnerships were diverse and shattered the heteronormative sexual and relationship orientations of settlers. There were practices of nonmonogamy, separation, divorce, and situations where both genders had more than one partner. These unchurched relationships were the subject of much settler surveillance.

Indigenous forms of gender construction and fluidity around gender had to be replaced with a rigid heteropatriarchal gender binary and strict gender roles. Indigenous peoples had to be removed from educating Indigenous children. The sexuality of Indigenous women and 2SQ people had to be removed from the public sphere and from the control of Indigenous women and 2SQ people, as normalized within Indigenous societies and contained within the white heteropatriarchal home.[28] This last point is critical to understanding the experience of Indigenous women today. Since we came from societies where sexual freedom and self-determination of our bodies was our birthright, the control of our bodies and sexuality became of critical importance to the colonizers. They reframed Indigenous sexuality within the confines of shame and modesty. They sanctioned it only on the terms and for the enjoyment of husbands and men within marriage. They removed it from the public sphere by labeling Indigenous women as promiscuous or prostitutes, and then criminalized their acts—all of which is a violent imposition on Indigenous self-determination and body sovereignty.

Officials were particularly focused on conformity to Christian forms of monogamous lifelong marriage and Euro-Canadian sexual prescriptions, and on the deterrence of nonmarital sexuality.[29] The rigidity of the colonial gender binary was a prominent part of policy and practice. The state had a strong interest in assimilating Indigenous bodies into the gendered roles of European females and males and infusing Indigenous families with the hierarchy of heteropatriarchy. This resulted in a near erasure of queer genders and sexualities, the confinement of women to the domestic sphere of the home, the ongoing criminalization of Indigenous women who trade or sell sex, and the continued criminalization of Indigenous women and queer people in urban, rural, and reserve spaces. It also resulted in the confinement of men to the roles of white patriarchal husbands and fathers, to the unskilled or the semiskilled working class, and to a colonial hierarchy of gender within Indigenous intimacies with men at the top, women in the middle, and nonconforming genders disappeared through individual and systemic violence.[30]

Nishnaabeg women skilled and adept in the practices of hunting, trapping, fishing, sugaring, ricing, gardening, and harvesting medicines were economically independent from the settler economy and therefore were less reliant on their husbands and Indian agents economically. This afforded them a higher level of freedom and autonomy that in turn posed a greater threat to assimilation. Thus, dismantling the power and influence of Indigenous women became important to the destruction of Indigenous nations. Domesticity—confining Indigenous women to heteropatriarchal marriage and the home—was an intense site of cultural genocide carried out by missions and educational institutions and through Indian Act policy and practice. Both missions and Indian agents actively regulated Indigenous women's sexuality and enforced obedience and compliance to Euro-Canadian models of "correct" gender expression.[31]

Non-Indigenous historian Joan Sangster has also documented examples of the sexual surveillance and punishment of Nishnaabeg women in Ontario under the Female Refuges Act, the Juvenile Delinquents Act, and the Training School Act. From 1919 to 1958, women in Ontario considered "idle and dissolute" were incarcerated under the Ontario Female Refuges Act. It targeted "women considered promiscuous, with illegitimate children, suspected of venereal disease, sometimes women involved with Asian or Black men."[32] This act also impacted Indigenous women, particularly because Canadian society in general already positioned Indigenous women as promiscuous and idle. In the early 1940s a young Indigenous woman was taken before the court by her Indian agent and the local RCMP for drinking and "dissolute" sexual behavior and was sentenced under the Female Refuges Act to a term at the Mercer Reformatory in Toronto.[33] Indigenous women were also convicted under this act for sleeping with men who were not their husbands, public intoxication, promiscuity, and prostitution, and the courts were highly influenced by the racist stereotypes of Indigenous women when sentencing.[34]

The threat of being sent to a reform school figured prominently in my own childhood growing up in the 1970s. My Michi Saagiig Nishnaabeg mother made it clear that if my sisters and I did not behave as good, young ladies—meaning polite, respectful (of male authority), and pure—we would be sent to reform school. In some ways this can be viewed as Indigenous women now taking on the role of the colonizer, or as Indigenous women's morals or values shifting to mirror that of the colonizer, but I think neither of these is true. I think my mom was trying to protect me from a racist, heteropatriarchal colonizing society that had the ability to punish me for behavior it deemed transgressive, and that this belief was something that seven generations of the Michi Saagiig Nishnaabeg women in my family had now faced. This also plays out in our communities in how we treat our relations who are pushed out of our community governance and decision making because they are perceived to fulfill and embody the stereotypes more overtly (people who are street involved, people with addictions issues, those who trade or sell sex, and queer people who "flaunt" their sexuality, for example).[35] Yet, within Nishnaabeg thought, every body is a political order and every body houses individual self-determination. The important work of the Indigenous Sex Sovereignty Collective reinforces this idea in their statement calling for centering the voices of people who trade or sell sex in Indigenous antiviolence organizing: "At a personal level, self-determination means the ability to choose how to identify one's experience, sovereignty over one's body, and respect for the decisions a person makes over their own lives today."[36] This idea is the very foundation of Nishnaabeg governance.

Native girls were also sentenced to the Ontario Training School for Girls, established in 1933 as a secular, state-supported reform school designed for girls under the age of sixteen, for a variety of misdeeds, including incorrigibility, sexual promiscuity, and running away under the Juvenile Delinquents Act and Training School Act of 1908. This could transpire without a court case, with only the recommendation of a child welfare agency, relatives, foster parents, guardians, or Indian agents, and the number of Indigenous girls incarcerated increased steadily after 1940s.[37] All of these acts, policies, attitudes, systems, and habitual practices were set up to control, undermine, and criminalize the self-determination of Indigenous women.

I notice that in the aftermath of the height of the Idle No More movement, there has been a significant amount of online activism toward eradicating stereotypes of Indigenous peoples and a significant lack of discussion and action about land issues. While it has become the practice for segments of Canadian society, particularly the more liberal and well-meaning segments, to condemn racist stereotypes, this same group is immobilized with regard to land issues. As a result, it is possible to get, for instance, music festivals to ban hipsters from wearing Native headdresses, or sports teams to change their name from the Nepean Redskins, or even the word *squaw* to be removed from maps. These efforts have my respect but also my worry. Changing stereotypes are easy wins right now. They are easy because they are acceptable to the oppressor, and they only give the illusion of real change. It is not acceptable to wear a headdress to a dance party, but it is acceptable to dance on stolen land and to build pipelines over stolen land. It is not acceptable to call Indigenous women "squaws," but it is acceptable to maintain all of the systems that target Indigenous women's minds, bodies, and spirituality and to continue to exclude those political orders from governance and decision making that we perceive to be embodying these stereotypes.[38] It is acceptable to undermine and attack our body sovereignty and self-determination. It is acceptable that we are not in control of how we want to use our bodies and our minds. It is acceptable that we are not free. In a sense, it is like the colonizer saying to me that colonialism, colonial gender violence, and Indigenous dispossession are now so entrenched in North America that we don't even have to use racist stereotypes to maintain these systems. They perpetuate themselves.

Let me be clear, from within Nishnaabewin, the decisions about how I use my body, my mind, my sexuality, my spirituality, and the relationship I'm embedded in are my decision and no one else's. The regulation of my body, my brain, and my sexuality are attacks on my body as a political order, my nationhood, and my freedom, regardless of intent. I do not consent to have my freedom restricted by those who believe they know best for me and my body. I refuse.

Indigenous Bodies as Political Orders

One of the most important interventions for me over the past few years related to gender, Indigenous nation building, and resurgence comes in the form of a talk by the brilliant Mohawk scholar Audra Simpson titled "The Chief's Two Bodies." One of Simpson's intellectual gifts is the ability to eloquently reframe the most important issues of our times out of a simplistic colonial realm and into truth—a layered and complex Indigenous reality. I am indebted to her for this. I've heard versions of "The Chief's Two Bodies" live. I've watched a recorded version several times. I've used the recording of her talk in classrooms across the country. I've forced graduate students to watch and to read her work before I'll work with them. Simpson is of course a celebrated and widely respected Indigenous scholar. For me, her work is some of the most important scholarship of our time because her analysis fully resonates with me as a scholar and with my experience as an Indigenous woman. I use my body, mind, spirit, and life in my writing as research and as a canvas, and rarely do the echoes of another scholar's work align with both my head and my experience. Simpson's does that.

In her talk, which I understand is part of a larger, new book project, Simpson maintains that the bodies of Indigenous woman are legal targets for death, disappearance, and elimination because we are signifiers of a political order that is a direct threat to the political legitimacy of settlement. I want to spend some time here exploring her talk and how I relate to it as an Nishnaabekwe because I think her intervention changes the way we are talking about gender (or not talking about it) in Indigenous Studies.

Simpson begins her talk stating that her paper makes two very simple arguments:

> That Canada requires the death and so-called disappearance of Indigenous women in order to secure its sovereignty; and this is a sovereign death dance that requires us to think hard about the ways in which we imagine not only nations and states but what counts as governance itself.[39]

What follows in Simpson's talk is a clear articulation of how the murdering, disappearing, and erasing of Indigenous women is necessary for Canada to secure and legitimize its sovereignty because they house and reproduce Indigenous political orders. This isn't true just for Indigenous woman, but it is also true for queer bodies and children because these Indigenous bodies have always housed and acted out Indigenous power, political and otherwise, that white women, queer people, and children did not have. This power resulted in the legally mandated disappearance of Indigenous women through the Indian Act, policy, and the criminal justice system; of transgendered people through the Indian Act, the criminal justice system, and residential schools; and of children, as our greatest potential, through residential schools and the child welfare system.

As a member of a neighboring nation to Simpson's, I've always been aware of the power and agency of Kanien'kehá:ka women, both political and personal, because I don't think there is a division between the two in Indigenous thought. Comparisons made between the two societies often note that Kanien'kehá:ka women's political power is well documented in Rotinonhseshá:ka politics and governance and recognized as having influenced white feminism, whereas Michi Saagiig Nishnaabeg society is positioned as a "hunter and gatherer" society, particularly by historians and anthropologists, with an assumption that Michi Saagiig Nishnaabeg women certainly did not enjoy the same power and influence the Kanien'kehá:ka women had.[40]

To begin with, this is a profound misunderstanding of Michi Saagiig political systems and governance. The governance and political systems of so-called hunter and gatherer societies in general and the Nishnaabeg in particular remain profoundly misunderstood. Our rhythmic, seasonal, traveling throughout the territory gets positioned as "nomadic," rather than as a political and governing structure and process that facilitated a gentle and sustainable use of our lands and waters, a decentralized national leadership, and an intensification of personal and political relationships with a diversity of human and nonhuman nations.

Our system of governance is often talked about, even among ourselves, as the clan system. The clan system is a way of organizing society into different responsibilities and of intimately connecting people to animal nations. To me, the clan system is actually a series of systems or networks of relationships that was also, when intact, territorial. In Michi Saagiig Nishnaabeg territory, the three main original clans were Eagle (Toronto area), Caribou (southeast shore of Lake Ontario), and Crane (Peterborough area), with each clan holding particularly responsibilities for governance and for relationships to the animal nation they were akin to.[41] The so-called leadership clans were the Eagle and Crane clans, but my understanding is that this type of leadership was an emergent structure that appeared when needed, particularly to deal with international issues or issues that concerned more than one clan, and was based on a generated grounded power, rather than an appointed authoritarian power.[42] Decisions were made by generated consensus of clans and clan leaders, and therefore the people had a stake in making new understandings through participatory practices that provided deep engagement with the issues. Individuals were at the base of the political system—people were the foundation of the Nishnaabeg politic. Individuals were accountable for their own self-actualization and self-determination in relation to the spirit world and their responsibilities to their relations. These values and processes guided families and then clans, and while the processes for decision making might get more complicated, the values and basic processes remained the same across scales. Leadership appears decentralized and family based, but this is a rather simplistic conceptualization of it. Nishnaabeg live in a world that is profoundly influenced by the spirit world, particularly at this time. All of our political structures are plugged into the essence and real power of life that exists across time and space as worlds of nonhuman beings, some of which are spiritual beings and some of which are our Ancestors. Decision making and leadership in a highly networked, diffuse political system that is grounded in relationship to spiritual power have to be actively generated, sustained, and maintained within Indigenous bodies and the relationships that forms these hubs. Different manifestation of leadership lies in all Indigenous bodies. To eliminate an Nishnaabeg political system, you can't just storm a building and execute the leader, because networked political systems recover from this loss, quickly and easily. Several other relationshiped bodies will hold all of the knowledge and skill embodied in this one leader. To eliminate an Nishnaabeg political system, you have to attack the nodes of the network and in particular the nodes of the network that continually regenerate the network itself: Indigenous bodies. Rotinonhseshá:ka and Nishnaabeg political systems are different, but women hold agency, power, and influence within both. Colonial governments and settler colonial governments require the taking of land from Indigenous peoples to propel their capitalist economies. Every year, Canada needs more land and more resources, and that comes domestically entirely from Indigenous lands.

Simpson's talk affirms my refusal of the ongoing victim narrative that neoliberalism creates, and it places my generated knowledge as kwe as a critical intervention in Indigenous scholarship and politics. My body sovereignty is not subject to attack just because it is an Indigenous woman's body. My body sovereignty is subject to attack because it exists as an Nishnaabeg political order "that threatens forms of sovereignty to settler states." Therefore, if you are engaged in political theory, political science, governance, resurgence, or nation building, you simple cannot ignore the fact that the performance of settler governmentality in Canada and the United States is strategically gendered. To ignore this fact represents an intellectual dumbing down of scholarship and action, and it serves the state, not Indigenous nations.

My mom was born in 1945, and so at this point in the historic record things become more intensely personal. But that's the trick of colonialism and white supremacy. The greatest violent acts were not carried out on unknown, nameless, and faceless Indigenous peoples. They were carried out on our children and siblings and parents and grandparents, and on us. This didn't happen in the past, it's happening as I speak, to our families in real time, in real life. Colonialism is by its nature gendered, and therefore the Radical Resurgence Project must also center the voices of Indigenous children, women, and 2SQ peoples and critically examine and act in ways that not just deconstruct but destroy the power of heteropatriarchy while building the alternative. We have to viciously throw off the lies fed to us through schools about the foundations of Canada and struggle to understand and feel the violence and pure evil that took our lands from us. We first have to survive in order to escape. And we first have to escape (enough) before we can mobilize.

EIGHT
INDIGENOUS QUEER NORMATIVITY

> To be queer and native and alive is to repeatedly bear witness to worlds being destroyed, over and over again.
>
> —Billy-Ray Belcourt, "Can the Other of Native Studies Speak?"

MY FAMILY REGULARLY PARTICIPATES in sweat lodge ceremonies. My kids have grown up in this ceremony. This past summer, we came together in community as we always had. At the time, my daughter was questioning her gender and how to express it in a truthful way. She was not wearing skirts, or lace, or pink, or anything that said "girl." She was asking about gendered pronouns and what it exactly it means or doesn't mean to be a girl. She was dressing in boys' clothes and wearing a boy's bathing suit. She's growing up in ceremony, and she is well aware of the accepted protocols in our wider community and our families' ceremonial practices. Typically, the accepted protocols are that women wear skirts, sit on a particular side of the lodge, have responsibilities around water and berries, and do not participate in the ceremony while menstruating. The morning of the sweat, she didn't pack a skirt but her boy's bathing suit. She helped me put the cedar in the lodge and the berries in a wooden bowl (in some ceremonial communities this is a woman's role), and she helped with the fire (in some ceremonial communities this is a man's role). When it came time to go into the lodge, she sat in the circle with the rest of us, in between the men and the women. When the pipes came around, she smoked them. This was all normalized for her.[1] There was no discussion ahead of time or after (although we've had plenty of discussion over all of this for the past fifteen years). We just did things as, for her, they had normally been done. I felt proud of my community and my family and also sad in the realization of how uncommon her experience is right now. I thought about how crushed she would have been if someone had tried to make her wear a skirt or had discouraged her from fire keeping. If that had happened, I know the pain and hurt she might have felt might have been enough for her to remove herself from ceremony, maybe forever. I also know from listening and reading the stories of queer Indigenous youth that her experience is incredibly rare.[2] Queer youth are telling me that most often they get crushed. The toll of crushing on bodies, minds, and spirits is accumulative, diminishing, and restrictive. It also eliminates. It eliminates queer bodies from Indigenous spaces. It eliminates Indigenous bodies as political orders.

Their *Indigenous* worlds get destroyed.

This is so unacceptable to me within the ethical frameworks of Nishnaabeg grounded normativity, and also so unnecessary. It is also infuriating because while there are a lot of things we cannot fix right now, this is one of the things that we can collectively take on and make better. Right now.

At the very foundation of this story is the idea that my child has the responsibility of figuring out a meaningful way to live in the world that is consistent with her most intimate realities. The job of everyone else is not to direct or control that but to support her. This is a relationship between her and the spirit world. No one else has the right to interfere with that, unless it is causing great harm to someone else.[3] This is true for all Nishnaabeg people regardless of gender. We all have the responsibility to figure out how to become contributing members of our society while honoring our deepest truths, our gifts and skills, our clan affiliations, and our names. Self-actualization is a relationship between ourselves and the spirit world, and it is supposed to take place in the context of family and community.

We all have a relationship to creation. Alex Wilson, a scholar from Opaskwayak Cree Nation, says, "We call the moon grandmother and the earth mother in English, but in Cree this is not the case. What is important is the relational aspect acknowledging some kind of kinship. In Cree, land (aski) is not gendered. . . . Same for water. It's not gender but it has spirit of life and it's fluid."[4]

This is true in Nishnaabewin as well: the earth is Aki; the moon, dibik-giizis; the sun, giizis; the sky, giizhik. Although there is a heteronormative imposed gender often projected onto creation, this is only one telling, a telling that is reflective in my view of a Christianized relationship to the earth, rather than one that is more deeply reflective of Nishnaabeg ethics and practices.[5] Perhaps one of the most powerful community-based tool kits ever written on the subject, *Violence on the Land, Violence on Our Bodies: Building an Indigenous Response to Environmental Violence,* produced by the Women's Earth Alliance and the Native Youth Sexual Health Network, provides a simple exercise that can be used to consider one's relationship to all aspects of creation without gendering them. The exercise begins by asking participants to choose one particular aspect of the land—a river, the sky, and so on—and talk about it and their relationship to it without gendering it. The exercise emphasizes that we all have a relationship to creation and that these relationships are not tied to certain body parts. It centers the idea that creating life comes in many forms, not just from the womb, and it creates a space where all genders can have valuable, ethical, consensual, meaningful, and reciprocal relationships with all aspects of creation—which I believe is the point.[6]

My spiritual world is also benevolent and intelligent. Spiritual beings see the complications of colonialism that have asymmetrically targeted queer bodies because they've lived through this *with us,* because many of them are queer in sexual orientation, and most of them come from a time when our nation embodied queerness in formation, as practice, ethics, and process. The violence of heteropatriarchy, heteronormativity, and transphobia changes our lived context. I believe our Ancestors love us unconditionally and are willing to work with us so no Indigenous bodies feel the pain and hurt of exclusion, shame, or outright violence in our most intimate spaces. Not only have they consistently provided us with stories, song, and ceremonies that embody the concepts of consent, body sovereignty, freedom, and individual self-determination, they have repeatedly emphasized the ideas of compassion, empathy, and caring in everything they do. I believe my Ancestors and the spiritual beings I am in relationship with are brilliant and complex, and they are not going to strike me down because I didn't follow a "rule" about how I should approach them—this to me is how Christianity works, not Nishnaabewin. I'm going to be someone's Ancestor at some point, and that's certainly not OK with me.

We simply cannot accept a singular, shallow interpretation of Nishnaabeg thought and use it to shame, exclude, and degrade members of our nations. Our thought systems within grounded normativity are fluid, dynamic, and responsive, and it is our responsibility to practice grounded normativity in the way it was intended: to build strong societies of individuals who are functioning as their best selves. They also come from the land—the land that provides endless examples of queerness and diverse sexualities and genders.[7] We collectively have a responsibility to figure out how to make our spirituality relevant to *all* our people. That's the philosophical and practical challenge each generation inherits. I strongly believe, then, that I have a responsibility to interpret and live these practices in ways that do not replicate homophobia, transphobia, heterosexism, heteronormativity, and heteropatriarchy. I think nation building and resurgence cannot be meaningful otherwise.

Alex Wilson has been working on this issue for decades now, from within her own Cree grounded normativity. She is from Opaskwayak Cree Nation in Manitoba, a community that normalized queerness when she was growing up. She writes,

"In my community, the act of declaring some people special threatens to separate them from their community and creates an imbalance. Traditionally, two spirit people were simply a part of the entire community; as we reclaim our identity with this name, we are returning to our communities."[8] Over the years, when I've asked different Nishnaabeg elders about queerness, they often say that we didn't have that. Then when I ask if two women ever lived together intimately, without men, they will remember stories of queer couples, not as queer people, but just people who lived like that, as something that wasn't a big deal, as if it were a normal inconsequential part of life. What these elders and Alex are describing is a gender variance that existed in many Indigenous communities prior to the strategic implanting of the colonial gender binary. This imposed an artificial gender binary as a mechanism for controlling Indigenous bodies and identity and sets out two very clear genders: male and female. It lays out two sets of rigidly defined roles based on colonial conceptions of femininity and masculinity.[9] It then places colonial concepts of maleness and masculinity as more important than female and femininity and erases any variance. This is what heteropatriarchy needs to operate, and the more that heterosexual cisgendered Native men and women buy into the hierarchy and choose to reproduce and enforce violence, exclusion, and erasure, the better it works to divide and destroy the fabric of relationships that make up our nations. Heteropatriarchy isn't just about exclusion of certain Indigenous bodies, it is about the destruction of the intimate relationships that make up our nations, and the fundamental systems of ethics based on values of individual sovereignty and self-determination. The more destruction our intimate relationships carry, the more destruction our political systems carry, and the less we are able to defend and protect our lands, and the easier it is to dispossess.

2SQ Indigenous peoples flourished in many Indigenous nations and were highly visible to the first European "explorers." The archival and Western historical record sets down this visibility and the anti-queerness of these explorers, translators, traders, and missionaries in the 1600 and 1700s. Samuel de Champlain, Jacques Marquette, Baron de Lahontan, Jesuit priest Pierre-François Lafitau, Pierre François Xavier de Charlevoix, military interpreter and writer John Tanner, David Thompson and Alexander Henry, Charles MacKenzie, fur trader Ross Cox, and, later, photographer George Catlin are a few examples.[10] In *Narrative of the Captivity and Adventures of John Tanner during Thirty Years Residence among the Indians in the Interior of North America*, John Tanner describes Ozawendib (Yellowhead), from Leech Lake, as a visible 2SQ man with several intimate partners, or "husbands."[11] Tanner records the term *agokwa* as one that was used to describe Ozawendib. He also describes an elder and the Nishnaabeg community around Ozawendib using the pronoun "she" to address Ozawendib and notes that her sexuality, relationship orientation, and gender were accepted as normal.[12] Tanner also records his own anti-queerness, as he describes this beautiful scene as "disgusting."[13]

Joseph-François Lafitau was a French Jesuit missionary and ethnologist working in Rotinonhseshá:ka territory in the early part of the 1700s. In his major and often cited work published in Paris in 1724, *Customs of the American Indians Compared with the Customs of Primitive Times*, Lafitau "congratulates" missionaries for "suppressing" Indigenous queer relationships. He describes the missionaries' success in prompting many queer Indigenous people and their relations to see their identity as "shameful." He was pleased to report that after seventy-five years of missionary work, people once "regarded as extraordinary men," had now "come to be looked on, even by the Indians, with scorn."[14] Jesuit missionaries also counseled Indigenous parents of children who were not conforming to the colonial gender binary to force conformity.[15] This is significant to me because the book was published 1724, before the height of the residential schools system and the Indian Act, after seventy-five years of intense targeting of 2SQ people in Indigenous nations and communities within the reach of Jesuit missions.[16] By 1724, the Jesuits were boasting about the deliberate elimination of queer Indigenous peoples from our nations. Of course they were incorrect, because 2SQ people clearly resisted and found ways of living invisibly to co-lonial powers, or I couldn't have written this chapter.

Scott Lauria Morgensen's *Spaces between Us: Queer Settler Colonialism and Indigenous Decolonization* makes the point that in other parts of the Americas 2SQ people were eliminated by death, but that by the mid-nineteenth century in French and British Canada and in postrevolutionary New England, 2SQ people were "less singled out for violence than subjected with their communities to military attack, containment or removal."[17] He goes on to say that colonial institutions such as Indian agencies, missionary churches, and boarding schools noticed sexual and gender variance but "without needing to exact brute force violence, these institutions used disciplinary education to try and break Native communities, languages and cultural knowledges."[18] Given the amount of surveillance of "unchurched" relationships among Indigenous men and women on reserves by clergy, Indian agents, and Christianized Natives, as discussed in the previous chapter, I find it difficult to believe that this wouldn't also be the case for 2SQ people in our communities, whether or not there is documented evidence in Indian Affairs archives.[19] I'm also unsure that I see the difference between brute force and the extreme forms of gendered, sexualized, physical, and emotional violence and abuse suffered by Indigenous children in residential schools, violence I can only imagine was amplified the more a child expressed variance from the strict colonial gender binary. We have no statistics on the number of queer children that died in residential schools, died escaping residential schools, committed suicide as a result of their residential school experience, or were forced to live an invisible life because of residential school homophobia and shaming. Nor have we fully investigated the intergenerational impacts of the infusion of anti-queer violence into our communities and its impact on our political systems and nationhood as a result of residential schools. Further, nearly four hundred years after Lafitau's book, queer Indigenous youth are telling us very clearly that anti-queer violence is still a tremendous, horrific force in their lives.

Two Spirit elder Ma-Nee Chacaby, in her autobiography *A Two-Spirit Journey: The Autobiography of a Lesbian Ojibwa-Cree Elder,* recounts her childhood in Ombabika, a community in northwest Ontario. Chacaby remembers her grandmother explaining to her that she had two spirits as a young child. She used the term *niizhin ojiijaak* to describe a male and female spirit living inside a girl.[20] She explained that Nizhiin Ojiijaak girls were often drawn to activities that boys like, and she said that Niizhin Ojiijaak could choose not to marry, could marry someone of the opposite sex, or could marry someone of the same sex. She explained that Nizhiin Ojiijaak couples would adopt children who had lost their parents, that they sometimes had special healing or ceremonial responsibilities, and that it was her responsibility to figure out how to live her own life. Her grandmother also told her stories of Nizhiin Ojiijaak—two men living and raising children together, another woman who was responsible for making navigational marks on rocks—and Chacaby remembers meeting other Nizhiin Ojiijaak in Ombabika.[21]

All of this evidence points to what Two Spirit and queer people have always known from living as 2SQ in settler colonialism: 2SQ bodies and the knowledge and practices those bodies house as Indigenous political orders were seen as an extreme threat to settler society, sovereignty, dispossession, and the project of colonization, colonialism, and assimilation. The powerful relationships queer bodies house—consent, diversity, variance, spiritual power, community, respect, reciprocity, love, attachment—were the very first thing colonizers sought to eliminate, and they began celebrating what they thought was the genocide of 2SQ people in my nation long before colonization reached nations on the West Coast or in the north.

I had the privilege of hearing Alex talk about queerness and Indigeneity in my class on self-determination at Dechinta last year. Alex talked about how normalized gender variance in Indigenous communities was attacked and the gender binary was violently enforced through residential schools, day schools, and sanitariums, where children were separated into boys or girls, their hair forcibly cut, and their clothes changed to skirts or pants, and where they were punished for normal, healthy expressions of sexuality and gender expressions outside of the rigidity of Victorian masculinity and femininity. The gender binary was also reinforced through the Indian Act: only men could run for chief and council until 1950, marriage was defined in a heterosexual, monogamous way, and the rules for status and property were gendered and binarized. Indian agents forced English names on us, which also upheld the gender binary; a binary was also reinforced in the church, by anthropologists studying roles, and later by narrow interpretations of our own thought systems. Indian agents prevented the use of Nishnaabemowin and therefore the gender variance encoded in our language, and they policed the intimacy of Indigenous peoples, as described in the previous chapter, to promote heterosexual, monogamous relationships between cisgendered men and women to the exclusion of all other intimate partnerships. I thought about this as an attempt to break the network of intelligent relationships housed in Indigenous bodies in order to prevent the replication of Indigenous freedom, in order to get land. This is one way heteropatriarchy dispossesses, but it's not the only way.

While these actions caused the power and agency of all genders to shrink, those that are farthest away from colonial ideals suffered most and continue to be targets of harsh colonial violence. Remember Audra Simpson's characterization of Indigenous bodies as political orders. Queer Indigenous bodies are political orders. Queer Indigenous bodies house knowledge, relationships, and responsibilities. Queer Indigenous bodies are a threat to settler sovereignty, which is why queer Indigeneity has been and is violently targeted by colonial and settler colonial powers in an ongoing way in order to dispossess. Queer Indigenous bodies therefore also house and generate a wealth of theory and critical analysis regarding settler colonialism that straight bodies cannot. Engaging in anti-queerness, therefore, in all its various manifestations is tantamount in my mind to us consenting to and participating in autogenocide.

Queerness from within Nishnaabeg Thought

Naming the gender binary as colonial is important because when I think about this binary from within Nishnaabeg conceptual thought or from within the reality of so-called hunting and gathering societies, it makes no sense in terms of the ethical systems grounded normativity sets up. Further, it is at odds with the practicality of life in the bush because it restricts and prevents relationships, productivity, and, in many aspects, actual survival. If I am to be able to take care of myself on the land, I need to have a reciprocal and respectful relationship with all aspects of creation. I need to have a proficiency in hunting, fishing, gathering, making shelter, traveling, ceremony, warmth, light, and feeding and clothing myself and those reliant upon me. I cannot restrict myself to an exclusively gendered workload and just expect to survive.

The word *matriarch* in reference to Indigenous conceptualizations of power and gender makes no sense to me within Nishnaabeg thought because it reinforces a gender binary, it reinforces anthropological social constructions of Indigeneity, and it reinforces authoritarian power, rather than authentic grounded power. Nishnaabeg "women" hunted, trapped, fished, held leadership positions, and engaged in warfare, as well as carrying out domestic tasks and looking after children, and they were encouraged to show a broad range of emotions and to express their gender and sexuality in a way that was true to their own being, as a matter of *both principle and survival.*[22] Nishnaabeg "men" hunted, trapped, fished, held leadership positions, engaged in warfare, and also knew how to cook, sew, and look after children. They were encouraged to show a broad range of emotions and to express their gender and sexuality in a way that was true to their own being, as a matter of both principle and survival. This is true for other genders as well. And while there was often a gendered division of labor (one that I believe was exaggerated by anthropologists), there were also a lot of exceptions based on individual agency. The degree to which individuals engaged in each of these activities depended upon their name, their clan, their extended family, their skill and interest, and most importantly individual self-determination or agency.[23] Agency was valued, honored, and respected because it produced a diversity of highly self-sufficient individuals, families, and communities. This diversity of highly self-sufficient and self-determining people ensured survival and resilience that enabled the community to withstand difficult circumstances. This diversity was seen in everything; for instance, there are a diversity of ways to harvest and process wild rice, which vary between individuals, families, communities, and regions. The *how* looks different for different individuals, but as long as the practices produce cured rice in an efficient and ethical manner, they don't need to be all the same. In fact, it is better for long-term sustainability if they aren't, so we have a variety of solutions and knowledge before any problems show up.

While the intersections between queer theory and Indigenous Studies are interesting, I am more drawn to recovering how Indigenous theory, in my case how Nishnaabeg theory, conceptualizes gender or can conceptualize gender and sexual orientation because my sense is that my Ancestors lived in a society where what I know as "queer," particularly in terms of social organization, was so normal it didn't have a name.[24] I've thought a great deal about Alex Wilson's words quoted early in this chapter, and in my fiction writing I try to create story worlds where queerness is normalized. This is consistent with stories I've heard from queer and straight elders.[25] It's led me to consider what straightness looks like in societies where queerness is normalized, where difference isn't difference but normal. Queerness provides for and celebrates variance, including straightness, whereas heteropatriarchy sets out to destroy, control, and manipulate difference into hierarchies that position white, straight, cisgendered males as normal, and everyone else as less.

This kind of thinking is now marginalized within Nishnaabeg intelligence, and I'm the first to offer that my thinking on this may be different than the majority of my nation. I want to begin by looking broadly at our values about diversity, consent, self-determination, and noninterference, building upon the discussion I started in *Dancing on Our Turtle's Back*. Nishnaabeg thought directs me to respect and celebrate individual self-determination and diversity. Coercion in this way of thinking is a kind of exploitation. Coercing someone into wearing something they are not comfortable wearing, using gendered pronouns that they do not want us to use, erasing queerness from every corner of the universe, is not consistent with any Nishnaabeg teaching I've ever heard. In this way, I believe that within Nishnaabeg intelligence, or grounded normativity, we have the concepts and ethics to build Indigenous nations where queer people have body sovereignty, self-determination, influence, and freedom and bear crucial political orders, and where homophobia, transphobia, heterosexism, and heteronormativity are unacceptable. I don't accept the narrow, singular interpretations of our knowledge systems that lead to "tradition" steeped in dogma, exclusion, erasure, and violence, and I am not willing to replicate that in the beautiful Indigenous worlds we will create in the present and in the future. I can't be part of a movement or a ceremonial community that is interested in building worlds that will continue to destroy queer Indigenous youth.

In 2011, Darryl Dennis hosted an episode of CBC's *ReVision Quest* on the theme of being Indigenous 2SQ people. I remember pulling over on the side of the highway and listening as he interviewed Nishnaabemowin (our language) expert Roger Roulette, Alex, and many others in his exploration of what it means to be "queer and Indigenous." Seven and a half minutes into the episode, Roulette explained some of the nonjudgmental terminology we have in Nishnaabemowin regarding queerness:

> wiijidaamaagan means s/he co-habits with a person;
> wiipemaagan means s/he sleeps with a person and
> wiijiiwaagan means a friend or companion; according
> to Roger's uncle . . . a gay person is described as wii-
> jininiimaagan—a man whose partner is another man;
> wiijikwemaagan is a woman with a female partner—the
> word has no judgment in it.[26]

Roulette also explained to the host that gender was not exclusively bound to certain roles in life, "it was determined more by
a child's natural inclinations rather than whether baby clothes
were pink or blue, and in some places these survived right up
into modern times."[27] I felt relieved that Roulette had confirmed
something that I had learned from a variety of elders but that
still somehow remains on the margins: that this rigid gender binary of male/female was brought to us under colonialism and
exists in tension to some of our core values and ethics, or at least
to some interpretations of our core values and ethics.[28] Similarly,
Nishnaabeg historian Anton Treuer writes:

> [Sex] usually determined one's gender and, therefore,
> one's work, but the Ojibwe accepted variation. Men
> who chose to function as women were called *ikwekaazo,*
> meaning "one who endeavors to be like a woman."
> Women who functioned as men were called *ininiikaazo,*
> meaning "one who endeavors to be like a man." . . . Their
> mates were not considered *ikwekaazo* or *ininiikaazo,*
> however, because their function in society was still in
> keeping with their sex [gender]. If widowed, the spouse
> of an *ikwekaazo* or *ininiikaazo* could remarry someone
> of the opposite sex or another *ikwekaazo* or *ininiikaazo.*
> The *ikwekaazowag* worked and dressed like women.
> *Ininiikaazowag* worked and dressed like men. Both were
> considered to be strong spiritually, and they were always
> honored, especially during ceremonies.[29]

Nishnaabeg playwright Waawaate Fobister uses the term recorded by Tanner, *agokwe,* in his critically acclaimed play of
the same name to describe gender variance and a gay male sexual orientation in a similar way. Waawaate translates the term
to mean a "wise woman," "two spirit," and "woman within a
man."[30] Some 2SQ people in the Nishnaabeg community also
use the term *agokwe-ininito* to refer to gender variance and a
lesbian sexual orientation, although my understanding of Nishnaabeg gender and sexual orientation is that we continue to express both qualities along a spectrum of variance.[31]

Later in the day, I returned home to my family and continued reading to my kids out loud from Nishnaabeg writer Louise Erdrich's Birchbark House series. This is Erdrich's juvenile fiction series and includes *The Birchbark House, The Game of Silence, The Porcupine Year,* and *Chickadee.* The series begins in the mid-1800s and follows an Nishnaabeg family living on an island in Lake Superior through three generations of living out an Nishnaabeg existence in an era of increasing settler surveillance and violence. Erdrich has carefully crafted a world that replicates the one so cherished in Nishnaabeg oral tradition, and this makes these novels both a gift and a masterpiece.

Erdrich's work is also an important reflection of the relationship between Nishnaabeg children and adults, and one that with a few exceptions is consistent with my understanding of this relationship coming through the oral tradition.[32] Children were afforded a lot of freedom and agency within their own lives. *The Porcupine Year,* for instance, begins with a story about two children, twelve-year-old Omakayas, the main character of the series, and her younger brother, Pinch, out night hunting for deer in a canoe. This in itself demonstrates a high level of skill (canoeing, firearms, navigation, hunting), self-determination (these two children are the decision makers), and trust from adults in their family. As in any good story, after the children are caught in the confluence of two rivers and whisked over rapids, they are forced to use their intelligence to take care of each other and make it back to their family.[33]

Similarly, the character Two Strikes clearly demonstrates that difference and diversity were both valued and fostered within Nishnaabeg practices. Two Strikes, while identified in the novels as a girl, takes up the responsibilities of hunting, trapping, and physically defending the family from a young age. The family, in fact, her extended family and community, not only makes room for her, but they support, nurture, and appreciate the gifts and contributions she makes to their community. She is an excellent shot and without question the best hunter and protector of her generation. She refuses to participate in the culture of women, whether its work, ceremonial responsibilities, or political responsibilities. She behaves and lives out the responsibilities of men, and rather than coercing or shaming her into the responsibilities of women, her family steps back and supports her expression of herself, in part because it is her responsibility to figure out how to live authentically in the world and in her family. Two Strikes chooses not to wear skirts and not to participate in girls' puberty rituals, because her path is different. Her relationship to the spirit world is a powerful one, which her family supports her in and influences, but they also have tremendous respect for her own agency within that relationship.

My daughter doesn't particularly like Two Strikes as a character, and neither do I, primarily because Two Strikes isn't written as a particularly lovable character. She is bossy, obnoxious, and mean, and she is also strong, uncompromising, and persistent. I wish the one gender "nonconforming" Nishnaabeg character my kid has read about was not written as someone who takes on the worst aspects of colonial masculinity as her queer identity, and I wish the gender fluidity that I know is part of my nation was written into all the characters. I wish my children were growing up surrounded by stories and literature written *by and for 2SQ people* that include trans kids as characters who are loving, brilliant queer Indigenous peoples.

Anti-Queerness as Autogenocide

This idea of supporting an individual's responsibility to self-actualize and find their own path with regard to their life's work, their gender expression, their sexual identity, their relationship orientation, and all other aspects of life is something I have repeatedly experienced within Nishnaabeg society, particularly among those practitioners who are engaged with the complexities of our ancient philosophies, as opposed to people, like myself, who are very much engaged in a process of reclamation and decolonization. I have also witnessed this in other Indigenous nations. When an individual asserts their identity, it is the community's job to make room and support that assertion. I have also of course seen the opposite of this, particularly directed toward women and 2SQ people, when rigidity and singular interpretations of protocols and rituals are used to exclude individuals and communities of people. Exclusion has been more common in my experience then inclusion. I find this extraordinarily problematic and inconsistent with my understanding of Nishnaabeg thought because while I am well aware of these teachings and protocols, there is another set of practices that are ignored when women and 2SQ people are excluded from ceremonies or pressured into wearing skirts. I understand that I am responsible for how I perform and interpret these practices and that responsibility is between me and the spirit world. I don't blindly accept that elders or ceremonial leaders can dictate that for me (nor do they ask me to). They can certainly offer perspectives and advice, but ultimately I am responsible for how I conduct myself, and this is dependent upon my own personal relationship with the spiritual realm. I might have a responsibility to share skirt wearing or moon time practices with other self-identified women, but it is up to them to determine which practices they will animate in their life, and if I'm upholding Nishnaabeg practices of love, gentleness, and respect for individual self-determination, then I must also practice an ethic of noninterference, nonjudgment, and nonshaming.

Resurgence, though, is not just about bringing queer individuals into straight Indigenous spaces. Queer Indigeneity cannot be reduced to just sexual orientation. It is about a web of supportive, reciprocal, generative relationships that we often do not have names for in English and that exist outside of the hierarchy and the imagination of heteropatriarchy—a hierarchy that places the relationship of cisgendered, married, monogamous men and women at the top, and de-emphasizes or erases all other relationships. Ceremonies, ritual, social organization, and mobilization that replicate this invisibility and hold up the hierarchy also center heteropatriarchy. Radical resurgence is then about the destruction of the colonial hierarchy that heteropatriarchy embeds in us, our communities, and our nations, and restoring all Indigenous bodies as political orders within our political systems and nationhood.

Centering Queerness in Resurgence

Two Spirit scholar Dana Wesley spent a considerable amount of time for her master's thesis, titled *Reimagining Two-Spirit Community: Critically Centering Narratives of Urban Two-Spirit Youth,* listening to Two Spirit youth. She concludes her work with a challenge to the broader Indigenous nation-building community:

> In my personal experiences during the beginning of the Idle No More movement, I noticed that it became a bit of a trend to include Two-Spirit when talking about women and children in relation to nationhood and sovereignty. At first glance it appeared to be a step in the right direction, in that there was recognition of Two-Spirit people (as well as of women and children) among Indigenous people who were challenging hetero-patriarchy and heteropaternalism in conversation with each other about nation building. Unfortunately, the conversation often stopped short of any kind of real engagement with Two-Spirit people. In my experience I did not witness any Two-Spirit people take part in Idle No More as representatives of Two-Spirit leadership. In Indigenous social and activist spaces, I have witnessed a pattern wherein Two-Spirit people are invoked by gestures to inclusion in the absence of any meaningful Two-Spirit involvement. Essentially, Two-Spirit has become a buzzword to include in speeches and presentations, but there is no follow-through on how to support Two-Spirit people within their own Indigenous communities. There is still no mention of Two-Spirit roles or of how essential they are to Indigenous communities. If Indigenous people want to have real conversations about nationhood, then there have to be serious efforts made to foster relationships between Two-Spirit people and wider Indigenous communities. If our leaders, academics, teachers, clan mothers, elders and medicine people

are serious about the idea that we are all related, and that nation-building is how we are going to decolonize our minds and communities, then there has to be more than just lip-service recognition of Two-Spirit existence. Creating real connections with Two-Spirit people means asking them what matters to them in relation to nation building.[34]

There are several important truths in this paragraph. Wesley is speaking back to a particular problem in Indigenous political mobilizations in general: the replication of anti-queerness through the erasure of 2SQ people from the leadership of these movements; the superficial gesturing toward 2SQ issues in organizing, presentations, and scholarship; and a lack of conversations with, or perhaps of listening to, the 2SQ community in nation-building exercises. She issues us a challenge. If nation building is how we are going to decolonize, then we have to ask 2SQ people what matters to them. I'd add that we need to do more than consult. We need to listen, hear, and center 2SQ people in nation building. To do otherwise is to dream Indigenous realities where we position queerness not as normal, as Alex Wilson practices, but as special and outside of the collective grounded normativity that generates us.

The contributions of Indigenous Two Spirit and queer organizers under the banner of Idle No More are also tremendous, and I want to be careful here to not erase the hard and often behind-the-scenes work of these organizers and the willingness of the Idle No More organization (www.idlenomore.ca) to address these issues within the organization. Several active chapters are led by 2SQ activists, the communications team of the organization includes many 2SQ leaders, the majority of Idle No More webinars have included 2SQ voices, and when INM was invited to meet with James Anaya (UN Special Rapporteur on the Rights of Indigenous Peoples), they used their entire allotted time to bring forward the issue of homophobia and suicide in the Two Spirit community. These are tremendous contributions to Indigenous movement building and organizing and are a result of years of hard work, sacrifice, and organizing on the part of the 2SQ community.[35]

I've thought a lot about the idea of queering resurgence and nation building throughout my life because I don't fit neatly into the colonial gender binary and the heterosexual, monogamous relationships it demands. It has never been the center of my work in part because I think there are brilliant queer Indigenous writers, scholars, and activists who are doing a better job of articulating these issues than I am, and because I've been in a long-term heterosexual relationship that bestows upon me privilege those in queer primary relationships do not have. I worry, though, that collectively we're not hearing or seeing the work of these brilliant queer Indigenous writers, scholars, and activists. I worry that Indigenous feminisms are sometimes too influenced by mainstream white, straight feminism. I worry that Indigenous masculinities reinforce the colonial gender binary, centering cisgendered straight men (who are already centered in everything) instead of dismantling heteropatriarchy, and that the binary set up between feminisms and masculinities casts queer people out, so they have to continually *come in*, because worlds have been constructed by straight Indigenous peoples that leave queer Indigenous thought out. I worry that Indigenous theory gets positioned in the past as unable to explain or generate queer Indigeneity in the present. I know that if we have to worry that we don't have enough queer voices on the panel or enough queer voices in the book, then we've already failed because we've constructed Indigenous worlds where 2SQ have to come in because anti-queerness placed 2SQ outside. This was clear to me at the 2015 meeting of the Native American Indigenous Studies Association annual meeting when hundreds of people showed up to hear the panel I was on, discussing *Red Skin, White Masks*, and a handful of people, who for the most part all knew each other, showed up to hear the queer Indigenous youth roundtable.

Queering resurgence begins for me by recognizing Alex's normalization of queerness within her community, by acknowledging, as Roger Roulette does, the normal descriptive terminology used to recognize queer relationships, and by looking at how gender is conceptualized and actualized within Nishnaabeg thought. I think Nishnaabeg thought is queer, and if we're doing it correctly, we shouldn't have to queer resurgence, because the political, ethical, and social organization that the 2SQ Indigenous community has held onto and protected so fiercely would already be centered. Queer Indigeneity has a place for straightness, and that's why we should center it.

The Skirt. Again.

The question I have been asked over and over again since the publication of *Dancing on Our Turtle's Back* is if I wear a skirt to ceremony. I deliberately didn't answer the question in that book because my point was to emphasize the process I went through to critically think about protocols and dogma in ceremonial practice, and to encourage others to do the same. I've made that point, and the repeated asking of this question tells me I need to be more clear.

I've been participating in Nishnaabeg ceremonies for about twenty-five years now across our territory. Different ceremonial leaders have different practices, which is part of the beautiful diversity of being us. I tend to think deeply about our practices and why we do the things we do. I think ceremony is everyone, and that every Nishnaabeg body and mind has a place in our circle, because I understand the point of ceremony to be to connect to the spiritual world in a good way, and to do so requires an open heart.

Over my life, I have seen us reclaiming our practices as Nishnaabeg. I think that's a beautiful thing to be doing. I think that's a critical thing to be doing. Knowing protocols is a way of showing we belong. But the more time I've spent language learning, on the land, and hanging out with elders, the less I think of rigid protocols and the more I think of relationships. In ceremony, I think the most important thing is that the group of people who have come together feel safe, respected, and openhearted as a necessary prerequisite to spiritual connection. That to me is the point of ceremony.

We have some important practices and stories in regard to skirt wearing for women. We have some ceremonial leaders that have very rigid protocols concerning gender. I have seen women and girls pressured into wearing skirts and excluded if they don't feel comfortable doing so. I have been pressured into wearing a skirt in order to participate. I have also seen the opposite. I have seen the skirt-wearing stories shared and ceremonial leaders adding that it is up to individuals to decide what they wear. In my own life, I mostly work with elders who believe that consent, respect for individual self-determination, diversity, and noninterference—basic Nishnaabeg values—are more important than rigid protocols.

Sometimes I think in our desire to reclaim what we've lost, we hold onto rules and protocols too tightly and forget that our way of life is about relationships—the practice of benevolent relationships. I often think of stories of ricing when I think about things like this. So-and-so used to rice from the back of the canoe. That family always sat in the front of the canoe. Old Kokum refused to use the sticks and only used her hands. Those guys used to duck hunt at the same time. Crazy old so-and-so built himself snowshoes and walked over the beds. We all did things slightly differently but in the context of shared values. I think ceremony is the same. Our communities hold so many, often hilarious stories of individuals doing things differently and being supported and cherished by the rest of the community. A particular incident also stands out in my mind from my experiences in Long Lake #58 First Nation. An elder told me that he didn't always have enough money to purchase tobacco when he went out hunting. Instead of tobacco, he would gift the animal whatever he had with him of value, which oftentimes, he explained, was a piece of his baloney sandwich. He felt that the animal spirit would understand his intent and accept this gift in the spirit it had been intended. These tiny rememberings are instructive to me.

In my own life, I don't always feel comfortable wearing a skirt, particularly if I am being pressured. Indigenous bodies, my body, have been a target for violence under colonialism and settler colonialism for four centuries. We were forced to wear skirts in residential schools, at church, and in missions in order to assimilate us from being Nishnaabeg women into the ideals of settler housewives. I was forced to wear a skirt or dress to church. Under colonialism the skirt has been and still is in many cases a tool of oppression. My body remembers this.

I believe that my Ancestors and the spiritual world are aware of this. I have been taught that they love us unconditionally and that they are brilliant. I believe that they are benevolent and that "tradition" can change and adapt to the needs of the people. I believe it is important to reclaim our foundational ethics of consent, noninterference, respect for self-determination, and diversity.

I have been in ceremonies where all genders are welcomed and cherished, where some people wear skirts and others do not, where trans people and gender nonconforming folks are normalized, and where community pipes are smoked by everyone. These have been some of the beautiful, powerful, and gentle places of my life. This to me is the purpose of ceremony. At every point in the day, there is a different amount of light—it is not just day and night. Our circles are not just men and women. There is an endless amount of diversity in our communities. I want us to stop policing and judging and excluding and start to build the kinds of communities that would make our Ancestors proud. Our philosophies are far more complex than you can't come to ceremony if you're not in a skirt.

I'm not going to take my kids into ceremonial places where their gender expressions are not honored and appreciated, and in my own life, I am committed to creating ceremonial spaces where all Indigenous bodies are celebrated. I think that's the intelligent decision. When I see women wearing pants at ceremonies, I believe that they are wearing teachings of diversity, consent, and respect for body sovereignty. When I see queer, transgendered, and gender nonconforming Nishnaabeg at ceremony, I am reminded of 2SQ political orders and brilliance. My favorite ceremonies are ones where I see women wearing skirts to honor those teachings, where I see women wearing pants to honor different teachings—where I see the full range of gender variance working together for a better future.

The heteropatriarchy of settler colonialism has regulated the bodies of Indigenous women and 2SQ people, and trans people particularly, to death. We live in a vat of heteropatriarchal violence. In this reality, gendered practices that once existed in a different context no longer generate the same intimate relationships in a settler colonial context, at the very least, not for everyone. In our current practices of Nishnaabewin, we simple do not publically regulate cisgendered heterosexual men's and boys' clothing or their bodies, particularly their reproductive body parts. Yet, we ask women and girls to publically exclude themselves when they are menstruating from many of our ceremonies, and we are continually regulating 2SQ bodies and relentlessly regulating trans bodies. The explanation for excluding menstruating women is that we are "too powerful" because we are cleansing ourselves. I've thought a lot about this over the years. No one, at any time, spiritual leader or otherwise, has ever asked me if I hold spiritual power when I am menstruating. I have felt and been spiritually powerful at several points in my life, so I am well aware of what that feels like. This isn't tied to menstruation for me. Further, I don't consent to discussing the intimate cycles of my body as a prerequisite for participating in a ceremony, particularly when men are not asked to do the same. I do know how this makes me feel, regardless of how this is explained to me. I do know that I do not feel valued, included, or powerful when my body is regulated. I don't feel respected when I'm honored as a "life giver" and not as an intellectual. For me, this regulation is a clear imposition on my own agency, sovereignty, self-determination, and freedom. It is a gendered regulation that controls women and 2SQ people and our spiritual power, and it prevents me from relating and attaching to the spiritual realm.

I understand the purpose of Nishnaabeg spiritual practices is to demonstrate respect to the spirits, to engage in rituals that infuse ceremony with meaning, to create a unity of purpose within the ceremonial group, and to engage with the spiritual world, and so sometimes I wear a skirt to ceremonies and sometimes I do not. Sometimes I can wear it and be open spiritually, and sometimes I cannot, because I have grown up a target of heteropatriarchy and the skirt is a loaded symbol of white male power for me. Sometimes I wear jeans because that's what I'm comfortable doing. Sometimes I wear jeans to demonstrate to youth that ceremony is about what is inside, not about what you wear, and to make space for them. Sometimes I wear pants so that I'm the person who has to negotiate with the women who have boxes of skirts in their cars or the ceremonial leader that is excluding, so younger people, including my kids, don't have to. When I am a visitor in other Indigenous peoples' territories, I tend to follow the practices of the people I am with because I believe it is their place, not mine, to find ways to practice their grounded normativities without holding up heteropatriarchy. I also have these discussions with my comrades in their territories, and they have often already figured out how to do this. In my own practice, I explain skirt and moon time practices to people new to our ceremony, and let them know that they will be supported however they choose to interpret these practices. I don't think anyone—straight or 2SQ—should be coerced into wearing skirts. I think it is actually *extremely easy* to remove the gender binary and exclusionary protocols from ceremonies and recenter them in practices of consent, diversity, noninterference, and intent, and I believe it is these practices and these relationships that should be the basis of our ceremonial life, our lives, our moments, and our nation building.

I don't like the word *protocols*.[36] Ceremony is our birthright, straight and queer. Protocols, like laws, are rigid rules. I like the word *practices* because practices are relationships. If we have not grown up with our practices, one of the first things we can reclaim is protocols: wear a long skirt, walk around the circle in a clockwise direction, don't blow out the sage, and so on. Enacting protocols is a way of belonging. It is a very simple way to say that "I know the rules" and therefore I belong. Which on one hand I like. I like it when people feel they belong; our people should feel like they belong. On the other hand, protocols make a lot of our people feel like they don't belong, including myself, and that's very problematic because it isn't congruent with the fundamental philosophical underpinnings of Nishnaabeg thought.

Breaking Indigenous peoples' spiritual connection to each other and to land is a critical part of dispossession. Breaking Indigenous peoples' social and spiritual mechanisms for processing trauma, for comfort, and for connecting to a higher power is critical in demobilizing our responses to colonial violence. This creates generations in some places of Indigenous peoples that have grown up without relationships to the implicate order, and we feel ashamed about that. As we re-embed ourselves in this system, we have to confront fear, shame, and anxiety and the idea that we are not good enough to be here among our ceremonial leaders. We have to confront the idea that we may be made to feel we don't belong, and we have to stop practicing interpretations of Nishnaabewin that cast people out. We don't exist unless we all belong. We all belong.

Cree poet and scholar Billy-Ray Belcourt recently shared this poem on his blog, *nakinisowin,* and I am sharing it here with his permission:

sacred

a native man looks me in the eyes as he refuses to hold my hand during a round dance. i pretend that his pupils are like bullets and i wonder what kind of pain he's been through to not want me in this world with him anymore. and i wince a little because the earth hasn't held all of me for quite some time now and i am lonely in a way that doesn't hurt anymore.

you see, a round dance is a ceremony for both grief and love and each body joined by the flesh is encircled by the spirits of ancestors who've already left this world. i ask myself how many of them never knew what desire tasted like because they loved their kookums more than they loved themselves.

i dance with my arm hanging by my side like an

appendage my body doesn't want anymore. the gap between him and i keeps getting bigger so i fill it with the memories of native boys who couldn't be warriors because their bodies were too fragile to carry all of that anger. the ones who loved in that reckless kind of way. you know, when you give up your body for him.

and i think about the time an elder told me to be a man and to decolonize in the same breath. there are days when i want to wear nail polish more than i want to protest. but then i remember that i wasn't meant to live life here and i paint my nails because 1) it looks cute and 2) it is a protest. and even though i know i am too queer to be sacred anymore, i dance that broken circle dance because i am still waiting for hands who want to hold mine too.[37]

My immediate response to reading this was heartbreak, and the line "too queer to be sacred" stayed with me. I wanted to shout "so queer, so sacred." Radical Indigenous resurgence and Indigenous life cannot destroy the worlds of queer youth. Our responsibility is to hold each other up. We have to be the safe place. We have to build that future. Queer Indigenous youth are our teachers and our most precious theorists, even though they shouldn't have to be. They have experiences with acute hetero-patriarchy as expansive dispossession. They hold part of the theory Indigenous nations need to escape settler colonialism. We need to listen.

NINE
LAND AS PEDAGOGY

OVER THE PAST FEW YEARS, I've spent a lot of time each March in the sugar bush. The practice of harvesting sap and making maple syrup has been a foundational experience for me and my family. The following Michi Saagiig Nishnaabeg story was told to me by Doug Williams. This is my own retelling of it, and it is one of the ways I tell it in March, when my family and I are in the sugar bush, making maple syrup. This story has been published by various authors over the years.[1] I have told different versions over the years. Nearly every time I tell it, I understand new meanings and make new connections.

The main character in this version of the story is Binoojiinh. Binoojiinh means child. Previous versions of this story have the main character as a boy and a girl.[2] This story is republished here with the main character a gender-nonconforming child choosing to use the pronouns *they* and *their*. This changes the context of the story. I am repeating this story here deliberately to make the point that it is crucial we tell stories in a way that draws every member of our community into the stories, and to demonstrate the intelligence we all miss when we continue to uphold the colonial gender binary.

Binoojiinh Makes a Lovely Discovery

Binoojiinh is out walking in the bush one day
It is Ziigwan[3]
the lake is opening up
the goon was finally melting
they are feeling that first warmth of spring on their cheeks
"Nigitchi nendam," they are thinking, "I'm happy."

Then that Binoojiinh who is out walking
collecting firewood for their Doodoom
decides to sit under Ninaatigoog
maybe just stretch out
maybe just have a little rest
maybe gather firewood a little later
"Owah, Nigitchi nendam nongom.
I'm feeling happy today," says that Binoojiinh.

And while that Binoojiinh
is lying down, and looking up
they see Ajidamoo up in the tree
"Bozhoo Ajidamoo! I hope you had a good winter."
"I hope you had enough food cached."
But Ajidamoo doesn't look up because she's already busy.
She's not collecting nuts.
Gawiin.
She's not building her nest
Gawiin, not yet.
She's not looking after any young.
Gawiin, too early.
She's just nibbling on the bark, and then doing some
    sucking.

Nibble, nibble suck.
Nibble, nibble suck.
Nibble, nibble, suck.
Nibble, nibble, suck.

Binoojiinh is feeling a little curious.
So they do that too, on one of the low branches.

Nibble, nibble suck.
Nibble, nibble suck.
Nibble, nibble, suck.
Nibble, nibble, suck.

MMMMMMMMmmmmmm.
This stuff tastes good.
It's real, sweet water.
MMMMmmmmmmmmmm.

Then Binoojiinh gets thinking
and they make a hole in that tree
and they make a little slide for
that sweet water to run down
they make a quick little container
out of birch bark, and
they collect that sweet water
and they take that sweet water home
to show their mama.

That doodoom is excited and they have three hundred
  questions:

"Ah Binoojiinh, what is this?"
"Where did you find it?"
"Which tree?"
"Who taught you how to make it?"
"Did you put semaa?"
"Did you say miigwech?"
"How fast is it dripping?"
"Does it happen all day?"
"Does it happen all night?"
"Where's the firewood?"

Binoojiinh tells their doodoom the story,
She believes every word
because they are her Binoojiinh
and they love each other very much.
"Let's cook the meat in it tonight,
it will be lovely sweet."

"Nahow."
"Nahow."

So they cooked that meat in that sweet water
it was lovely sweet
it was extra lovely sweet
it was even sweeter than just that sweet water.

The next day, Binoojiinh takes their mama
to that tree and their mama brings Kokum
and Kokum brings all the Aunties, and
there is a very big crowd of Michi Saagiig Nishnaabe-
    kwewag
and there is a very big lot of pressure
Binoojiinh tells about Ajidamoo
Binoojiinh does the nibble nibble suck part.

At first there are technical difficulties
and none of it works.
but Mama rubs Binoojiinh's back
she tells Binoojiinh that she believes them anyway
they talk about lots of variables like heat and temperature
    and time
then Giizis comes out and warms everything up
and soon its drip, drip, drip, drip.
those Aunties go crazy
Saasaakwe!
dancing around
hugging a bit too tight
high-kicking
and high-fiving
until they take it back home
boil it up
boil it down
into sweet, sweet sugar.

Ever since, every Ziigwan
those Michi Saagiig Nishnaabekwewag

collect that sweet water
and boil it up
and boil it down
into that sweet, sweet sugar
all thanks to Binoojiinh and their lovely discovery,
and to Ajidamoo and her precious teaching
and to Ninaatigoog and their boundless sharing.

Given Lovingly to Us by the Spirits

Nishnaabe scholar Wendy Makoons Geniusz translates the word *gaa-izhi-zhaawendaagoziyaang* as "given lovingly to us by the spirits."[4] This describes the gift of maple sap and the process of making sugar so perfectly. This spring, while tapping a stand of maple trees, I remembered that the story of Binoojiinh is one of my favorite stories. It's one of my favorites because nothing violent happens in it. At every turn, Binoojiinh is met with very basic, core Nishnaabeg values—love, compassion, and understanding. They center their day around their own freedom and joy. I imagine myself at age seven running through a stand of maples with the first warmth of spring marking my cheeks. I imagine everything good in the world. My heart, my mind, and my spirit are open and engaged, and I feel as if I could accomplish anything. I imagine myself grasping at feelings I haven't felt before, that maybe life is so good that it is too short, that there really isn't enough time to love everything.

In reality, I have to image myself in this situation because as a child, I don't think I was ever in a similar situation. My experience of education from kindergarten to graduate school was one of coping with someone else's agenda, curriculum, and pedagogy, someone who was not interested in my well-being as a girl, my connection to my homeland, my language or history, or my Nishnaabeg intelligence. No one ever asked me what I was interested in, nor did they ask for my consent to participate in their system. My experience of education was one of continually being measured against a set of principles that required surrender to an assimilative colonial agenda in order to fulfill those principles. I distinctly remember being in grade three at a class trip to the sugar bush and the teacher showing us two methods of making maple syrup: the pioneer method, which involved a black pot over an open fire and clean sap, and the "Indian method," which involved a hollowed-out log in an unlit fire with large rocks in the log to heat the sap up—sap that had bark, insects, dirt, and scum. The teacher asked us which method we would use, and being the only Native kid in the class, I was the only one who chose the "Indian method."

Things are different for this Binoojiinh. They have already spent seven years immersed in a nest of Nishnaabeg intelligence. They already understand the importance of observation and learning from our animal teachers when they watch the squirrel so carefully and then mimic its actions. They understand embodiment and conceptual thought when they then take this observation and apply it to their own situation—by making a cut in the maple tree and using a cedar shunt. They rely upon their own creativity to invent new technology. They patiently wait for the sap to collect. They take that sap home and share it with their family. Their mother, in turn, meets her child's discovery with love and trust. Binoojiinh watches as their mama uses the sap to boil the deer meat for supper. When they taste the deer and the sweetness, they learn about reduction, and when their mama and they go to clean the pot, they learn about how sap can be boiled into sugar. Binoojiinh then takes their elders to the tree, already trusting that they will be believed, that their knowledge and discovery will be cherished, and that they will be heard.

Binoojiinh learned a tremendous amount over a two-day period—self-led, driven by both their own curiosity and their own personal desire to learn. They learned to trust themselves, their family, and their community. They learned the sheer joy of discovery. They learned how to interact with the spirit of the maple. They learned both *from* the land and *with* the land. They learned what it felt like to be recognized, seen, and appreciated by their community. They *came to know* maple sugar with the support of their family and elders. They come to know maple sugar in the context of love.

To me, this is what coming into wisdom within a Michi Saagiig Nishnaabeg epistemology looks like. It takes place in the context of family, community, and relation. It lacks overt coercion and authority, values so normalized within mainstream, Western pedagogy that they are rarely ever critiqued. The land, Aki, is both context and process. The process of coming to know is learner led and profoundly spiritual in nature.[5] Coming to know is the pursuit of whole-body intelligence practiced in the context of freedom, and when realized collectively, it generates generations of loving, creative, innovative, self-determining, interdependent, and self-regulating community-minded individuals. It creates communities of individuals with the capacity to uphold and move forward our political practices and systems of governance.

I am using Binoojiinh's story here in the same way it is used within Nishnaabeg intelligence, as a theoretical anchor whose layered and diverse meanings are revealed over time and space within individual and collective Nishnaabeg consciousness. A "theory" in its simplest form is an explanation of a phenomenon, and Nishnaabeg stories in this way form part of the theoretical basis of our intelligence. But theory also works a little differently within Nishnaabeg thought. "Theory" is generated and regenerated continually through embodied practice and within each family, community, and generation of people. Theory isn't just an intellectual pursuit. It is woven within kinetics, spiritual presence, and emotion. It is contextual and relational. It is intimate and personal with individuals themselves holding the responsibilities for finding and generating meaning within their own lives.

Most important, theory isn't just for academics; it's for everyone, and so the story of maple sugar gets told to (some of) our kids almost from birth. Theory within this context is generated from the ground up, and its power stems from its living resonance within individuals and collectives. Younger citizens might first just understand the literal meaning. As they grow, they can put together the conceptual meaning, and with more experience with our knowledge system, the metaphorical meaning.

Then they start to apply the processes and practices of the story in their own lives (when I have a problem, I'll call my aunties or my grandparents), and "meaning-making becomes an inside phenomenon."[6] After they live each stage of life through the story, they then can communicate their lived wisdom through six or seven decades of lived experience and shifting meaning. This is how our old people teach. They are our geniuses because they know that wisdom is generated from the ground up, that meaning is for everyone, and that we're all better when we're able to derive meaning out of our lives and be our best selves.[7] Stories direct, inspire, and affirm an ancient code of ethics.[8] If you do not know what it means to be intelligent within Nishnaabeg realities, then you can't see the epistemology, the pedagogy, the conceptual meaning, or the metaphor, or how this story has references to other parts of our oral tradition, or how this story is fundamentally, like all of our stories, communicating different interpretations and realizations of an Nishnaabeg worldview.

It is critical to avoid the assumption that this story takes place in precolonial times because Nishnaabeg conceptualizations of time and space present an ongoing intervention to linear thinking. This story happens in various incarnations all over our territory every year in March when the Nishnaabeg return to the sugar bush. Binoojiinh's presence (and the web of kinship relations that they are composed of) is complicated by their fraught relationality to the tenacity of settler colonialism,[9] and their very presence simultaneously shatters the disappearance of Indigenous women and girls and Two Spirit and queer people from settler consciousness. They also escape the rigidity of colonial gender binaries by having influence and agency within their family, while physically disrupting settler colonial commodification and ownership of the land through the implicit assumption that they are supposed to be there. Their existence as a hub of intelligent Nishnaabeg relationality may be threatened by land theft, environmental contamination, residential schools and state-run education, and colonial gender violence, but Binoojiinh is there anyway, making maple sugar as they have always done, in a loving compassionate reality, propelling us to re-create the circumstances within which this story and Nishnaabewin takes place. Propelling us to rebel against the permanence of settler colonial reality and not just "dream alternative realities" but to create them, on the ground in the physical world in spite of being occupied. If we accept colonial permanence, then our rebellion can only take place within settler colonial thought and reality, and we also become too willing to sacrifice the context that creates and produces cultural workers like Binoojiinh. What if Binoojiinh had accepted the permanence of settler colonialism as an unmovable reality?

What if Binoojiinh had no access to the sugar bush because of land dispossession, environmental contamination, or global climate change?

What if they were too depressed or anxiety ridden from being erased from Canadian society, removed from their language and homeland, and targeted as a "squaw" or a "drunken Indian." Or too depressed or anxiety ridden from being bullied for not neatly fitting into the colonial gender binary?

What if the trauma and pain of ongoing colonial gendered violence had made it impossible for their mama to believe them, or for their mama to reach out and so gently rub their lower back at that critical point? What if that same trauma and pain pre vented their aunties and elders from gathering around them and supporting them when there were technical difficulties? What if settler-colonial parenting strategies positioned the child as "less believable" than an adult?

What if Binoojiinh had been in a desk at a school that didn't honor at its core their potential within Michi Saagiig Nishnaabeg intelligence? Or if they had been in an educational context where having an open heart was a liability instead of a gift? What if they had not been running around, exploring, experimenting, observing the squirrel . . . completely engaged in Michi Saagiig Nishnaabeg ways of knowing? What if they hadn't been on the land at all?

What if Binoojiinh lived in a world where no one listened to trans kids? Or where they had been missing or murdered before they ever made it out to the sugar bush?

It Comes *through* the Land

For me, this story is a critical intervention into current thinking about Indigenous education, because Indigenous education is not Indigenous or education from within our intellectual practices unless it comes through the land, unless it occurs in an Indigenous context using Indigenous processes.[10] To re-create the world that compelled Binoojiinh to learn how to make maple sugar, we should be concerned with re-creating the conditions within which this learning occurred, not just the content of the practice itself. Setters easily appropriate and reproduce the content of the story every year when they make commercial maple syrup in the context of capitalism, but they completely miss the wisdom that underlies the entire process because they deterritorialize the mechanics of maple syrup production from Nishnaabeg intelligence, and from Aki. They appropriated and recast the process within a hyperindividualism that negates relationality. The radical thinking and action of this story are not so much in the mechanics of reducing maple sap to sugar but lie in the reproduction of a loving web of Nishnaabeg networks within which learning takes place.

For countless generations, Nishnaabeg children grew up within the milieu of Nishnaabewin, not the institution of school. Many of our children still do, thanks to parents, grandparents, and communities. Like governance and leadership and every other aspect of reciprocated life, education comes from the roots up. It comes from being enveloped by land. An individual's intimate relationship with the spiritual and physical elements of creation is at the center of a learning journey that is lifelong.[11] You can't graduate from Nishnaabewin; it is a gift to be practiced and reproduced. And while each individual must have the skills and knowledge to ensure their own safety, survival, and prosperity in both the physical and spiritual realm, their existence is ultimately dependent upon intimate relationships of reciprocity, humility, honesty, and respect with all elements of creation, including plants and animals.

Nishnaabeg-Gikendaasowin, or Nishnaabeg knowledge,

originates in the spiritual realm, coming to individuals through dreams, visions, and ceremony and through the process of gaa-izhi-zhaawendaagoziyaang—that which is given lovingly to us by the spirits.[12] This makes sense because this is the place where our Ancestors reside, where spiritual beings exist, and where the spirits of living plants, animals, and humans interact. To gain access to this knowledge, one has to align oneself within with the forces of the implicate order through ceremony, ritual, and the embodiment of the teachings one already carries.[13]

Within this system there is no standard curriculum because it is impossible to generate a curriculum for "that which is given to us lovingly from the spirits," and because it doesn't make sense for everyone to master the same body of factual information. Nishnaabeg society in its fullest realization requires a diversity of excellence to continue to produce an abundance of supportive relationships. Within the context of humility and agency, decisions about learning are in essence an agreement between individuals and the spirit world. Nishnaabewin fosters and cherishes individuals with particular gifts and skills as a mechanism for growing diversity, and childhood is an excellent time for individuals to focus in on those particular gifts and hone them into excellence. Just as it is unthinkable within an Nishnaabeg worldview for a leader to impose their will on their people, it is unthinkable to impose an agenda onto another living thing—in essence the *context is the curriculum,* and land, Aki, is the context.[14]

In addition to the land (including the spiritual world), the context for Nishnaabewin is profoundly intimate. Gaa-izhi-zhaawendaagoziyaang requires long-term, stable, balanced warm relationships within the family, extended family, the community, and all living aspects of creation. Intelligence flows through relationships between living entities. Gaa-izhi-zhaawendaagoziyaang requires love, the word *zhaawen,* a part of the word *Gaa-izhi-zhaawendaagoziyaang,* means to have complete "compassion for another in one's thoughts and mind. It has a connotation of bestowing kindness, mercy, and aid. It includes ideas of pity, empathy and deep unconditional love."[15] Nishnaabeg scholar John Borrows explains:

For instance, my friend Kekek notes that zhawenjige is
another derivation of zhawenim. It means to hunt. We
hear the word used in hunting and harvesting songs.
When we sing zhawenim izhichige it means "you will be
pitied, or have mercy placed upon you in your actions
and what you are doing." The idea behind this word
is that when we acknowledge our relations with the
world, and our responsibilities to each other, then we
will all be blessed or find love and compassion. We will
be nourished, sustained and taken care of. The idea of
zhawenjige is said to be part of an old treaty the Nishnaabeg made with the animals. As long as we love them
they will provide for us, and teach us about love and
how to live well in the world.[16]

Meaning, then, is derived not through content or data or even
theory in a Western context, which by nature is decontextual-
ized knowledge, but through a compassionate web of interdependent relationships that are different and valuable because of
difference. Individuals carry the responsibility for generating
meaning within their own lives; they carry the responsibility for
engaging their minds, bodies, and spirits in a practice of generating meaning. Within Nishnaabewin, I am responsible for my
thoughts and ideas. I am responsible for my own interpretations,
and thus you'll always hear from our elders what appears to be
qualifying their teachings with statements that position them as
learners, position their ideas as their own understandings, and
place their teachings within the context of their own lived experience. This is deliberate, ethical, and *profoundly* careful within
Nishnaabewin because to do otherwise is considered arrogant
and intrusive with the potential to interfere with other beings'
life pathways.[17] Although individuals have the responsibility to
self-actualize within this system, intelligence in this context is
not an individual's property to own. So once an individual has
carried a particular teaching to the point where they can easily
embody that teaching, they also then become responsible for
sharing it according to the ethics and protocols of the system.
This is primarily done by modeling.

Continually generating meaning is often, but not exclusively, done in ceremony and involves ongoing ethical systems of accountability and responsibility, particularly for emotional trauma and healing.[18] Individual generated meaning is an authentic and grounded power. These meanings in all of their diversity then become the foundation of generated collective meanings and a plurality of truths.[19] This collective process, operationalized within Nishnaabeg political practices, for example, generates a series of collective meanings, including dissension, that make sense within broad and multiple interpretations of Nishnaabeg values and philosophies.[20]

Nishnaabeg Intelligence Is Diversity

There are unseen forces or spiritual elements that hold power and influence in the story of maple sugar that are only alluded to within the narrative at least in part because older Nishnaabeg teachers culturally talk about these things as if they are sitting beside us in a room, rather than coming directly at them.[21] There is an implicit assumption in this story that Binoojiinh offered tobacco to the maple tree before they cut the bark to collect the sap. They do this as a mechanism to set up a relationship with the maple tree that is based on mutual respect, reciprocity, and caring. By placing the tobacco down, they are speaking directly to the spirit of the maple tree. I understand it as their spirit speaking directly to the spirit of the maple tree, entering into a balanced relationship of mutuality. The maple tree does not have to produce sap for Binoojiinh; the tree has agency over this act. Binoojiinh also has agency; they have chosen to act in a way that aligns themselves with actions their people know promote more life and interconnection within Kina Gchi Nishnaabegogamig.[22] There are also several other spiritual interactions involved in this story of lovingly coming to know: the spirit of the squirrel, the spirits of their family that supported them, and the spirits of their Ancestors. Within an Nishnaabeg epistemology, spiritual knowledge is a tremendous, ubiquitous source of wisdom that is the core of every system in the physical world. The implicate order provides the stories that answer all of our questions. And the way we are taught to access that knowledge is by being open to that kind of knowledge and by being engaged in a way of living that generates a close, personal relationship with our Ancestors and relations in the spirit world through ceremony, dreams, visions, and stories. The implicate order does not discriminate by gender, by age, by ability, or by any of those things. The implicate order only cares if you believe, if you're living your life in an engaged way. If we are open to this, then knowledge will flow through us based on our own actions, on our name, clan, and helpers, and on our own self-actualization, as long as we uphold these responsibilities.

Binoojiinh already lives in a reality where the spiritual world has tremendous presence in each moment. Binoojiinh is a vessel of resurgence. They are a leader. They embody the core teachings and philosophies of Michi Saagiig Nishnaabeg culture. They paid attention to our creation story—the one that says Nishnaabewin have both intellectual knowledge and heart knowledge, the one that says you have to be fully present in all aspects of your physical and spiritual body to access the gift of knowledge from the spiritual world.[23] Binoojiinh very clearly represents this kind of citizen capable of upholding the tenets of our nation in spite of settler colonialism. They are in essence the goal of community: the re-creation of beings that continually live lives promoting the continuous rebirth of life itself.[24] In the context of Nishnaabeg resurgence—the rebuilding of Indigenous nations according to our own political, intellectual, and cultural practices—we need to reestablish the context for creating a society of Binoojiinh because we need to re-create a society of individuals who can think and live inside the multiplicity of our culture and our intelligence.

This presents Michi Saagiig Nishnaabeg people with a critical task. If we do not create a generation of people attached to the land and committed to living out our culturally inherent ways of coming to know, we risk losing what it means to be Nishnaabeg within our own thought systems. We simply cannot bring about the resurgence of our nations if we have no one that can think within the emergent networks of Nishnaabeg intelligence. We cannot bring about the kind of radical transformation we seek if we are solely reliant upon state-sanctioned and state-run education systems. We cannot carry out the kind of decolonization our Ancestors set in motion if we don't create a generation of land-based, community-based intellectuals and cultural producers who are accountable to our nations and whose life work is concerned with the regeneration of these systems rather than meeting the overwhelming needs of the Western academic industrial complex or attempting to "Indigenize the academy" by bringing Indigenous Knowledge into the academy on the terms of the academy itself. Our Ancestors' primary concern in "educating" our young people was to nurture a new generation of elders—of land-based intellectuals—philosophers, theorists, medicine people, and historians who embodied Nishnaabeg intelligence in whatever time they were living in because they had lived their lives through Nishnaabeg intelligence.

They embodied Nishnaabeg intelligence because they were *practitioners* of Nishnaabeg intelligence.

Nishnaabeg intelligence has been violently under attack since the beginning days of colonialism through processes that remove Indigenous peoples from our homelands, whether those processes are education in residential and other forms of state-run schools, outright dispossession, the destruction of land through resource extraction and environmental contamination, imposed poverty, heteropatriarchy, or colonial gendered violence. Our peoples have always resisted this destruction by engaging in Nishnaabewin whenever and wherever they could. I would not exist and be writing this chapter today if it were not for the physical survival of several generations of Nishnaabeg women in my family and the heartbreaking sacrifices of my elders in resisting colonial educational practices in their commitment to teaching others, the vast majority of the time in the absence of compensation or deep reciprocity, and outside of the provincial education and the postsecondary education system. Not one time has an elder told me to go to school to learn Indigenous Knowledge. Not one time has an elder told me to go and get a degree so that I can pass Indigenous Knowledge down to my children, yet we place tremendous pressure on our youth to gain

Western academic credentials. This seems highly problematic to me because we desperately need a new generation of thinkers who are articulate and brilliant from within Nishnaabewin, a generation that can think within our philosophies and enact those philosophies as a living and breathing imposition to colonialism, as every generation has done in some capacity before us. Otherwise we risk losing being Michi Saagiig Nishnaabeg. To create a nation of Binoojiinh—to survive *as Nishnaabeg*—we shouldn't be just striving for land-based pedagogies. The land must once again *become* the pedagogy.

Intelligence as Consensual Engagement

Binoojiinh very clearly embodied the idea of land as pedagogy as they went about their day learning with and from maple trees, among many other beings. Binoojiinh had already grown up in a community where the adult practitioners of Nishnaabeg intelligence were teaching them through modeling how to interact with all elements of creation. So on one hand, Binoojiinh was just doing what they had seen the adults in their life do every day over and over again in a variety of different activities. On a deeper level, Binoojiinh was also teaching us by "modeling"; their story aligns itself with our embodied theory, our Creation stories.

Gzhwe Manidoo in the very beginning of the cosmos and in the continual creation of Nishnaabeg ontology, axiology, and epistemology set up the context for Nishnaabeg reality.[25] That context was the earth Gzhwe Manidoo created, and as we know by now, Nishnaabeg conceptualizations of Aki are at their core profoundly relational. Borrows explains it this way:

> The Nishnaabeg have long taken direction about how we should live through our interactions and observations with the environment. People regulate their behavior and resolve their disputes by drawing guidance from what they see in the behavior of the sun, moon, stars, winds, waves, trees, birds, animals, and other natural phenomenon. The Nishnaabeg word for this concept is

gikinawaabiwin. We can also use the word akinoomaage, which is formed from two roots: Aki: noomaage. "Aki" means earth and "noomaage" means to point towards and take direction from. As we draw analogies from our surroundings, and appropriately apply or distinguish what we see, we learn about how to love, and how we should live in our lands.[26]

Aki includes all aspects of creation: landforms, elements, plants, animals, spirits, sounds, thoughts, feelings, and energies and all of the emergent systems, ecologies, and networks that connect these elements. Knowledge in akinoomaage flows through the layered spirit world above the earth, the place where spiritual beings reside and the place where our Ancestors sit.[27]

In the Nishnaabeg creation stories told and discussed in *Dancing on Our Turtle's Back,* the process in which Gzhwe Manidoo created the world is the process by which Nishnaabeg people come to know. Coming to know is a mirroring or a reenactment process where we understand Nishnaabeg epistemology to be concerned with embodied knowledge animated, collective, and lived out in a way in which our reality, nationhood, and existence are continually reborn through both time and space. This requires a joining of both emotional knowledge and intellectual knowledge in a profoundly personal and intimate spiritual context. Coming to know is an intimate, unfolding process of relationship with the spiritual world.

Coming to know also requires complex, committed, *consensual* engagement. Relationships within Nishnaabewin are based upon the consent—the informed (honest) consent—of all beings involved. The word *consensual* here is key because if children learn to normalize dominance and nonconsent within the context of education, then nonconsent becomes part of the normalized tool kit of those with authoritarian power. Within the context of settler colonialism, Indigenous peoples are not seen as worthy recipients of consent, informed or otherwise, and part of being colonized is engaging in all kinds of processes daily that given a choice, we likely wouldn't consent to. In my experience of the state-run education system, my informed consent was never required. Learning was forced on me using the threat of emotional and physical violence. In postsecondary education, consent was coercive: if you want these credentials, this is what you have to do, and this is what you have to endure.[28] This is unthinkable within Nishnaabeg intelligence. In fact, if there isn't a considerable amount of demonstrated interest and commitment on the part of the learner, learning doesn't occur at all. Raising Indigenous children in a context where their consent, physical and intellectual, is not just required but valued goes a long way to undoing the replication of colonial gender violence.

In the context of resurgence, which is in essence an emergent process mitigated by spiritual forces, physical and intellectual *engagement* with the struggle of nation building within specific cultural contexts is the only way to generate new knowledge. Being engaged—deeply and consensually—in the physical, real-world work of resurgence, movement building, and nation building is the only way to generate new knowledge on how to resurge from within Nishnaabeg intellectual systems. We cannot just think, write, or imagine our way to a decolonized future. Answers to how to rebuild and how to resurge are therefore derived from a web of consensual relationships that is infused with movement (kinetic) through lived experience and embodiment. Intellectual knowledge is not enough on its own. Neither is spiritual knowledge or emotional knowledge. All kinds of knowledge are important and necessary in a communal and emergent balance.

This creation story also emphasizes that Nishnaabeg people embody all the necessary knowledge for resurgence. We are enough because if we are living our lives out in an Nishnaabeg way (as many of us are), we can access all the knowledge that went into creating the universe. In my experience as an Nishnaabeg person in the context of centuries of gendered violence and ongoing occupation of my homeland, part of my knowledge base is a critical attunement to settler colonialism and generated theories of resistance as well as resurgence and liberation, both coming from within my own knowledge system and through the sharing of the liberatory politics of Indigenous peoples and people of color who have also been forced to live through oppression. Aki is also liberation and freedom—my freedom to establish and maintain relationships of deep reciprocity within a pristine homeland my Ancestors handed down to me. Aki is encompassed by freedom, freedom that is protected by sovereignty and actualized by self-determination.

Once this context is reestablished, even if it begins as only a dream or a vision, even held just by a few individuals, the fetishization of theoretical approaches to realize that context becomes counterproductive.[29] If Dionne Brand or Fred Moten speaks to my heart as an Nishnaabekwe, as both do, then Nishnaabeg intelligence compels me to learn, share, and embody everything I can from every teacher that presents themselves to me in a mutually ethical, consensual, and reciprocal way. Nishnaabeg intelligence *is* diversity—Nishnaabeg intelligence *as* diversity.[30]

Nanabush. Period.

Nanabush is widely regarded within Nishnaabeg thought as an important teacher because Nanabush mirrors human behavior and models how to (and how not to) come to know. I think it's important to point out that Nanabush does not teach at a university, nor is Nanabush a teacher within the state school system. Nanabush also doesn't read academic papers or write for academic journals. Nanabush is fun, entertaining, sexy, and playful. You're more likely to find Nanabush dancing on a table at a bar than at an academic conference. If Nanabush had gone to teachers' college, Nanabush would have been fired in the first three months of his first teaching gig.[31] This is precisely why Nanabush is an outstanding teacher. Nanabush not only teaches me self-compassion for the part of me that may dance on bars in celebration of life and love and all things good, but Nanabush comes with inevitable contradictions held within the lives of the occupied. Nanabush also continually shows us what happens when we are not responsible for our own baggage or trauma or emotional responses. The brilliance of Nanabush is that Nanabush stories the land with a sharp criticality necessary for moving through the realm of the colonized into the dreamed reality of the decolonized, and for navigating the lived reality of having to engage with both at the same time.

In the spirit of Nanabush, part of me is being facetious in that last paragraph, and part of me is not. The academic industrial complex does not and cannot provide the proper context for Nishnaabeg intelligence without the full, valued recognition of the context within which Nishnaabeg intelligence manifests itself: the *practice* of Aki—freedom, sovereignty, and self-determination over bodies, minds, and land. The academy does not and cannot provide the proper context for Nishnaabeg intelligence without taking a principled stand on the forces that are currently attacking Nishnaabeg intelligence: colonial gendered violence, dispossession, erasure, and imposed poverty. The academy does not and cannot provide the proper context for Nishnaabeg intelligence without the full recognition of the system that generates this intelligence and the people who have dedicated their lives to growing, nurturing, and living that system—our elders and knowledge holders. The academy does not and cannot provide the proper context for Nishnaabeg intelligence without fully funding the regeneration of Indigenous thinkers as a matter of restitution for the damage it has caused and continues to cause the Indigenous Knowledge system through centuries of outright attack.[32]

I imagine myself talking about postsecondary education with Nanabush right now, and he immediately asking me why I think spending sixty hours a week indoors in a classroom or on a computer is Indigenous education at all. Point taken. I've just spent several hours writing all of this down when my Ancestors have always understood this, and in fact, I think my kids understand most of it. Several Nishnaabeg elders are embodying all of these teachings right now, and any Indigenous person with motivation to learn to think inside the land should be interacting with their own elders and experts in their own homelands instead of reading me. So while I could ask Nanabush what Nishnaabeg education is, I'd have to be ready for him to flip the table. He's not known for his patience, for one thing, and for another, he's spent eternity trying to demonstrate that with his own life. It's not Nanabush's fault we aren't paying attention.

One person who is paying attention is Binoojiinh, because in going back to the sugar bush, Binoojiinh models their day on an important Nanabush story. Shortly after the creation of the world and the birth of Nanabush, Nanabush took a trip around the world as a way of learning about the world. That's the first lesson. If you want to learn about something, you need to take your body onto the land and do it. Get a practice.[33] If you want to learn about movement building, get yourself outside involved with people that are building movements. That doesn't mean don't read books or don't talk to people with all kinds of intelligences. It doesn't mean don't find mentors. It does mean get out, get involved, and get invested. After Nanabush had completed his first journey around the world, he embarked on a second journey around the world, this time with wolf as a companion. At this point, we should all recognize pretty clearly that the learning changes when the relational context changes. Nanabush did a tremendous amount of visiting on both of his trips—he visited with Nokomis, he visited with the West Wind, he visited with plants and animals, mountains, and bodies of water. Visiting within Nishnaabeg intelligence means sharing oneself through story, through principled and respectful consensual reciprocity with another living being. Visiting is lateral sharing in the absence of coercion and hierarchy and in the presence of compassion. Visiting is fun and enjoyable and nurtures the intimate connections and relationship building. Visiting is the core of our political system (leaders visiting with all the members of the community), our mobilization (Tkamse and Pontiac visited within and outside of their own nations for several years before they expected mobilization), and our intelligence (people visiting elders, sharing food, taking care). Binoojiinh knew this. This is why they were visiting the maple tree in the first place.

At several points in Nanabush's journey, Nanabush sought spiritual guidance through dreams, visions, and ceremonies. At one point he had to learn to build a canoe to cross a large body of water. He experimented until he figured it out. This was both time consuming and frustrating. When he finally got a structure that would float, he had no way to propel it. This was also time consuming and frustrating. Eventually by calming down and watching a beaver, he was able to fashion a paddle inspired by the beaver's tail and continue across the body of water.

In this story, Nanabush models how to come to know for Binoojiinh. He *shows* us land as pedagogy, without yelling "LAND AS PEDAGOGY," or typing "land as pedagogy" into a computer fifty times. Sometimes when I am teaching PhD students, I say that in this story Nanabush is teaching us how to be students, teachers, and researchers. He is giving us theory and methodology, but it's really much bigger than that. Nanabush is teaching us how to be full human beings within the context of Nishnaabeg intelligence. Nishnaabeg intelligence is for everyone, not just students, teachers, and researchers. It's not just pedagogy, it's how to live life.

Resurgent Education

Being engaged in land as pedagogy as a life practice inevitably means coming face-to-face with settler colonial authority, surveillance, and violence, because this practice places Indigenous bodies in between settlers and their money.[34] The practices of hunting, fishing, and living off the land within my territory have been a direct challenge to settler colonialism since 1923 and the imposition of the Williams Treaty.[35] Being a practitioner of land as pedagogy and learning in my community also mean learning how to resist this imposition. It's a process of learning how to be on the land anyway.

There are countless stories that I could tell here about settler surveillance, criminalization, and violence that occur on the land while Michi Saagiig Nishnaabeg are engaged as practitioners in Nishnaabewin,[36] but the story I want to leave you with is one that comes from someone who has invested greatly in my intelligence as an Nishnaabekwe.

Over the past fifteen years or so, I have spent a large amount of time on the land learning from Doug Williams. Doug and I have hunted, fished, trapped, picked medicines, conducted ceremonies, harvested birch bark, made maple syrup, canoed ancient routes, and harvested wild rice throughout our territory. This represents the most profound educational experience of my life, and I hope that it is far from over. During our extensive time on our land, Doug has taught me the history of Michi Saagiig Nishnaabeg, an oral tradition passed down to him from his uncles, who would have learned it from their parents and grandparents. He has taught me the political practices of our people and the ceremonies, philosophies, and values they carried with them. He has taken me to every sacred site in our territory and has shared songs, seamlessly moving between the roles of best friend, father, and elder. He has patiently listened to me. He has patiently answered every question I've brought to him. He has told me hundreds of stories cataloging the fierce resistance of our Ancestors to our way of life. He has healed me.

It is this relationship more than any other that has created in me the same fierce resistance my Ancestors carried with them and that has fostered a responsibility in me to our territory. It is this relationship more than any other that has made me Michi Saagiig Nishnaabeg. Doug has invested more time in my spiritual, emotional, and intellectual education than anyone else in my life. Yet it is completely unrecognized, unsupported, and disregarded by academic institutions.

Being out on the land with Doug living our Michi Saagiig Nishnaabewin means we run up against colonial authorities regularly, whether that is the police, game wardens, or settlers providing their own homegrown surveillance for the settler colonial authorities. To be honest, most of this is fairly normalized, and unless there is a particular aggression or violence involved in the incident, I often don't even notice. But Doug reminds me continually through story that being tied to land also means being tied to an unwritten, unseen history of resistance:

> The 1923 Williams Treaty was devastating to my people. I witnessed the trauma and the fear that was put on my people that were trying to live on the land. They lived daily watching over their backs and trying to maintain

their lifestyle as Michi Saagiig Nishnaabeg. The government with the implementation of the "basket clause" was a sneaky way to get rid of us as people who enjoyed this part of our great land.[37] These old men I hung around with such as Madden and Jimkoons Taylor lived a life where they had to live by sneaking around and feeling like they were "poachers." They resorted to catching other animals and harvesting those things that the government did not feel were part of the things they need to "protect" from us. These things included small animals, such as the groundhog and the porcupine; the muskrat for meat and other things were also eaten because we were forbidden from hunting deer (which was our staple). Michi Saagiig Nishnaabeg were also prohibited from fishing from October 15 to July 1 every year under provincial statutes. These colonial restrictions were devastating to people that lived on the land. They posted game wardens in the tri-lakes area—Buckhorn, Chemong, and Pigeon—to enforce these restrictions. We faced starvation.

It was particularly difficult to obtain food in the wintertime, and since fishing was prohibited, it became a time of great suffering. People had to run up an account at the Whetung General Store to tide them over until the muskrat season opened in April. So it was November to April that was quite difficult. Some people still had to fish and would do it at odd hours and would have to sneak around and not be seen. This is a very difficult thing to do in the winter. Anyone standing on the ice can be seen for miles, and this is what the game warden would look out for and go out and chase my people. There were many stories told of how my people escaped the game warden. There were many stories of our people being caught and going to court in Peterborough to be given fines for fishing out of season. Imagine the indignity on our people when they came in front of the Canadian courts for being Michi Saagiig Nishnaabeg in our own territory!

Our people were incredibly strong and resilient. We were able to survive even though we were forced to live in an undignified way of living off the land. There is a story told of one of the young men—Shkiin, short for Shkiininini meaning "young man." Shkiin had the ability to escape the game warden by putting on these skates you tied onto your feet. The only problem was the skates had no brakes, so it was impossible to stop. One day, the game warden showed up with modern tube-type skates. He saw Shkiin fishing out on the ice, put on those speed-skating skates, and went after Shkiin. Shkiin tied on his skates and took off. After awhile, the game warden started to catch up. Shkiin thought, "uh oh I'm in trouble." Just then he saw some open water. He thought he would skate as fast as he could and jump over the open water because he knew the game warden couldn't follow. So he skated as fast as he could, took the leap—it was about twenty feet—and he made it. He landed, looked around, and the game warden had to put on the brakes. Shkiin turned around, waved at him, and gave him that Saasaakwe sound. The old people used to tell about that story and how Shkiin became a legend in getting away from game wardens.

I admire the resilience of my people very much. One of the ways they kept up their spirit was with humor. Many stories are told of the klutzy game wardens that were posted on the lakes to watch out for us. There are also some sad stories. Old Sam Fawn after many years of carving axe handles, saving up money, and making other items like that. With his little bit of money he was able to afford a cedar-strip canoe from Peterborough. He went fishing on Fox Island out of provincial season. He was seen by the game warden, who chased him. Sam beat him and came across from Fox Island to the mainland at Curve Lake. He put his canoe up on shore, turned it over, and walked home. Everyone did that back in those days. Everyone knew each other's canoes. The game warden was watching him from Fox Island, and he sneaked over and seized that canoe. The canoe has never been seen again. Poor Sam Fawn, worked hard his whole life, trying to live off the land. I remember him as being one of the most gentle human beings that lived in Curve Lake. The trauma created by the 1923 Williams Treaty will be long-lived. It lives in our hearts. The government can never repay us for what the damage they have caused. The damage is done. Many of the people that lived through this trauma have now passed on. I remember them dearly, and I hope that somehow there are no game wardens in the Happy Hunting Grounds.[38]

This story serves as an important reminder: by far the largest attack on Indigenous Knowledge systems right now is land dispossession, and the people that are actively protecting Nishnaabewin are not those at academic conferences advocating for its use in research and course work, but those who are currently putting their bodies on the land. In many ways, the fight for Nishnaabewin is not taking place in parliament, on social media, or on the streets in urban centers; rather, it lies with communities like Grassy Narrows and those on the ground who are active practitioners of Nishnaabewin or who are actively protecting their lands from destruction.

When I was a PhD student at the University of Manitoba in the late 1990s, there was a considerable amount of discussion among academics on how to ethically and responsibly bring Indigenous Knowledge into the academy, as a way of legitimizing the knowledge of Indigenous peoples as an intellectual system on par with Western traditions, as a mechanism to attract Indigenous students to the academy, and as a means to preserve Indigenous Knowledge.[39] An effort was made to produce more Indigenous scholars so they would have a stronger presence within the colonial system. When I first held a tenure-track position in an Indigenous Studies department, there were two elders on faculty, both women, who had gained tenure on the basis of their expertise in Indigenous Knowledge, not on Western credentials. Fifteen years later the same university has no tenured elders, only Indigenous and non-Indigenous academics primarily hired on the basis of Western credentials.

The problem with this approach then and now is that it reinforces colonial authority over Nishnaabeg intelligence by keeping it reified and fetishized within a settler colonial approach to education designed only to propel settler colonialism. This serves to reinforce asymmetrical power relationships between Indigenous Knowledge and Western knowledge, and between Indigenous and non-Indigenous peoples. It sets both Indigenous Knowledge holders and Indigenous learners up in a never-ending battle for recognition within that system, when the academy's primary intention is to use Indigenous peoples and our knowledge systems to legitimize settler colonial authority within education used as a training ground for those who would legitimize settler colonial authority over Indigenous peoples and our nations in Canadian society.[40]

The thing for Nishnaabeg to do is to stop looking for legitimacy within the colonizer's education system and return to valuing and recognizing our individual and collective intelligence on its own merits and on our own terms. Withdrawing our considerable collective efforts to "Indigenize the academy" in favor of a resurgence of Indigenous intellectual systems and a reclamation of the context within which those systems operate goes much further toward propelling our nationhood and reestablishing Indigenous political systems because it places people back on the land in a context that is conducive to resurgence and mobilization. The academy has continually refused to recognize and support the validity, legitimacy, rigor, and ethical principles of Nishnaabeg intelligence and the system itself, so we must stop begging for recognition and do this work for ourselves. This colonial refusal should be met with Indigenous refusal—refusal to struggle simply for better or more inclusion and recognition within the academic industrial complex.[41] As Jarrett Martineau and Eric Ritskes state in their discussion of decolonial aesthetics, "This means the task of decolonial artists, scholars and activists is not simply to offer amendments or edits to the current world, but to display the mutual sacrifice and relationality needed to sabotage colonial systems of thought and power for the purpose of liberatory alternatives.[42] This is true in politics, art, cultural and intellectual production, and education because these systems are seamlessly woven together within our intelligence. If the academy is concerned about not only protecting and maintaining Indigenous intelligence but also revitalizing it on Indigenous terms as a form of restitution for its historic and contemporary role as a colonizing force (of which I see no evidence), then the academy must make a conscious decision to become a decolonizing force in the intellectual lives of Indigenous peoples by joining us in dismantling settler colonialism and actively protecting the source of our knowledge: Indigenous *land*.

I am not saying that Indigenous peoples should forgo learning Western-based skills altogether, but we currently have a situation where our greatest minds, our children and youth, are spending forty hours a week in state-run education systems from age four to twenty-two if they complete an undergraduate degree. Next to none of that takes place in an Nishnaabeg context, and although many Indigenous parents and families do everything they can do to ensure their children are connected to their homelands, this should be the center of the next generation's lives, not the periphery. To foster expertise within Nishnaabeg intelligence, we need people engaged with land as curriculum and in our languages for decades, not weeks. Shouldn't we as communities support and nurture children who choose to educate themselves only within Nishnaabewin? Wouldn't this create a strong generation of elders? Don't we deserve learning spaces where we do not have to address state learning objectives, curriculum, credentialism, and careerism, where our only concern for recognition comes from within? Are the state-run education system and the academic industrial complex really a house worth inhabiting?[43]

Nishnaabewin did not and does not prepare children for successful career paths in a hypercapitalistic system. It is designed to create self-motivated, self-directed, community-minded, interdependent, brilliant, loving citizens who at their core uphold our ideals around family, community, and nationhood by valuing their intelligences, their diversity, their desires and gifts, and their lived experiences. It encourages children to find their joy and place it at the center of their lives. It encourages children to value consent. This was the key to building nations where exploitation was unthinkable. But don't our children have to live in a hypercapitalistic system? Well yes, and if we are going to survive this as Nishnaabeg, we need to create generations of people who are capable of actualizing radical decolonization, diversity, transformation, and local economic alternatives to capitalism.

The beauty of culturally inherent resurgence is that it challenges settler colonial dissections of our territories and our bodies into reserve/city or rural/urban dichotomies. All Canadian cities are on Indigenous lands. Indigenous presence is attacked in all geographies. In reality, the majority of Indigenous peoples move regularly through reserves, cities, towns, and rural areas. We have found ways to connect to the land and our stories and to live our intelligences no matter how urban or how destroyed our homelands have become. While it is critical that we grow and nurture a generation of people who can think within the land and have tremendous knowledge and connection to Aki, this doesn't have to take away from the contributions of urban Indigenous communities to our collective resurgence. Cities have becomes sites of tremendous activism and resistance and of artistic, cultural, and linguistic revival and regeneration, and this comes from the land. Whether urban or rural, city or reserve, the shift that Indigenous systems of intelligence compel us to make is one from capitalistic consumer to cultural producer. Radical resurgent education is therefore at the heart of the Radical Resurgence Project because it rebelliously replicates nation-based Indigeneity. Binoojiinh reminds me that "the freedom realized through flight and refusal is the freedom to imagine and create an elsewhere in the here; a present future beyond the imaginative and territorial bounds of colonialism. It is a performance of other worlds, an embodied practice of flight."[44] For me, Binoojiinh as fugitive to within provides the fire, the compassion, and the loving rebellion to do just that.

TEN
"I SEE YOUR LIGHT"
RECIPROCAL RECOGNITION AND GENERATIVE REFUSAL

INDIGENOUS SCHOLARSHIP has recently experienced crucial interventions into how we account, frame, and tell the truths of the political and cultural lives of Indigenous peoples that move away from a constriction of our intelligence within the confines of Western thought and the dumbing down of the issues for the non-Indigenous outside to a meticulous, critical, robust, and layered approach that accurately contextualizes and reflects the lives and the thinking of Indigenous peoples on our own terms, with the clear purpose of dismantling colonial domination.[1] In my mind this approach isn't just important in the academy, this is also important in the Indigenous practices of resurgent organizing, mobilization, and struggle.

As a first step, this requires a clean break from mobilizations and organizing that occur in direct response to the state and that are entwined with the politics of recognition. Glen Coulthard's meticulous discussion in *Red Skin, White Masks* of recognition, reconciliation, resentment, and the Dene nation's own mobilization in the 1970s demonstrates the pitfalls of this approach. Coulthard demands that we stop seeking recognition from the state of our cultural distinctiveness, of our inherent rights to self-government, of the state's treaty obligations under the domination of settler colonialism. He uses Fanon's critique of Hegel's master-slave dialectic and the experience of his own Dene nation to challenge the assumption that Indigenous peoples will achieve any sort of peaceful coexistence through the politics of recognition. He maintains that instead these politics serve only to entrench settler colonial power. He points to resurgence, a *radical* resurgence in my mind, as a more effective set of politics to dismantle colonial domination.[2] The first tenet then of radical resurgent organizing is a refusal of state recognition as an organizing platform and mechanism for dismantling the systems of colonial domination.

The second tenet requires us to refuse the state's framing of the issues we organize around, and respond to and re-embed these issues within Indigenous political contexts and realities and within the place of productive refusal as a mechanism for building unity within the struggle. I want to revisit the way Audra Simpson reframes memberships here in terms of resurgent organizing. In *Mohawk Interruptus* Simpson re-embeds membership issues into a living Rotinonhseshá:ka matrix of relatedness and tension over membership and belonging in Kahnawà:ke by naming the root: *fear of disappearance*—a basic, terrifying, omnipresent reality of being Indigenous and particularly of being an Indigenous woman or queer person and occupied by Canada. She re-embeds belonging in a *productive* place of refusal, which I read as a spectacular animation of Mohawk theory as Mohawk life and Mohawk land. A productive place of refusal is one that generates grounded normativity. If we mobilize around "fear of disappearance" rather than encoding that fear into policy in the form of a membership code, what does that mobilization look like? This is important to consider because when we encode fear into policy, we inevitable create hurt, pain, and ultimately divisions within our own communities. Membership issues in this light, actually most Indigenous issues, are ultimately about

Indigenous peoples very existence as Indigenous peoples. All of us want our communities and nations to continue, and I'm confident in saying that because all of us have in various ways been fighting to survive assimilation for centuries now. This shift in framing from identity politics to fear of disappearance enables us to organize around the root, instead of the symptom, and it allows for multidimensional nation-based approaches. For example, what if we had refused the gender discrimination of the Indian Act from a productive place of refusal when we first began to mobilize around this issue in the late 1980s? What if we had seen this issue as an attack on our nation, as a mechanism to accelerate assimilation, as a strategy to weaken our resistance, as a colonial strategy to get more land and destroy Indigenous families by attacking Indigenous women, many of whom were moms? What if we had mobilized as nations to love and physically support those women that lost faux status, as our nations have always done, and used this issue to build unity and to strengthen ties within communities? What if we had organized outside of the politics of recognition, refused identity politics, and categorically refused the heteropatriarchy of the Indian Act? What if our leaders saw heteropatriarchy as an attack on our nations and refused to uphold it as an act of sovereignty and self-determination, and we focused intensely on taking care of our own and having each other's backs?

What if no one sided with colonialism?

What happens, then, when we build movements that refuse colonial recognition as a starting point and turn inwards, building a politics of refusal that is generative? Well, you get things like the Dene Declaration, and you get things like the Iroquois Nationals refusing to participate in the World Lacrosse League Championship tournament in Manchester because the UK refused to recognize their sovereignty as demonstrated through their Mohawk passports.[3] You can sign a petition and stage a demonstration because you don't want a Canadian passport, or you can make your own passports and travel on them. The latter to me represents resurgent organizing. It is organizing based on a refusal of settler colonialism coupled with the embodiment of the alternative, an alternative that amplifies grounded normativity. Radical resurgent organizing refuses both settler colonialism and its many manifestations. It does not allow settler colonialism to frame the issues facing Indigenous peoples, and this is critical because settler colonialism will always define the issues with a solution that reentrenches its own power. Radical resurgent organizing refuses the politics of recognition as a mechanism to bring about change, and it is generative; that is, it is organizing and mobilizing that takes place within nation-based grounded normativities.

In the next three chapters, I explore the potentialities of organizing and mobilizing within a radical resurgent politic by beginning to reconceptualize these concepts within Indigenous intelligence or within the diverse nation-based practices of grounded normativity. I see a relocalization of place-based, nation-based issues and alternatives within a network of other Indigenous nations doing the same, a focus on people and relationships, the prioritizing of resurgent-based education, and the strengthening of networks of bodies that house Indigenous intelligence. Indigenous resurgent organizing might look like a network of Indigenous intellectuals giving talks in the prison system in a coordinated, nation-based way across Canada; it might look like a network of urban breakfast programs highlighting Indigenous food systems and alliances between reserves and cities within Indigenous nations; it might look like a network of land-based freedom schools for all ages; it might look like co-ops, trade agreements, and economies that prioritize Indigenous modes of production and sharing; it might look like a series of coordinating, rotating blockades and camps across Turtle Island that challenge the extractivism. Resurgent organizing takes place within grounded normativity and is necessarily place based and local, but it is also necessarily networked and global.

Building movements that reject the politics of recognition and center generative refusal inherently creates Indigenous bodies more connected to each other and the land, and that act out, through relationality, Indigenous thought. In a sense both books asked the same question to me as a reader: What is the best way to ensure we do not disappear as unique distinctive Indigenous peoples and place-embedded nations? How do we build movements with strong enough personal relationships to withstand settler colonial pushback? Or asked another way, how do I live as an individual and as part of a collective in a way that ensures I recognize my great-great-great-grandchildren as Indigenous peoples?

The Act of Recognizing

My favorite part of Simpson's *Mohawk Interruptus,* the part I've thought the most deeply about, is a tiny moment shared between two Mohawk nationals in a bar in Greenwich Village. The researcher, Simpson, asks her interviewee, "What is the ideal form of membership for us? What do you think makes someone a member of the community?" He looks her squarely in the eye and doesn't answer. Instead he says, "When you look in the mirror, what do you see?"

Genius.

Every time I get to this part of this book, I stop reading. This time, I've stopped reading for three weeks now, because there is so much to think about in his answer.

Obviously, the interviewee does a brilliant job of reflecting the academy and the researcher back onto us, and that's very enjoyable to me because our people have been refusing the framings, the constraints, and the outright lies, and misinformation of the academy. But he also refuses the agonizing over whether someone else belongs and asks Simpson, asks me, asks us to consider how we belong. Couple this with the underlying question that haunts membership and citizenship codes, how do we ensure our survival as Indigenous peoples, and he is ultimately asking me to consider, perhaps critically, how I reflect, act, model, and embody my belonging back to my family, community, and nation.

How do I recognize myself as a Michi Saagiig Nishnaabekwe? Do my Ancestors recognize me as one of their own? How does Simpson as a Mohawk woman recognize me as a Michi

Saagiig Nishnaabeg woman? How are we related? When I am hunting, does the spirit of the moose see me and recognize me in the same way she recognized my Ancestors? Does the moose see me as someone who is seeking her consent through my offerings, prayers, and practices to harvest her body so that my family can live? Does that moose see me as someone who is engaging with her in the relational terms set out in our diplomacy? Does she feel respected and that she has sovereignty and agency over the act of harvesting? Or have my actions made her feel like a resource? Does she see me as the enemy? Does she feel exploited? Unseen? Unrecognized? Hunted?

What makes me a member of my nation? What am I contributing? How am I living Nishnaabewin? How am I embodying consent and diversity in an Nishnaabeg way? How I am contributing to resurgence? What practices am I carrying along to the next generation? What am I doing in my daily life and practices of being Nishnaabeg that are ensuring the next generation will be Nishnaabeg, that is, substantively living different lives than their Canadian neighbors?

What do I see when I look in the mirror? A list of negative stereotypes? The positive attributes? A mixture? Do I see a network of intimate relationships rotating through time and space in all directions across human, plant, and animal nations and in the context of a spiritual cosmos? How do I, how do we reflect back the Indigeneity of our unique nations? How do I both see my reflection and act as a mirror? Do I, like Simpson, see a nice person? How do I recognize my relations? How am I recognized?

What if the driving force in Indigenous politics is self-recognition rather than a continual race around the hamster wheel of settler colonial recognition?

Recognition in Nishnaabewin

Let's talk about how relationality plays out in Indigenous contexts. Part of being in a meaningful relationship with another being is recognizing who they are, it is reflecting back to them their essence and worth as a being, it is a mirroring. Positive mirroring creates positive identities; it creates strong, grounded individuals and families and nations within Indigenous political systems. So at the same time I am looking into the mirror, I also am the mirror. What do I mirror back to my kin? Dysfunction? Criticism? Cynicism? What do these two books mirror back to Dene and Mohawk peoples? That's easy: they mirror back strength, pride, connection, beauty, love, fierceness, courage, bravery, and the very best parts of being Dene or Mohawk.

Michi Saagiig Nishnaabeg greet each other by saying the word *Aaniin,* which is a way of saying hello that is common for Michi Saagiig Nishnaabeg people to use. I spent some time with Doug last week, sitting around a fire talking about Nishnaabeg conceptualizations of recognition. We talked about the word Aaniin. He told me the Ah sound places us in a spiritual context, in the context of the Nishnaabeg universe. The Ni is "a taking notice as sound." When put together, he understands the word to be asking, how do you see yourself in all of this? Or put another way, taking in all the thought and feeling of your journey in the universe, how do you see or recognize yourself? Aaniin then can also mean "I see your light," or "I see your essence," or "I see who you are." To me, seeing someone else's light is akin to working to see the energy they put into the universe through their interactions with the land, themselves, their family, and their community. Aaniin isn't an observation but a continual process of unfolding; it is a commitment to the kind of relationship where I have dedicated myself to seeing the unique value in the other life as a *practice.*

Why, then, do we continually seek recognition from Canada when we know it never ends well? Why is internal reciprocal recognition so important within Indigenous thought? Recognition within Nishnaabewin is a lovely practice that builds resilient relationships. My people recognize through song when spirits enter our lodges and ceremonies. We recognize our family members who have passed on to the Spirit World through particular ceremonies. We recognize and greet the sun every morning, and the moon each night through prayer and ceremony. We recognize when particular animals return to our territory in the spring, and when plants and medicines reappear after winter rests. Recognition for us is about presence, about profound listening, and about recognizing and affirming the light in each other as a mechanism for nurturing and strengthening internal relationships to our Nishnaabeg worlds. It is a core part of our political systems because they are rooted in our bodies and our bodies are not just informed by but created and maintained by relationships of deep reciprocity. Our bodies exist only in relation to Indigenous complex, nonlinear constructions of time, space, and place that are continually rebirthed through the practice and often coded recognition of obligations and responsibilities within a nest of diversity, freedom, consent, noninterference, and a generated, proportional, emergent reciprocity.

Reciprocal recognition is a core Nishnaabeg practice. We greet and speak to medicinal plants before we pick medicines. We recognize animals' spirits before we engage in hunting them. Reciprocal recognition within our lives as Nishnaabeg people is ubiquitous, embedded, and inherent. Consent is also embedded into this recognition. When I make an offering and reach out to the spirit of Waawaashkesh before I begin hunting, I am asking for that being's consent or permission to harvest it. If a physical deer appears, I have their consent. If no animal presents itself to me, I do not.

This kind of Indigenous collective self-recognition is a core, place-based practice. It is a core, living concept of Nishnaabeg grounded normativity because it is a mechanism in which, despite environmental destruction and settler colonial strangulation, we continually throughout our lives and throughout the day reinsert ourselves in the network of living relationships that give us meaning. Indigenous internal, reciprocal self-recognition is a mechanism through which we reproduce and amplify Indigeneity.[4] When another Indigenous person recognizes and reflects back to me my Nishnaabeg essence, when we interact with each other in an Nishnaabeg way, my Michi Saagiig Nishnaabewin deepens. When my Indigeneity grows, I am more connected. I fall more in love with my homeland, my family, my culture, and my language and more in line with the thousands of stories that demonstrate how to live a meaningful life, and I have more emotional capital to fight and protect what is meaningful to me. I am a bigger threat to the Canadian state and its plans to build pipelines across my body, clear-cut my forests, contaminant my lakes with toxic cottages and chemicals, and make my body a site of continual sexualized violence.

Nanabush is the original teacher of reciprocal recognition.

Recall from chapter 4 and from the previous chapter on education, Nanabush's journey around the world.[5] I want to revisit this story one last time. In my PhD theory and methodology classes, I often position Nanabush as the first researcher because the purpose of this journey is to learn about the world.[6] I point out that Gzhwe Manidoo doesn't give Nanabush a reading list or a stack of books. Gzhwe Manidoo doesn't make him write a proposal, come up with a research question or objectives, or go through an ethics review. Students laugh at the absurdity of that, but to me it isn't absurd; it is a critical political intervention that says that Nishnaabeg intelligence is brilliant in its own right and that after Gzhwe Manidoo transferred all of the knowledge from the creation of the universe into our bodies, after Gzhwe Manidoo showed us the potential of combining potential energy and kinetic energy as a creative force, after the Nishnaabeg world of being was created, we had access to the entire universe through our practices.[7] This is Nanabush's theory—this is the relational foundation that Nanabush interprets and derives meaning from. There is some fluidity to this theory—it's not necessarily the same for everyone. People's interpretations change as they wear these stories through their lives. Lived experience leads to transformation. But there is a limit to the fluidity, and that's the web of ethical relationships that working in cohesive manner with each other, create more life and propel the continuous rebirth of mino bimaadiziwin.[8]

Nanabush sets off on foot on a trip around the world. Nanabush *visits* with every aspect of creation: the rivers, the lakes, the oceans, the plants, the animals, the spirits, the mountains, the prairies, the northlands. Nanabush greets and *recognizes* every aspect of creation, and Nanabush names each of those beings in each of those nations. Nanabush develops a deep relationship of reciprocity with each of these, many of which are recorded in our oral stories. Nanabush introduces the Nishnaabeg to the practices of consent, recognition, and reciprocity. Nanabush listens. Nanabush shares of himself. Nanabush learns about the plants, for instance, and therefore learns about himself. Nanabush doesn't interview anyone or hand out surveys. Nanabush visits. Nanabush observes. Nanabush reflects. Nanabush does ceremony. Nanabush listens. Nanabush shares and receives stories. Nanabush actively participates. Nanabush experiments. Nanabush prays, sings, and dances. Nanabush struggles. Nanabush dreams. Nanabush participates.

When Nanabush returns, Gzhwe Manidoo asks him to go around the world another time. This time with Ma'iingan, the wolf, as his companion. Relationality gives birth to meaning. Repeating the journey again in relation to another being shifts and deepens understandings. For the journey to go well, Nanabush has to engage in reciprocal recognition with Wolf as a daily practice because the journey will challenge their strength and the strength of their relationship on every level.

These practices are Nanabush's methodology, to use an academic term. These practices are the basis of Nishnaabeg political, economic, spiritual, and intelligence systems. They are the base of reality. Nanabush's trip stories the landscape with relational knowledges. When Nishnaabeg see a birch tree, we recognize a library of stories involving birch. When we see a lady's slipper, or moss on rocks, or cranberries, or maple trees, or a woodpecker, or beaver, more libraries. Nanabush's character is a reflection of Nishnaabewin and of Nishnaabeg themselves, and in our practice of Nishnaabewin we are both mirror and reflection to ourselves and our communities. Nested into each practice is the practice of reciprocal recognition.

Reciprocal recognition, the act of making it a practice to see another's light and to reflect that light back to them, forms the basis of positive identity, self-worth, and dignity in the other being. This in turn creates strong individuals and strong families, the building block of Nishnaabeg political systems.

In our language, Basil Johnson uses the term *Maa maa ya*

wen du moowin to mean the process or the art of recognizing, of understanding, of fully comprehending, of being aware, cognizant, and enlightened; literally it means the blending of all thoughts and feelings into recognizing another being. When I took this word to Doug, he talked about the *wendamoowin* part meaning "what is your thought process as you move through life?" He talked about the first *maa* in maa maa ya meaning "it's in my heart." He made a distinction between *Baamaaya*, meaning searching for recognition, and *maamaaya*, meaning having it, finding, fully understanding yourself or another being.[9]

I want to think about that for a minute. Recognition within Nishnaabeg intelligence is a process of seeing another being's core essence; it is a series of relationships. *It is reciprocal, continual, and a way of generating society*. It amplifies Nishnaabewin— all of the practices and intelligence that make us Nishnaabeg. It cognitively reverses the violence of dispossession because what's the opposite of dispossession in Indigenous thought again? Not possession, because we're not supposed to be capitalists, but connection, a coded layering of intimate interconnection and interdependence that creates a complicated algorithmic network of presence, reciprocity, consent, and freedom.

When another Native person recognizes and mirrors back to me my Nishnaabeg essence, my Indigeneity grows. When my Indigeneity grows, I fall more in unconditional love with my homeland, my family, my culture, my language, more in line with the idea that resurgence is my original instruction, more in line with the thousands of stories that demonstrate how to live a meaningful life, and I have more emotional capital to fight and protect what is meaningful to me. I am a bigger threat to the Canadian state and its plans to build pipelines across my body, clear-cut my forests, contaminant my lakes with toxic cottages and chemicals, and make my body a site of continual sexualized violence.

I See Your Light

One of the mechanisms settler colonialism applies to destroy Indigenous systems of reciprocal recognition is shame. Shame is a powerful tool of settler colonialism because it implants the message in our bodies that we are wrong. Think back to the list of negative stereotypes the class listed at the beginning of chapter 6. The primary message in these stereotypes is *you are wrong*, not even *you've done something wrong* but *you are wrong*. This is the overwhelming and pervasive message of our participation in Canadian culture unless we are fully and utterly assimilated, and even then, our appearance is still wrong because it is not the right hue. The impact of being immersed for several generations now in continual, daily messages to varying degrees of *you are wrong* is that individually and collectively we carry large amounts of shame inside of us.

I first started thinking seriously about shame after rereading Fanon's *Black Skin, White Masks* while teaching the same group of students I described earlier at the Dechinta Centre for Research and Learning. A few weeks after we had done the exercise on gender stereotypes in the Indigenous self-determination course I was teaching, Dene filmmaker Amos Scott visited the class. I had asked Amos to work with me on a music video for a song that was being released on a record of poetry and music. Amos agreed, and we decided to use the project as a filmmaking workshop with the students.

I introduced the students to the poem.

I went through each line, explaining my intent and the Nishnaabeg references. I played them the poem-song.

Amos then asked each of them to say in one word how they felt. We recorded the list of feelings. He then asked them to translate that emotion into a visual image, and we recorded those. Then we went through each line and created a storyboard.

Then we talked about intent.

In essence, the students wanted the film to be a mirror. They wanted the film to be an exercise in reciprocal recognition, although they didn't use those terms. They wanted other Native people, particularly Native youth, to see themselves in the film in a positive way—smiling, participating in "ancient" Dene practices in "contemporary" times. They wanted the genders to show a range of emotions. They wanted to show skin, love, connection, and drinking without shame. They wanted to create a piece of work where Indigenous audiences would *feel that they were right*. They wanted to make a film where they were presented without being shameful.

In showing the film to Indigenous audiences over the past few months and leading discussions about the experience of watching the film, I have seen that the overwhelming emotion produced is pride. Watching the film is an emotional experience for Native people, and there are often tears. They see beauty. One audience member commented that it is "all the best parts of us in two and a half minutes." Although the film is Dene at its core in that it depicts mainly Dene people on their land practicing their way of life, Indigenous peoples from other nations still recognize themselves and their practices in the film. Audiences feel good.

Intellectually and artistically, this is an extremely simple intervention and one that is often a driving force in Indigenous art making and the self-representation of Indigenous story in the media. In terms of Indigenous audiences though, it is still a powerful intervention. It is still new. It still carries tremendous meaning to see our communities and families and ourselves reflected back to us in a positive light. The film is saying just that "I see your light."

My kids had a much different reaction to the film. They had trouble positioning it as a film at all. They thought it was boring. They didn't understand why we would make a film that just recorded normal life where nothing happens. "That is just us doing what we normally do. Why would anyone want to watch that?" That feedback made me very happy. They think being Nishnaabewin is normal. They aren't ashamed to the degree they can't even imagine feeling ashamed about that. It has taken my family over six generations to get here.

This experience led me to reflect more deeply on the role of shame as a tool of settler colonialism. We are made to feel ashamed for being Indigenous. This shame leads to disconnection from the practices that give us meaning. It elicits pain. To cope with that pain, either we turn inward, amplifying and cycling messages of shame leading to self-harm, drugs, alcohol abuse, or depression and anxiety; or we turn our shame outward into aggression and violence. We are then made to feel ashamed—dysfunctional, wrong, "damaged goods"—because of how we cope with the pain of shame and violence, which in turn amplifies and perpetuates shame. We also shame ourselves over not knowing our languages, not protecting our lands well enough, not organizing effectively enough, for always being on the losing end of colonial violence. Shame cages resurgence in a very basic way because it prevents us from acting. Radical resurgent organizing, then, must generate the escape routes out of shame and into grounded normativity.

Right now to a great degree in Indigenous life, we are looking into the colonizer's mirror, and that mirror is reflecting back that we are shameful, that we are not good enough, that we are not smart, or successful, or rich enough, or white enough, or Canadian enough, or together enough to organize. And what is reflected back is much, much worse if we are Indigenous women or 2SQ.

But why is the colonizer our mirror? Because the colonizer will always reflect back to us what the state wants to see: an "Aboriginal" that shops at the Gap, votes in the election, skips happily to Revenue Canada on income tax day, perhaps knows her language and participates in a ceremony instead of church on Sunday, perhaps even attends a vigil for missing and murdered Indigenous women, because wow, those poor Indigenous peoples just can't get their shit together. But they certainly do not reflect back anything that has to do with land, sovereignty, or my power as kwe.

Yet, collectively we still keep looking and begging, and educating and appealing to the morality of benevolent Canada. *If only they knew better.*

Look where that has gotten us.

Resurgent organizing, then, has to be concerned with building a generation of Indigenous nationals from various Indigenous nations who think and act from within their own intelligence systems; who generate viable Indigenous political systems; who are so in love with their land, they are the land; who simply refuse to stop being themselves; who refuse to let go of this knowledge; and who use that refusal as a site to generate another generation who enact that with every breath, birth, and political engagement and in every moment of their daily existence.[10] Resurgent organizing must create a future generation that never has to ask how to live free, because they've never known anything else—a generation that does not know shame, because they are embedded in each other's light.

ELEVEN
EMBODIED RESURGENT PRACTICE AND CODED DISRUPTION

IN "EVERYDAY DECOLONIZATION: Living a Decolonizing Queer Politics," Kwagiulth (Kwakwaka'wakw) scholar and resurgence theorist Sarah Hunt and non-Indigenous scholar Cindy Holmes ask, "What does decolonization look and feel like, what does it entail, in our daily actions as queer women? What is decolonization beyond something to aspire to as allies to Indigenous struggles for self-determination or as Indigenous queers who want to align various aspects of our Two-Spirit identities?"[1] They ask us to actively take up decolonization in intimate spaces—with friends and family and in our homes—and encourage us to engage in critical conversations within these spaces as a mechanism to see, hear, and think differently. They challenge us to embody our decolonial politics and practice them in our daily lives. If we are members of Indigenous nations, they propel us to live in our bodies as Indigenous political orders in every way possible. They ask us to re-create Indigenous political practices inside our homes, right now, every day, including a criticality about the replication of heteropatriarchy. This to me is a powerful movement and a powerful way of embodying radical resurgence.

Cherokee scholar Jeff Corntassel's research on Indigenous pathways of resurgence focuses on identifying "everyday practices of renewal and responsibilities within native communities today" by asking the simple question, "How will your ancestors and future generations recognize you as Indigenous?"[2] His challenge is for individuals and communities to reject state affirmation, recognition, and the performativity of the rights-based discourse and to move beyond political awareness and symbolic gestures to grounding ourselves and our nations in everyday place-based practices of resurgence. He warns against the politics of distraction—states' attempts to move us away from the renewal of place-based practices by distracting us with politics that are designed to reinforce the status quo rather than deconstruct it. He encourages us to center our individual and communal lives around renewal. I see power in Hunt and Holmes's and Corntassel's work as flight paths out of the cage of violence and shame that colonialism traps us in.

The combination of living decolonial queer politics in intimate spaces and everyday acts of resurgence can be a force for dramatic change in the face of the overwhelming domination of the settler colonial state, particularly on microscales.[3] This kind of thinking has inspired diverse nation-based principled action, particularly among Indigenous youth, all over Turtle Island. The generative and emergent qualities of living in our bodies as political orders represent the small and first steps of aligning oneself and one's life in the present with the visions of an Indigenous future that are radically decoupled from the domination of colonialism and where Indigenous freedom is centered. This embodiment draws us out of the politics of distraction and away from continually positioning ourselves and structuring our movements in a response to the politics of distraction. We then become centered in our Indigenous presents, rather than centered in responding to the neoliberal politics of the state.

This is so crucial in the context of resurgence. My Ancestors are not in the past. The spiritual world does not exist in some mystical realm. These forces and beings are right here beside me—inspiring, loving, and caring for me in each moment and compelling me to do the same. It is my responsibility with them and those yet unborn to continuously give birth to my Indigenous present. This spatial construction of time is crucial and is encoded in Nishnaabemowin. Nishnaabeg artist Susan Blight recently explained this to me using the word *biidaaban*. This is commonly translated as "dawn." Blight, learning from elder Alex McKay from Kitchenuhmaykoosib Inninuwag, broke down the word as follows. The prefix *bii* means the future is coming at you; it also means the full anticipation of the future, that you can see the whole picture. *Daa* is the verb for living in a certain place or the present. *Ban* or *ba* is a verb used for when something doesn't exist anymore or someone who has passed on. Biidaaban, then, is the verb for when day breaks, the actual moment daylight appears at dawn, not as a prolonged event but the very moment.[4] My own interpretation of this is that the present, then, is a colliding of the past and the future. Everyday embodiment is therefore a mechanism for ancient beginnings.[5] Engagement in these practices unlocks their theoretical potentialities and generates intelligence. It is this present, this *presence,* that will create flight paths out of colonialism and into magnificent unfolding of Indigenous place-based resurgences and nationhoods. I was reminded of this by a short video from the Polynesian Voyaging Society's journey of the Hōkūle'a when one of the knowledge holders comments, "you can't go anywhere if your canoe is tied to the dock."[6]

Embodiment compels us to untie our canoes—to not just think about our canoes or write about our canoes but to actually untie them, get in, and begin the voyage. Embodiment also allows individuals to act now, wherever they are, city or reserve, in their own territory or in that of another nation, with support or not, in small steps, with Indigenous presence. These acts reinforce a strong sense of individual self-determination and freedom and allow individuals to choose practices that are meaningful to them in the context of their own reality and lives. On an individual level, people are taking it upon themselves to learn their own nation-based Indigenous practices. This can mean everything from becoming vitally attached to land and place; to learning language, songs, dances, stories, and artistic practices; to renewing ceremonies; to engaging in land and place-based practices and ethics; to revitalizing our systems of politics, governing, caring, education, and service; to reclaiming birthing, breastfeeding, and parenting practices and death rituals; to regenerating the responsibilities and positions of the 2SQ community. At first glance, these acts seem to have the most transformative power within individuals. But as I've witnessed this unfolding in various manifestations, these individual everyday acts of resurgence are starting to also become organized and collectivized, and it is in relationship to each other that we can enact and renew our political and governing practices. I am thinking here of the Dene students at Dechinta, spending significant time on the land with elders mastering Dene thought through the practice of Dene bush skills. I am thinking here of the Onaman Collective regularly hosting language immersion houses, building canoes and snowshoes, making maple syrup, and fund-raising to buy land for a permanent cultural camp; and the Ogimaa Mikana Project in Toronto restoring original names and inserting Nishnaabemowin into the urban spaces of downtown cores. I am thinking of the Kwi Awt Stelmexw language institute for Skowmish immersion. I am thinking of the tireless peer-to-peer work on sexual health and addictions done by the Native Youth Sexual Health Network.[7] I am thinking of young moose-hide tanners in Denendeh whose work might start out as individual everyday acts of resurgence but then grow as they connect with hunters, expert hide tanners, tool makers, story, and Ancestors and as they embody and generate theory.[8] I am also thinking of the resurgent organizing and daily embodiments of Indigenous practices taking place on the land around occupations such as the Unis'tot'en Camp and the ongoing blockade at Grassy Narrows.[9] I am interested in thinking about how to build upon these place-based resurgent mobilizations to build a network of resurgent struggle. Everyday acts of resurgence tie us to original creative processes that create networks across time and space and generate doorways for new theoretical understandings to emerge. They are the kinetics in Edna's creation story. They are the *how*.

Refusing Colonial Spatialities

Everyday acts of resurgence sound romantic, but they are not. Put aside visions of "back to the land," and just think land—some of it is wild, some of it is urban, a lot of it is ecologically devastated. Everyday acts of resurgence are taking place as they always have, on both individual and collective scales on Indigenous lands irrespective of whether those lands are urban, rural, or reserve. Every piece of North America is Indigenous land regardless of whether it has a city on top of it, or it is under threat, or it is coping with industrial development. I am uncomfortable with the continued settler colonial positioning of reserve versus urban communities as a mechanism to reinforce division. Reserves are colonial constructs, as are urban communities. Urban Indigenous communities are often sites of tremendous opportunity and action in terms of political alliance building, governance (because urban Indigenous collectives and organizations are not under the thumb of the Indian Act), language revitalization, local Indigenous economic and food initiatives, urban land reclamation and renaming, artistic renaissance, political education, and community organizing, as are reserve communities, and I believe many Indigenous peoples are attached and in love with our homelands regardless of where we live. Indigenous women and 2SQ people have particularly long histories of activism in Canadian cities as a result of the expulsive heteropatriarchal policies of the Indian Act. We have a network in cities of Friendship Centres, shelters, theaters, health care programs, organizations that support the families of missing and murdered Indigenous women and girls, and schools because of these actions, not to mention the decades of 2SQ movement building and organizing that has taken place in urban environments, and this unfortunately too often goes unseen.

In *Mark My Words: Native Women Mapping Our Nations*, Seneca scholar Mishuana Goeman asks us to question the acceptance of colonial spatialities, and she challenges us to construct deeper understandings of ourselves by examining our own relationships to place and to each other outside of the spatial constructs of settler colonialism.[10] Goeman speaks of her family's mobility in a manner that enables me to see that they are mapping aspects of their Seneca grounded normativity through spatialities as intervention, as a mechanism through which to maintain their dignity and self-sufficiency as Indigenous people. Through connections with other Indigenous people outside of their reservation, they created tiny islands of Indigeneity, in spite of these settler colonial spatialities. They created refuges. They escape into Indigeneity. Goeman uses the concept of (re)mapping, drawing on Gerald Vizenor, to "connote the fact that in (re)mapping, Native women employ traditional and new tribal stories as a means of continuation."[11] This makes sense to me. Mapping, storytelling, and continuation have always been a part of our grounded normativity, even shattered grounded normativity. Vizenor defines survivance as "an active sense of presence, the continuance of native stories, not a mere reaction, or a survivable name. Native survivance stories are renunciations of dominance, tragedy, and victimry."[12] Within Nishnaabeg thought, stories throughout time have always been a renunciation of dominance, tragedy, and victimry, and so to me, the lens of resurgence resonates more than the lens of survivance. I don't experience a division between "tribal" and "new." I don't just renounce. I refuse and I continue to generate. Tools do not necessarily define process, and while we have added "new" tools for storytelling within our embedded practices, we can also remain rooted in our deeper philosophical and aesthetic understandings to generate meaning. There is no hybrid. Mobility shatters and refuses the containment of settler colonialism and inserts Indigenous presence. This is an asset.

Indigenous mobility under the domination of settler colonialism as process is complicated and layered with multiplicity. I see at least four kinds of mobility: mobility within grounded normativity as an embedded Indigenous practice, mobility as a response to colonialism as resistance, mobility as a deliberate and strategic resurgence, and mobility as direct or indirect forced expulsion, relocation, and displacement and the creation of Indigenous diaspora. Indigenous movement can be any one of those things or a fluid combination of any or all of those elements. Indigenous peoples and our mobility can certainly be an expression of agency and self-determination within even shattered grounded normativity. Given the reality of settler colonialism, many of us continually reevaluate where we live, whether it is a city or a reserve, in our own territory or not, as a process to figure out how to live with as much dignity as possible. Our answers change as we move through the stages of life. I see this as a theoretical intervention. I see this as us using our mobility as a flight path out of settler colonialism and into Indigeneity. I see mobility imbued with agency as resurgence.

Mobility and the diplomacy and community building inherent in it are a practice of many Indigenous nations. We've always moved throughout our territories and through the territories of others with the practice of diplomacy, moving with the consent of other nations. Most of us have lived or will live in a variety of places throughout our lives, and we travel back and forth maintaining connection wherever possible and whenever we have the means. This in my mind does not necessarily dilute our Indigeneity, nor does it dilute our demands for a land base. In resurgence practice we should be working to strengthen the connections between our communities and building upon our strengths rather than falling into the colonial trap of urban versus reserve. Everyday acts of resurgence are one mechanism that can be used to build a more united resurgence movement that strengthens nationhood and works outside of the colonial spatial constructs the Indian Act has created to keep us divided, particularly when everyday acts are collectivized and done in relationship or community with other Indigenous people. Indigenous makers—those who live Indigenous practices inside of Indigenous spaces—hold onto these practices. When we start to link up with other individuals and communities engaged in everyday acts of resurgence by refusing the divisions of colonial spatialities, networks, or constellations, emerge.

The Indigenous artistic community is a site where this has always occurred, and I'd like to think about these contributions as a mechanism for moving from individual acts of resurgence to collective ones.

Creative Combat:
Resurgent Artistic Practice

In his extraordinary dissertation "Creative Combat: Art, Resurgence, and Decolonization," Jarrett Martineau begins to consider what happens when everyday acts of resistance become collectivized. Martineau uses the artistic practices of a diverse series of Indigenous provocateurs to examine the decolonizing potentiality of art making to disrupt and interrogate forms of settler colonialism and advance the project of resurgence and Indigenous nation building.[13] Using the practices of the artist collectives Post Commodity, Walking with Our Sisters, and Skookum Sound System, among many others, for examples, Martineau not only examines potentiality but artists and artist collectives engaged in radically resurgent production processes that result in art not as a product or even as an event but as an organizing structure of their lives—for their collectives and for the audience that participates with them.[14] Martineau argues that they are engaged in *affirmative refusal,* a refusing of forms of visibility within settler colonial realities that render the Indigenous vulnerable to commodification and control. He frames these creative practices as against representation, arguing that resurgent practice (he uses "artistic practice"; I would argue all resurgent practice) acts as "noise to colonialism's signal"; that is, resurgent practice is a disruptive and a deliberate act of turning away from the colonial state. But these practices aren't *just* disruptive. They are grounded in a coded articulation, like Martineau's dissertation itself, of Indigenous intelligence as theory and process and as affirmative refusal, resulting in the creation of not just points of disruption but collective constellations of disruption, interrogation, decolonial love, and profound embodiments of nation-based Indigeneity. They are artistic processes based in the infinite creative wealth of grounded normativity.

In a sense, the artists that Martineau draws upon and Martineau himself are making alternatives and are creating islands of colonial disruption in the present.

While Martineau's work makes crucial interventions in and across the fields of Indigenous studies, Indigenous contemporary art and aesthetics, performance studies, critical theory, political philosophy, sound studies, and hip-hop scholarship, the dissertation itself is also elegantly engaged in an affirmative refusal. I see a foundational use of Indigenous intelligence in Martineau's dissertation, yet to someone without extensive experience inside Indigenous knowledge systems, his work appears theoretical (only) in a Western sense of the word. This is because Martineau is refusing to visibilize Indigenous intelligence or grounded normativity and therefore make it vulnerable to commodification and control by settler colonialism, and by those that have not done the work within Indigenous intelligence systems to carry the knowledge in the first place.[15] It is an elegant level of protection and disruption, and it is a reminder that one does not become educated within Indigenous intelligence systems by reading books or obtaining degrees. My experience of this dissertation was not of a linear, logical work that moves from A to B, but of a spiraling into and then out of a core series of arguments, much like the movement of spiritual energy in ceremony. I interpreted this as a profound coded expression of Martineau's own Cree and Dene grounded normativity. In moving from individual acts of resurgence to connecting with networks of resurgence, coded communication and articulation are important because they protect the network from co-option, exploitation, and manipulation, and the sovereignty of the network remains in the hands of its Indigenous makers. This is perhaps one of the greatest lessons I continually learn from Indigenous artists: coded disruption and affirmative refusal through the use of Indigenous aesthetic practices. As a writer, my biggest struggle is often to speak directly to Indigenous audiences without the manipulation of settler colonial publishing, editing, and distribution. How do we speak to each other and build relationships with each other on our own terms?

Indigenous Aesthetics: Coded Disruption and Affirmative Refusal

The use of Indigenous aesthetics in artistic practice is one mechanism Indigenous creators use to code their work, to "disrupt the noise of colonialism," to speak to multiple audiences, and to enact affirmative and generative forms of refusal. It is also an everyday act of resurgence and a practice in and of itself that becomes collectivized when Indigenous peoples recognize the shared code. In my own writing, I rely on Nishnaabeg aesthetic principles to speak to multiple audiences through my own artistic and intellectual practices. This began a few years ago when I was at a talk by Monique Mojica at Nozhem Theatre in Peterborough, Ontario.[16] She was explaining her artistic process in working with a Kuna visual artist and in writing a play in pictographs. She talked extensively about Kuna aesthetics: *repetition, duality, multidimensionality,* and *abstraction.*

This resonated with me because I saw those aesthetic principles and theory underlying all kinds of things in Nishnaabeg thought, from ceremony, to storytelling, to art making of all kinds, and I recognized that I was already using them in my practice and wanted to deepen this practice. I thought carefully about each principle.

Repetition is interesting for a writer, because editors unfamiliar with Indigenous aesthetic principles hate repetition. Repetition is a bad thing whether you are writing nonfiction or fiction. Editors look for it because the assumption is that the reader will get bored, yet rhythmic repetition is at the base of Nishnaabeg intelligence. We hear variations of the same creation story for our entire lives, and we are expected to find meaning in it at every stage of life, whether that meaning is literal (when we are kids), metaphorical, conceptual, or within the constellation of our collective oral traditions or that meaning comes from lived experience. Our way of life is repetitive. Every fall we collect wild rice. We don't take a year off because we are bored, because aside from that being ridiculous, if we are not continually and collectively engaged in creating and re-creating our way of life, our reality, our distinct unique cultural reality doesn't exist. If you're bored, frankly you're not paying attention.

Duality is another principle that confuses Western thinkers because they get it mixed up with dichotomy. Duality again is present in all of our stories and our ceremonies and our daily lives, but it is not an either-or situation. I understand it really as holism. Every year, we all experience the fall and spring equinoxes, when there is the same number of hours of darkness and light everywhere on earth. Now that's not what really happens. Our experience of an equinox is mitigated by weather, for one thing, but even if we understand that one day as a dichotomy, there are 363 other days of shadowlands, and all of it is part of a complex whole—a whole that is constantly in motion and constantly changing. Yet there is a clear dichotomy between night and day, and you know what? I'm not a postcolonial critical theorist, so I don't experience dichotomy as a problem.

I like writing *multidimensionality* into my work not because I'm trying to write speculative fiction but because that's how Indigenous worlds work. There is an organization of time and space that's different than the colonial world's—different plans of reality. The implicate order, if you want to use that term, is influencing and intertwined within our own continually created physical reality. I was recently asked to write Indigenous science fiction, which coming from Indigenous aesthetics didn't make much sense to me. Our stories have always talked about the future and the past at the same time. They've always coinhabited the spiritual realm; the birthright of the storyteller has always been to make the stories that come through them relevant to the current generation. A lot of what science fiction deals with—parallel universes, time travel, space travel, and technology—is what our Nishnaabeg stories also deal with.

Abstraction is also a grounding principle in Nishnaabeg aesthetics. Again, I think Western thinkers get this confused with extraction. Indigenous abstraction is different because it comes from our grounded normativity. Extraction is a cornerstone of capitalism, colonialism, and settler colonialism. It's stealing. It's taking something, whether it's a process, an object, a gift, or a person, out of the relationships that give it meaning, and placing it in a nonrelational context for the purposes of accumulation. Abstraction within the context of grounded normativity is shifting the relationality to change meaning or to illuminate a different meaning.[17]

I also now see *layering* as an aesthetic through which makers weave multiple and coded meanings, and these can be literal, conceptual, metaphorical, and theoretical meanings layered into their artistic practice and the art they produce. This became very clear to me in working with Kanien'kehá:ka dancer and choreographer Santee Smith on her piece *Re-Quickening*. *Re-Quickening* blurs the lines between performance art, dance, and theatre and is a call for a reawakening of the intact feminine. As an audience member, I experienced the performance through movement, sound, and embodied kinetic conceptual knowledge that centered the truths of Indigenous women and our relationships in spite of the strangulation of various settler colonial insurgencies. It was grounded in Kanien'kehá:ka internationalism, as Santee worked with Maori, Zapoteca, and Kuna artists.[18] Two years before the world premiere, I was invited by Santee to her parents' home at Six Nations to talk about women, sovereignty, and violence along with four Indigenous artists: Christi Belcourt, Monique Mojica, Marina Acevedo, and Frances Rings. What unfolded was a very honest, complicated conversation about our experiences being Indigenous women that was highly influential in my development of parts of this book because I was so struck by the raw truths that come out in the intimate spaces Indigenous women and 2SQ people create and by the fact that these truths are so (still) rarely written. I am tremendously grateful for Santee's willingness to honor and center my experience and our collective experience as strength. In Santee's collaborative process the themes discussed at this meeting became an embodied performance ritual with multiple meanings mapped over objects, wardrobe, movement, sound, text, and the relationships between the performers themselves. This is an echo of what happens in my own creative work around layering meanings within storytelling, and I see it as ultimately an Indigenous mechanism for packaging and revealing knowledge in different contexts throughout a person's life. This to me is how ceremonial knowledge works: one can experience it on literal, conceptual, metaphorical, emotional, physical, spiritual, and intellectual levels through time and space but only if one deeply engages with the work with an open heart.

I have also learned a great deal about the Nishnaabeg aesthetics of *reenactment* and *presencing* from watching the performances of Nishnaabeg performance artist Rebecca Belmore and Nishnaabeg artist Robert Houle. From Belmore, I've learned that my voice, my body, and my physical presence are interventions in a settler colonial reality, in a similar way to the work of Audra Simpson, but in this case not intellectual, or not just intellectual, but as a physical presence. Belmore's body is her art, as my body is research. When Belmore enters a space to perform or even to give an artist talk, she does so in a way that emanates Nishnaabeg sovereignty and self-determination to a degree that I've only witnessed in elders. She comes into space with grounded power as a provocateur and agent who is not a victim. She is intervention. She is theory. She is both the presence and the doorway, and in her performances she often gives birth to the flight paths out of settler colonial reality and then literally takes those flight paths in front of the audience as witness.

A good example of this occurred in Belmore's performance in Queen's Park, Toronto, on Canada Day 2012. The space was marked with four pots of niibish, or nibi (water), and three large plastic bottles of water marking the front of the space, telling me that this performance was going to be about women. Nibi within Nishnaabeg philosophy carries within it many complex teachings and is also a strong reference to women. There are four female spirits responsible for the water in the oceans, the fresh water, the water in the sky, and the water within our bodies. Nibi is the responsibility of women. Nibi is women's sovereignty.

Belmore began by leading her three shkaabewisag (helpers) around the mitigomizh (oak tree), which would become the focal point for the work. Over the next hour, large sheets of brown kraft paper were unrolled, moistened with spray bottles of water, and carefully wrapped around the tree over and over. They used nibi to hold the sheets together. At first, the tying of the brown paper around the tree seemed like a marker to me. My attention was exclusively on mitigomizh. It was the elder, the grandmother Nokomis in the park. I imagined the destruction Nokomis had witnessed over the course of her life. I thought of all the water held by her roots and in her body. I thought of all the black oak trees and black oak savannas that are no longer in Michi Saagiig Nishnaabeg territory. I noticed the hordes of people walking by the tree, not noticing, on their way to see the horse statue and the legislature. For an hour, we sat or stood, talking and laughing quietly with our friends, eating and drinking and looking at Nokomis, the old oak tree in the context of water. We watched as our water was used to hold together the paper, methodically being wrapped around our grandmother.

I remembered the murdered, the missing, the stolen, the disappeared, and the erased. I remembered generation after generation after generation after generation of our warrior women and 2SQ. I remembered the generations yet to come. When mitigomizh was wrapped with the paper, it reminded me of a sexy, strapless party dress, with ruching from top to bottom and one asymmetrical strap coming across her shoulder, where Belmore had attached the gown to the tree (by initially throwing the paper tied to a yellow rope over a very tall branch).

Mitigomizh for me had become sexualized through no choice of her own. She was aesthetically beautiful, but then she was also aesthetically beautiful before the performance began. I had just forgotten to notice.

Then, one of the shkaabewis, dressed in her own black party dress and with long, flowing black hair, sat in the lap of mitigomizh. Belmore took the wig off the shkaabewis's head and placed it over her face. Then she continued to wrap the shkaabewis into the tree with the paper. All the while, our sacred water was being used as the glue. Eventually, the Indigenous woman disappeared.[19] Belmore then sat on the ground in front of the pots of water, facing the mitigomizh and the disappeared woman.

That in and of itself was emotionally moving.

Then, the pinnacle.

The peace was suddenly and without warning shattered by the sound of gunfire. I immediately thought of Oka and the sounds of bullets terrorizing the pines. The violence of the explosion vibrated through my body and the ground.

The twenty-one-gun salute felt like the brutal targeting and assassination of Indigenous women disguised as a salute and an honoring, which speaks to the insidious and manipulative nature of colonialism, helping, and reconciliation and the dangers of perpetually placing Indigenous women in the context of victimhood. The audio also included casual chatting, as if nothing was happening. As if it was all so normal, because violence against Indigenous women and 2SQ people is normalized. The layers of paper on mitigomizh's body made the stereotype of "easy squaw" came alive for me as the paper now became the layers of sexism, racism, and heteropatriarchy slowly and seemingly gently, but fiercely and persistently, wrapped around my body, replacing my own context of sacred being, good in her own right, with one of violence and attack, directly in the line of fire with people who are not afraid to pull the trigger. The water, my own fragmented power being used to hold me down, hold me back, to make me disappear.

This is the collective story of Indigenous women and 2SQ people in Canada.

We all to varying degrees face the daily firing squad, disguised as a reconciliatory salute. Our young girls are slowly but surely wrapped in heteropatriarchy and racism. Our bodies are never our own but always the focal point of the gaze, receptacles of violence. And then there are our grandmothers, carrying the water inside them, rooted to the land, their bodies magnificent archives of story.

The brilliance of Belmore's work is always for me in its apparent nuanced simplicity, which hours and days later becomes more and more complex. It is the very best of Indigenous storytelling grounded in the very same processes that have brought meaning to the lives of our Ancestors: multidimensionality, repetition, abstraction, metaphor, and multiple sites of perception.

In short, a multilayered conversation whose meaning shifts through time.

At the end of the performance, Belmore took the wig off her shkaabewis's face and helped her out of the wrappings and down off the tree. The image of Belmore extending a hand to Cherish Violet Blood and Blood bursting through the bonds of five hundred years of oppression with a huge smile on her face is one of the images seared into my memory from that day. The others, I'll carry with me, and every time I pass by a mitigomizh, wherever I am in the world, I will now remember the fierce, gentle, beautiful, nurturing nation-building spirit of Indigenous women.

Rebecca Belmore is presence. She takes (back) her (our) space (land) in the world, and her work compels me to take (back) my (our) space (land) in the world. On Canada Day in 2012, she took every mitigomizh in my territory back, no matter where they grow. She embedded the story of Nishnaabekwewag into their bark, and in doing so she liberated the story of Indigenous women from the bonds of victimhood. Belmore constructs a constellation between the missing and the murdered, the erased and the present, and she does so on the terms of kwe, not so much as performance but as reality. I experienced Belmore's intervention as radical resurgence.[20] After reading Martineau's work, I also understand it in terms of affirmative refusal. In reconsidering it here, years after the original performance, I see it is a coded intervention that disrupts the heteropatriarchy of settler colonialism and generates and then reinserts kwe as theorist and kwe as revolutionary.

Robert Houle's *Paris/Ojibwa* is another intervention that is generative encodement and carries within it an expression of Nishnaabeg aesthetics.[21] When I first stood in front of Houle's reconstruction of a 1840s Parisian salon, I had tears in my eyes thinking about my Michi Saagiig Nishnaabeg relatives from the Credit River at the center of the installation. I felt the horrific pain and despair of Uh wus sig gee zhig goo kway, a young Michi Saagiig Nishnaabeg mother and artist who watched her children die of smallpox in Europe while completely isolated from her land and family. Standing in the gallery some 170 years later, I could feel my heart break, imagining the moment when she realized that she would lose her own life and leave her remaining children motherless in a foreign and hostile land. This is the brilliance of Houle—his ability to create islands of decolonial love in their full richness while also evoking raw emotional responses, and in the process collapsing the perceived gap between artist and audience.

Paris/Ojibwa is a contemporary, multifaceted response to the story of a group of Michi Saagiig Nishnaabeg artists who traveled to Paris in 1845 to entertain French nobility as part of George Catlin's "Indian Museum." The artist collective included a family: Maungwedaus (see also chapter 4), his wife Uh wus sig gee zhig goo kway, their children, and various other family members. The early and brutal first stages of colonialism had foisted upon them a set of complex circumstances that led to their collective resistance and artistic response—one that took form through dance, performance, and the writings of Maungwedaus himself. I experience Maungwudaus and Uh wus sig gee zhig goo kway as rebel artists refusing colonial recognition at a time when Maungwudaus's brothers were (already) actively engaged in the politics of recognition as a mechanism to improve the social conditions of our people. Maungwudaus's journal invokes this. He was irritated and critical of his audience. He was not uncritically performing for white people. When he wrote in his journal lines like "The English women cannot walk alone; they must always be assisted by the men. They make their husbands carry their babies for them when walking," he is providing us with a rare written critical account of English life through the eyes of a Michi Saagiig Nishnaabeg writer and artist.[22] To me, he was a performance artist in the same vein as Belmore, giving a performance as coded intervention and affirmative refusal.

Houle's installation is a reconstructed Parisian salon with four painted panels of figures returning to their homeland: a shaman, a warrior, a dancer, and a healer. Below each panel is an image of the smallpox virus. Above the panels are the names of the dancers, cycling in reference to Nishnaabeg honoring practices.[23] I loved that Houle's language and visual imagery speak directly to our community: in the bowl of sage in the front corner of the salon, in the "sound of water, which changes to drums and finally an honor song, fills the entire space," and in his respect for our practices of honoring the spirits of those who have passed on by not speaking their names, but cycling them in text at the top of the exhibit.[24] *Paris/Ojibwa* represents a liberation, a homecoming, and an honor song both to the Michi Saagiig Nishnaabeg artists in Catlin's "Indian Museum" and to contemporary Nishnaabeg.

Originally shown in Paris as part of a series of performance reenactments, *Paris/Ojibwa*'s Canadian premier was at the Art Gallery of Peterborough in the heart of Michi Saagiig Nishnaabeg territory. The initial Parisian enactments are a crucial part of this story. In 2006, Houle and artist Barry Ace traveled to various locations in Paris, following the footsteps of Maungwudaus's performance collective, reenacting Michi Saagiig Nishnaabeg dance and performance for the crowds of Paris.[25]

The installation installed in Michi Saagiig Nishnaabeg territory at the Art Gallery of Peterborough now becomes to me about resurgence. I like the irony of a Parisian salon in the heart of Kina Gchi Ogamig, nested in Nishnaabewin, as a physical intervention of the Nishnaabeg internationalism discussed in chapter 4. Houle shifts the gaze from "Indians as objects in a museum" to the politics of power and representation that allow us to exoticize and objectify "Indians" in the first place, while also illuminating the resistance and resilience of the Nishnaabeg. Through *Paris/Ojibwa,* Houle delicately transforms the history of Maungwudaus and Uh wus sig gee zhig goo kway from tragedy into a beautiful, sacred story of the Nishnaabeg kind.[26] This idea of *reenactment as aesthetic* combined with abstraction becomes a way of empathizing across time and space with Maungwedaus and Uh wus sig gee zhig goo kway by creating and then living a different ending.

This reenactment as aesthetic became a part of my own artistic practice with the making of the poem, poem-song, and video "Leaks." The poetry is a response to a racist encounter with a white county worker while picking wild leeks with my daughter, who was five at the time. This was her first encounter with white racism. I felt guilty for not being able to protect her and initially wrote the poem as a way of processing the traumatic experience for myself. I sent the poem to Cree/Nishnaabeg singer-songwriter Tara Williamson, and she sent a song back. Over the course of a few months of performing the piece in Peterborough, we were approached by Métis filmmaker Cara Mumford, who wanted to make a video of the poem-song and to have my daughter dance in the film. Cara's process involved going back to the site, like Houle, and reenacting to some degree (in a child-appropriate manner) what had happened but this time in a different context—the context of a loving, supportive, funny group of Indigenous women artists. This process of art making through reenactment was not only healing but produced a moving short film.[27]

All of these works involved an initial tragedy or experience with colonial violence, and all three use the processes of Nishnaabewin to lead artist collectives and eventually audiences through a different ending of the story. *Paris/Ojibwa* ultimately restores honor and dignity to those lost through colonial violence, on our own terms. *Paris/Ojibwa* in particular operationalizes the story of Maungwedaus and Uh wus sig gee zhig goo kway but through an opaqueness rather than through the consumptive eyes of the colonizer. While the Parisian audience is consuming Ace's dance performance, *Paris/Ojibwa* is also consuming them under the gaze of the Michi Saagiig Nishnaabeg. While I am walking through the Parisian salon installed in my territory, I am part of a speaking back to colonialism. *Paris/Ojibwa* is a disruption to colonialism's gaze, it is a generative refusal, it is opaque—a visible but largely unreadable or differently read installation and experience to those outside of Nishnaabewin.[28] In a sense, Houle has built a network or a constellation across time and space, transforming Maungwedaus and Uh wus sig gee zhig goo kway from skeletons in unmarked graves in Europe to sacred beings.[29] He then links them as Ancestors to us, to me and my community, to himself and his community, to how we are represented, and to the audience who walks into a constructed Parisian salon as spectacle, embedded in opaque Michi Saagiig grounded normativity. For me, as a Michi Saagiig audience, he set up a constellation as a flight path to my Ancestors, Maungwedaus and Uh wus sig gee zhig goo kway, their family, and their affirmative refusal, centuries before that was even a concept.

TWELVE
CONSTELLATIONS OF CORESISTANCE

STARS, IN EDNA MANITOWABI'S TELLING of the Seven Fires creation story, represent the thoughts of Gzhwe Manidoo.[1] In the first attempt at creating this world, Gzhwe Manidoo's thoughts and ideas went out into the universe in perpetuity because there was no physical structure to embody them. That's the first layer of knowledge that stars carry. They are a reminder that thought (the sound of the rattle) has to be combined with heart and motion (the sound of the drum) in order to have energy and influence. These are the sounds of the skyworld holding the universe together, because sound creates and maintains relationships that embody both intellectual and emotional knowledge, otherwise known in Nishnaabeg thought as knowledge.[2]

The skyworld is an important space in Nishnaabeg thought. I know of Nishnaabeg creation stories of spontaneous creation, creation from the earth below us, creation from the water, and of course, there are several origin stories about creation from the skyworld.[3] To me, the skyworld in the peopled cosmos of the Nishnaabeg holds the present because it carries the events and beings of the past, and the events and beings of the future. We are born from the skyworld, and we return there when our time in the physical world is done. The spirits live there. Knowledge is held there. One of the primary responsibilities and beautiful struggles of physically being Nishnaabeg is that we have to strive and commit to maintaining deep everyday relationships with this world when we are physically on the earth.

Collections of stars within Nishnaabeg thought are beacons of light that work together to create doorways, like Bagone'giizhig, into other worlds.[4] On a conceptual level, they work together to reveal theory, story, and knowledge representing a mapping of Nishnaabeg thought through the night sky and through time. It takes the light of the stars a great deal of time to reach the earth, so when we look at stars, we are actually looking from the present back into time and space. When my children were being born, Edna Manitowabi told my partner and me to watch the sky for information of what this new being's name might be, because birth is an act of coming through the doorway between the spiritual and physical world. The people around me, supporting me, were in this way a constellation opening a doorway to the spiritual world to give physical presence to a new being. I am also a new hunter, and this comes with great responsibility. The taking of life is similar for me to the giving of living because they both involve transformations between worlds, and those transformations occur through doorways. The act of hunting requires an animal's consent to return to the spirit world by appearing and then physically dying, allowing its spirit to travel through the doorway back to the spirit world.

Constellations are not just physical doorways to other worlds; they also act as conceptual doorways that return us to our core essence within Nishnaabeg thought. Constellations are constantly in motion shifting with the seasons, serving as signposts indicating when it is time to tell winter stories, when the ice is no longer safe, or when it is time to move to the sugar bush. Some constellations are ceremonies, like the sweat lodge or shaking tent formations, while others are animals of the clan system. Constellations are coded mappings for Nishnaabeg for those with star literacy.[5] They are what Jarrett Martineau describes as opaque—visible to everyone all night and unreadable theory and imagery to the colonizer or those who aren't embedded in grounded normativity. Just as birds and other animals look to stars as guides in migration, the Nishnaabeg looked to the skyworld for knowledge and flight paths out of settler colonialism. The constellated and emergent relationships from within grounded normativity between radical resurgence, generative refusal, and reciprocal recognition, for instance, might create the potential for heightening nationhood, Indigeneity, and freedom. Similarly, Martineau writes of a slightly different conceptual constellation as a mechanism to open up flight and fugitivity in the context of radical resurgence:

> Thus far I have explicated becoming other as a strategic movement away from the terms of subjection and subjectivity, considered through strategic refusals mobilized in abjection, disidentification, détournement, and opacity. Taken together, this resistant constellation can be understood as a modality of flight, both away from identity and identity politics as such, and in anticipation of an arrival to an elsewhere that is already here, if hidden from view. This elsewhere is a decolonial turn away from the romantic rhetoric of revolutionary subjectivity *represented* in direct contestation against Empire.[6]

This is an important intervention into the use of ideas of escape, fugitivity, and flight. Indigenous thought doesn't dissect time into past, present, and future.[7] The future is here in the form of the practices of the present, in which the past is also here influencing. When Martineau suggests resistant constellations as flight paths to the future, he is really talking about the opaque Indigenous worlds that Indigenous peoples to varying degrees are already living within—flight paths to Nishnaabewin, flight paths to an amplified and centered grounded normativity. This works because constellations are place-based relationships, and land-based relationships are the foundation of Indigenous thought. Aki is the foundation of Nishnaabeg thought.

This conceptual layer of constellated intelligence is also seen in Nishnaabeg theory. The Gchi Ojiig formation, known as the Big Dipper, is to me about these same constellated relationships, overcoming hardship, struggle, and resolution, and in a radical resurgence context, it is a mapping of flight or fugitivity turning inwards and away from settler colonialism. Indigenous fugitivity is always flight inwards.[8] The story takes place in a time where the world was engulfed with darkness—there was no sun. Let's say the story takes place exactly right now, as all of our stories do, because faced with the strangulation of settler colonialism that results in children as young as ten years old committing suicide, it certainly feels like I live in a place where there is no sun.

Ojiig (fisher), lynx, wolverine, and otter embark on a journey to the skyworld to see if they can get the sun back because sustaining life was so difficult in constant cold and darkness. The four beings travel to the skyworld, where life is very good and the sun's warmth brings forth a continual bounty of new life. It is warm with lush vegetation and a pristine lake. Wolverine and Ojiig decide to work together to make the hole in the sky bigger so the warmth of the skyworld will flow down to their mother. I wonder if they forgot to ask the sky people for consent. No one has ever told that to me, but still I wonder. It doesn't seem right. They aren't in their own territory, except for Wolverine because she is also a star person, she is also a member of both worlds.[9] Maybe it's not consent that's missing. Maybe it is collective decision making.

After they work for a long time, the snow on earth starts to melt, the waters start to flow, and the world begins to wake up. At some point, the people of the skyworld show concern that the hole is taking all of their sun and warmth. They confront the four animals. Wolverine is so startled that she falls through the hole and back to the earth. Some of the sky people and fisher, lynx, and otter negotiate to make the hole the right size so that both worlds can share and benefit from the light and heat of the sun. Other sky people aren't able to understand, and they kill fisher with an arrow. Gzhwe Manidoo watches all of this. Honoring her for her work, Gzhwe Mnidoo picks up Ojiig and places her in the stars for trying to help everyone on earth. Every winter Ojiig is struck by the arrow and falls over on her back, but during the summer she rolls onto her feet to bring warmth back to her people.[10]

This story is about mistakes, struggle, mobilization, sacrifice, love, negotiation, and sharing. To fully understand the coded conceptual meanings of this story, one has to consider all of the knowledge and story held by the four animals, the skyworld, the people of the skyworld, and the grounded normativity within which this story takes place. The lynx, otter, and fisher are all members of the larger Martin Clan, a clan that is concerned with providing the necessities of life to the nation, including protection.[11] In that way, the journey to the skyworld is a collective action in the fulfillment of their larger responsibilities to the nation.

Constellations are also an original code. When Canadians look up in the sky, they see the Big Dipper. When Nishnaabeg people who live within Nishnaabeg intelligence look up, they see Gchi Ojiig, they see their version of this story—an actual flight path out of darkness. They see a story and a series of relationships between otter, fisher, wolverine, lynx, and the sky people. They see a negotiation and a treaty. They see a problem, action, and solution. They see honoring and remembrance, and thanks to Martineau's work, I now also see opacity. The land itself is a coded representation of Nishnaabewin that is visible to those who live within Nishnaabewin but is opaque to those who do not. This is fundamentally why engagement with land-based practices generates theory within Indigenous contexts. Being on the land is a highly intellectual practice that is a living interaction between heart, mind, and movement.

Fugitive Intervention

Constellations exist only in the context of relationships; otherwise they are just individual stars. When individual star people or thoughts come together, they create doorways into Nishnaabewin. In the section of "Creative Combat" titled "Decolonial Constellations of Love and Resistance," Martineau details the concept of constellations as opaque, fugitive theoretical interventions in the universe of settler colonialism. Martineau and I have been talking about constellations as Indigenous intelligence, as theory, and as an organizing concept for years now, and what follows is highly influenced by both these conversations and his published work.[12] The concept of constellation provides a different conceptual way of collectively ordering beyond individual everyday acts of resurgence, and Martineau provides several examples of this formation as a mechanism operating in the context of the artist collective. This gestures toward the constellation as an organizing value in resurgent movement building, one that I started to see glimpses of during Idle No More with small collectives of people coming together to organize a particular event, or to create or hold Indigenous presence that in some way was disruptive to settler colonialism. Martineau writes,

> The artist collective, I claim, embodies Indigenous values of individuated creation and collaborative, interdependent communality. In the transdisciplinary work of artist collectives including Postcommodity, Skookum Sound System, A Tribe Called Red, and the Black Constellation, collectivization becomes a means of instantiating micro-communal forms of relationality, governance, and creation. In the case of Métis artist Christi Belcourt, for example, the *Walking With Our Sisters* "exhibit" becomes a collectively-produced and collaboratively authored work that self-generates structures of creative Indigenous women's and queer leadership and accountability. As the exhibit travels between communities, it creates locally-organized, lasting relationships between co-creators and collaborators.[13]

The idea of a constellation of amateurs is the process that has driven my own artistic work through the production of the album *f(l)ight* (RPM Records, 2016). Starting with a series of poems, I worked with a collective of Indigenous and non-Indigenous musicians and artists to produce songs, a recorded album, and a performance. This constellation grew each time the record was performed live in various incarnations from a site-specific installation and durational performance with Tanya Lukin Linklater to more standard musical performances. This constellation grew again through the creation of a series of music videos with a diverse group of emerging Indigenous filmmakers (leannesimpsonmusic.com).

The idea of artist collectives creating space for instantiating microcommunal forms of grounded normativity and Indigenous intelligence is rich and fertile Indigenous space across Turtle Island and extends beyond artistic practice. Collectives allow people with common goals to come together, produce, act, and then disband, reform, or continue as needed. They are an opportunity to govern ourselves using Indigenous processes, to challenge heteronormativity in our ceremonial practices, to critically examine how our movements erase and marginalize 2SQ and replicate transphobia. Individuals can and should have their own practices of production, but these collective spaces can be used to generate resurgence modes of production in addition to their own work, and when these collectives start to develop relationships with other collectives, constellated organizing intensifies across orders of magnitude. This organizational structure seems to have relevance to radical resurgent organizing.

Constellations then become networks within the larger whole. Individual stars shine in their own right and exist, grounded in their everyday renewal of Indigenous practices and in constellated relationships, meaning relationships that operate from within the grounded normativity of particular Indigenous nations, not only with other stars but also the physical world and the spiritual world. Constellations in relationship with other constellations form flight paths out of settler colonial realities into Indigeneity.[14] They become doorways out of the enclosure of settler colonialism and into Indigenous worlds. They can be small collectives of like-minded people working and living together, amplifying the renewal of Indigenous place-based practices. They can be larger Indigenous nations working within their own grounded normativity yet in a linked and international way. When these constellations work in international relationship to other constellations, the fabric of the night sky changes: movements are built, particularly if constellations of coresistance create mechanisms for communication, strategic movement, accountability to each other, and shared decision-making practices.

Mobilization within Grounded Normativity

A few years have passed since Idle No More, which represented the largest mass mobilization of Indigenous peoples that I've witnessed in my lifetime. I want to now spend some time thinking about this mobilization, how we organized, and what we achieved. I think these conversations are important, and while I know we're having them in small groups, with our most trusted friends and colleagues, I don't think those involved with the many facets of the movement are having them on the scale of the movement. My consideration of these issues here is primarily based on my own experience from within the mobilization. Many, many others will have different experiences and perspectives, and in my consideration, I mean no disrespect to the tremendous contributions of the organizations, leaders, and people that I struggled alongside with during the winter of 2012–13. There were several beautiful and effective moments in our collective action. My discussion here is also by no means a comprehensive review of Idle No More, and I am using the term "Idle No More" in the broadest sense and in a temporal sense as well; that is, I am referring to the diverse movement that was at its peak during the winter of 2012–13. I am not referring to the organization Idle No More (www.idlenomore.ca) nor the ongoing work that has continued to occur under the banner of Idle No More to the present day. I focus on primarily three issues here: our use of the Internet, how we built the movement, and our relationship to allies. These issues in a sense are not specific to Idle No More but are relevant to thinking through mobilizations in the age of the Internet. I will be upfront: I have a lot of observations and few answers. This section is based largely on my personal experiences and observations during 2012 and

2013 in Ontario, and there is certainly regional diversity within the movement. I have not been involved with Idle No More as an organization, and I have not organized under the banner of Idle No More since 2013. I'm not sure any of us have answers at this point, because the Internet and mobilizing in Indigenous contexts are so new. I do, however, think we need to take stock and remember how to organize and mobilize within grounded normativity in a way that is effective in the present.

At the beginning of Idle No More, I *felt* like I was part of a community. I felt like I was part of something bigger. I remember being excited about being a part of something with a group of like-minded people who wanted to change and were willing to make sacrifices to do so. I worked with people I had met online and never met in person, editing blogs, organizing protests and events. There was a sense of unity that I enjoyed, and even though I knew that politically I might not agree on everything with the organizers I was working with, we could agree on enough to trust each other and work together on some issues. I thought that I was part of a community, and in a sense I was. And on the other side of that, there was shallowness to my online relationships that would only later reveal itself.

During the editing of *The Winter We Danced*, a collection of key writings from the winter of 2012–13, it became clear to me that there were three distinct but interrelated Indigenous political strains coming together: a rights-based approach that was interested in changing the relationship between Indigenous peoples and the state through policy, bills, and electoral politics; a treaty rights approach that included using the numbered treaties to change the relationship between Indigenous peoples and the state; and a nationhood approach that involved the rejection of recognition and rights-based politics and a turn toward Indigenous resurgence and that was anticapitalist in nature.[15] In many ways, the divisions weren't as clear as I am making them, and many individuals saw and see merit in all three approaches, while others simply do not. There was also a fourth strain, which involved lifelong organizers, those who had been organizing as activists through years of work, many of whom were involved in the environmental movement or had long activist résumés of participation in community-based actions. The movement was young in the sense that a lot of my mentors, those Indigenous people who had decades of experience in struggle, were participating from the sidelines. Many of the voices and leadership emerging were new to political activism. This was both inspiring and frustrating, as basic organizing and media literacy at times was lacking. It is often said that the movement was led by women, and I think this is true, but I also think most resistance movements throughout Indigenous history have been led in various ways by women. There were also ally voices—predominately but not exclusively white. Social media played a critical role in providing a vehicle to bypass Indigenous representations in the mainstream media and self-represent our interest, our voices, and our movement to the Canadian public directly. But we didn't use social media just for self-representation. We used it as a tool through which to amplify, to organize, and to *build* the movement. Although the vast majority of actions during Idle No More took place on the ground, in the real world, the organization of those events took place using social media. In a sense, the movement, like other mass movements at the time, for the first time was built to some degree in cyberspace.

On one hand, that last statement isn't the full truth, and I need to be more nuanced. The Indigenous community, particularly the segment of our community that is engaged politically, is small. To some degree we know each other. More than once, I asked friends and family who so-and-so was, and most often they knew a friend or a cousin of the person I was asking about. In a sense, the networks that social media created between individuals were an overmapping of kinship networks that already existed, but not entirely. Indigenous agitators of the past, such as Nahnebahnwequay, Pontiac, Tkamse, and Yellowhead, spent large amounts of time, years in fact, movement building. Movement building was relationship building, and it involved traveling large distances to create a physical connection with other human and nonhuman beings. This privileged the power of human connection and intimacy and of being fully present in the moment. Walking a great distance to spend significant time with people and the land builds empathy, trust, and the ability to give each other the benefit of the doubt. It connects bodies to land, and bodies to Ancestors. I was reminded of this during the great walks of Idle No More, with youth undertaking epic physical journeys to Ottawa, stopping to meet and visit communities of people along the way. The Nishiyuu walkers created a moment of unity in the movement because they physically walked on the land and connected to other Indigenous peoples.[16] These Cree youth, like Theresa Spence, did something *real*.

This movement-*building* step is critical in all movements, but it is particularly crucial to think this through in the age of the Internet, when a seemingly easy shortcut exists. Seemingly, because on a very basic level, I wonder how the Internet, as another structure of control whose primary purpose is to make corporations money, is at all helpful in building movements. I wonder if the simulated worlds of the Internet are *simulations* that serve to only amplify capitalism, misogyny, transphobia, anti-queerness, and white supremacy and create further dependencies on settler colonialism in the physical world. I wonder if this creates further alienation from oneself, from Indigenous thought and practices, and from the Indigenous material world. I wonder if this is a *digital dispossession* from ourselves because it further removes us from grounded normativity. The Internet is the ultimate Cartesian expression of mind and mind only. There are no bodies on the Internet. There is no land. Insertion of Indigeneity in cyberspace is not insertion of Indigeneity in the physical world. As much as it pains me to admit, grounded normativity does not structurally exist in the cyber world, because it is predicated on *deep,* spiritual, emotional, reciprocal, real-world relationships between living beings. Dispossessed from our Indigenous material worlds, our thought systems and our practices, are we losing the ability to be makers and to solve problems, or at the very least are we accelerating this loss because most of our time is spent on screens connected to the Internet? How are we generating theory as practice on the Internet? How are we building a movement that centers Indigenous makers when Internet access is so unevenly distributed across our territories? How is the Internet anything more than a house of cards when the next distraction is just one second away? How would my Ancestors feel about me being so fully integrated into a system of settler colonial surveillance and control when I have very little knowledge of how any of this technology works? I can't "fix" my phone. I don't know how to set up alternative digital communication systems. I don't know how to protect myself from state surveillance. I do know how to do exactly what larger corporations—Facebook, Apple, Twitter, and Google—want me to do to make them money, and I do it for the most part uncritically. I do know how to engage in apps and software. I can even be a content provider, but I have no ability to *structurally intervene*. Yet, almost more than any other structure, the Internet has structurally intervened in my life. There is a tremendous asymmetry here. The Internet and digital technologies have become a powerful site for reinforcing and amplifying settler colonialism, and I see losing the ability to structurally intervene as highly problematic. Code and algorithms are controlling our (digital) lives, and capitalism is controlling code. For Indigenous peoples, this takes place in the wider context of colonialism as the controlling structure in Indigenous life. Every tweet, Facebook post, blog post, Instagram photo, YouTube video, and e-mail we sent during Idle No More made the largest corporations in the world, corporations controlled by white men with a vested interested in settler colonialism, more money to reinforce the system of settler colonialism. Our cyber engagements were also read, monitored, collected, surveyed, and archived by the state. They were also read, monitored, collected, and surveyed by the segment of Canadian society that hates us, and they used these to try and hurt us. This worries me. I think we must think critically and strategically about adopting digital technologies as organizing and mobilizing tools. What are we gaining? What are we losing? How do we refuse the politics of recognition, engage in generative refusal, and operate with opaqueness on the Internet? Can we operate from a place of grounded normativity on Facebook when the algorithm attacks its very foundations?

When I think of the consequences of Internet organizing, I return over and over to January 11, 2013—Indian Act chiefs in boardrooms, people on the streets. It was at this point that I began to realize that Idle No More wasn't a movement that we could sustain. Most of my comrades I had never met in person. While there were small groups of people meeting and strategizing about specific actions and events, we had no mechanism to make decisions as a movement because at this point social media had replaced organizing. Disagreements over analysis or actions occurred online, and because we had shallow cyber relationships, instead of real-world ones, the larger structure fell apart quickly. We tried to build a movement online through social media, and when we needed to trust each other, when we needed to give each other the benefit of the doubt, when we needed empathy and a history together that we could trust, we couldn't. When we were sold out by leaders who didn't represent us, we were not able to regroup and relaunch the movement.[17] This was the first significant pushback from the state, and it crushed us, and maybe without the state doing anything at all, we would have crushed ourselves. I wonder in hindsight if maybe we didn't build a movement, but rather we built a social media presence that privileged individuals over community, virtual validation over empathy, leadership without accountability and responsibility, and unchecked liberalism that has now left us more vulnerable to the superficial recognition of the neoliberal state.

I've returned a few times in this book to Nanabush's first journey around the world as a way of showing the relationship between place and internationalism within Nishnaabeg thought, and to explore how Nanabush is original, reciprocal recognition. Nishnaabeg leaders, organizers, those concerned with mobilizing our people throughout history, have also considered this story, particularly the visiting aspect of it. Nanabush visited with, that is, created, a personal, intimate relationship with all aspects of global creation as a prerequisite for the work Nanabush came to do on earth. Leaders, whether Tkamse, Pontiac, Nishnaabeg water walkers, or the Nishiyuu youth, re-created this journey when they physically and personally traveled to each community in our territory to mobilize the nation. This act of visiting and recognizing was repeated over and over again through virtually every Indigenous mobilization up until Idle No More. Social media gave us an opportunity to skip the hard work of being present, of doing ceremonies together, of sharing food, and of standing face-to-face with our people, even when we disagree. I'm not sure it's an opportunity we should have taken.

Social media in many ways is the antithesis of Indigenous life. It is appealing, attractive, addictive, and apathetic. It amplifies fear, ego, and anxiety. It centers individuals within a corporate, capitalist, coded algorithm—an algorithm that we have no control over and that most of us don't even know how it works. It creates a false sense of power and influence. It scans our digital lives and then markets them back to us. Every piece of cyber resistance makes *them* more money and consolidates *their* power. The Internet creates false communities of like-minded individuals without presence, empathy, or trust. A relationship is not accepting a friend request and scrolling through photos and posts. A Facebook page is not a person, and a Facebook friend isn't a real friend.

Use of social media also has serious consequences for leadership within movements. Idle No More, at least initially, enjoyed a decentralized leadership model. This allowed for a diversity of tactics, politics, and localized actions that produced high levels of engagement. Decentralized leadership though, a cornerstone of Nishnaabeg leadership in the past, requires larger amounts of trust and truthful communication, shared accountability, and collective decision making. So again, if this kind of leadership is to be effective, the first steps of building a movement cannot be skipped, because in this process communications networks are built that enable secure, collective, principled decision making within the ethical processes of grounded normativity. The communication network in decentralized leadership models needs to be even stronger and more robust than in more centralized models. Conversations about leadership and strategy cannot take place online, because social media is *public* and Indigenous peoples are spectacle, criminal, and easy targets for exploitation and violence in settler colonial public. In the absence of both movement-generated leadership and robust private communication networks, social media creates a vacuum. Its spectacle sparks and then amplifies infighting and lateral conflict. It allows white liberals to crown leaders for us through likes, shares, followers, and protest selfies, and spokespersons for our movements are chosen without regard to the movement itself, let alone grounded normativity.

It isn't quite as easy as saying the Internet is pure capitalist evil though, is it? Social media proved to be a power tool to amplify the movement. Social media enabled us to get bodies on the ground in real life quickly. Social media and blogging were also critical in the education of Canadians during Idle No More, by providing a direct link between Indigenous peoples and our audience, unmitigated by the mainstream media, and this is evidenced through the plethora of writing—writing that took place during the mobilization. We wrote the movement in real time from our own perspectives in an unprecedented act of self-representation.[18] This was the first time that this happened on such a grandiose scale. Blogging, podcasting, and spreecasting became critical tools of representing ourselves and our issues on our own terms, en masse, to the Canadian public. When we don't have content that accurately reflects our lives, being a content provider is important. This was powerful, maybe even if it was making the bad guys more money. It influenced, to some degree, the way the mainstream media reported on Idle No More and in the years now following, on Indigenous issues in general. It increased our visibility in Canadian society, at least on the terms that Canadian society was willing to afford us recognition.

In the aftermath of Idle No More, the wealth of Indigenous reporting, writing, analysis, and opinion has propelled at least some Indigenous voices, arguably those that conform to neoliberalism most easily, into the mainstream media. While that has certainly benefited individual Indigenous peoples, most of whom were not in it for career advancement or notoriety, myself included, I'm not sure how or if this has benefited us collectively. We are certainly more visible in 2016 then we were in 2012. More Canadians read my work. There are more Indigenous peoples engaged in federal politics, and more Indigenous politicians in positions of power. We have more media celebrities. We have more Twitter followers and Facebook friends that have produced faux leaders that speak on our behalf with no accountability, and in some cases, no actual knowledge of the issues. I'm not sure, however, that I see evidence that we have advanced a decolonial political agenda, that is, a "radical decoupling of Indigenous life from the state's control and from the conditioning wrought by colonial society; a collective practice oriented toward the total reclamation of Indigenous life and land; a struggle for freedom."[19] I'm not sure I see that we've made much progress in terms of fundamentally shifting our relationship with the state, particularly in terms of a nationhood approach and in terms of resurgence. I'm not sure.

Again and again, it matters to me how change is achieved.

If I think back to my creation stories—whether it's the Seven Fires story, the story of Nanabush and the turtle's back, the story for Kinomagewapkong, the people that were created from the ocean, those spontaneous humans—the creation of the world within Nishnaabeg thought comes from struggle.[20] It was never easy. Mistakes were made. Prototypes were built. It came from a being or beings, fully engaged in a creative process that was a process of struggle. This is in stark contrast to Christian creation stories, where the world was made in seven days and then given to humans. Nishnaabeg worlds were created, collectively, out of struggle, and the process of creating and creation was given to us, not the results of that. The process, not the results.

The crux of resurgence is that Indigenous peoples have to recreate and regenerate our political systems, education systems, and systems of life from within our own intelligence. We have to create Indigenous worlds, not on the Internet but in physical reality. Our movements must respond to the basic social needs of our communities: relief from crushing poverty, clean drinking water, listening to youth and then doing what they tell us to create meaningful existences for them in their communities right now, supporting harm reduction approaches to addictions, dismantling children's aid and supporting people recovering from the damage it has caused, setting up alternative accountability structures for gender violence so 2SQ people, women, and children are safe, and supporting midwifery, breastfeeding, and families with children. These "social issues" are not social. They are political. They are a direct result of state violence in the form of settler colonialism that maintains and accelerates dispossession. Organizing to support urban and reserve communities on these issues in a politicized way must be part of any radical resurgence project because within Indigenous grounded normativity, these are our first responsibilities. This means we collectively have a tremendous amount to learn from Indigenous youth because they are disproportionately impacted by all of these social issues and because they are therefore experts on the way out.

This isn't something any state government can do for us. If we don't want our communities to be governed by the Indian Act, we need to build our alternative. If the state education system is failing our kids and not reproducing Indigenous intelligence, then what is the alternative (freedom schools, language houses)? If capitalism is killing the planet, then how do we create for ourselves a material means through which to build nations (local, place-based, integrated Indigenous economies)? How do we eradicate gender violence and create systems of accountability outside of the police and inquiries? And we must not just ask what is the alternative: we need to do the alternatives over and over until we get it right. This is the work of decolonization and resurgence, and it is not work the state can do for us, because we are the experts, because we are self-determining. Coming to state power with working alternatives in place, with strong nations, is coming to the state with grounded, authentic Indigenous power. More important, engaging in the resurgent process of creating based on individual and national Indigenous intelligence builds stronger relationships between our peoples and our lands. The struggle, even if it is not successful according to the dominate colonial narratives of success, creates more connection, more engagement with Indigenous thought, a seeking out of Indigenous expertise, and a stronger Indigenous present. These are the necessary prerequisites for an Indigenous future because the act of presencing is the act of creating the future.

If Indigenous peoples were engaged in resurgent organizing and mobilizing right now at the intensity they were at the height of Idle No More, through the election and through the first years of Trudeau power, if neoliberalism's electoral politics hadn't gutted the resistance, what would the landscape look like now? What's clear to me is that the work that goes into building relationships in the real world, building a movement of empathetic, caring Indigenous peoples, is how long-term mobilization was achieved in the past. It's the reason any of us exists today.

Constellations of Coresistance

In almost every classroom I find myself in and at the end of almost every talk, there is always a white person that asks the Indigenous instructor or speaker what they can do to help. It is usually an honest question with good intentions. It is not the worst question we all have to answer. I want to take a step a back from that question for a moment. I'm interested in thinking about who we are seeking solidarity from within the context of grounded normativity. Who should we be in constellation with? White "friends" and allies are seen as the promised land of the changed. If we can just get more white people to see that we are human, to see the state of poverty and inequality, they will pressure their governments and do the work they need to do in their own lives to bring about change. If the issue impacts everyone, maybe we can all be on the same side.

I think resurgent mobilization necessarily points us in a different direction because there is virtually no room for white people in resurgence. Whiteness is not centered in resurgence. If we recognize settler colonialism to be dispossession, capitalism, white supremacy, and heteropatriarchy, that recognition points us to our allies: not liberal white Canadians who uphold all four of these pillars but Black and brown individuals and communities on Turtle Island and beyond that are struggling in their own localities against these same forces, building movements that contain the alternatives. These are our allies, yet during Idle No More, we had almost no relationship with any of these communities, not because these communities weren't interested in us, but primarily because, again, we hadn't done the work of relationship building before mobilizing.

I have been influenced throughout my life by Black feminists and womanists and by the Black Radical Tradition. As a second-year biology student at the University of Guelph, I took two courses in Black history taught by Dr. Clarence Munford, who introduced me to Black Marxist traditions and Black liberatory movements. Professor Munford gave me a tremendous wake-up call. He propelled me to find out who I was and live it. Dr. Munford mentored me and a group of Black students and students of color for three years when we were on the university's presidential task force for antiracism, and he had a formative influence on my learning how to organize. He taught me how to speak back with fire.

Is there a basis for coresistance and solidarity between radical resurgence and the Black Radical Tradition? Black feminists and womanists? Black queer organizers and thinkers? How can Indigenous resurgence and nationhood make sure we are not replicating anti-Blackness without solid, reciprocal relationships with Black visionaries who are also cocreating alternatives under the lens of abolition, decolonization, and anticapitalism? Doesn't grounded normativity compel us to figure out how to act in solidarity with these comrades?

This is heightened for me in my own nation. Again, *how* is a pretty important concept in Indigenous thought because it reminds us that the outcome is different if Indigenous peoples create the alternatives on our own terms, on the ground, rather than by relying on the state. It also matters *with whom* we achieve liberation. Toronto, or Gchi Enchikiiwang, exists within Michi Saagiig Nishnaabeg territory.[21] The largest community of Black people in Canada live in Toronto—the home of fierce and beautiful acts of diverse forms of Black people's resistance to white racism, erasure, and ongoing police violence, to name just a few. Yet, the lines of segregation between the resisting

Indigenous and Black communities for the most part remain intact, and in fact, I think are being reinforced by the mainstream
Indigenous response to the Trudeau government.[22]

How am I accountable to the struggle of Black peoples in
Kina Gchi Nishnaabeg ogamig? How am I responsible to them
within the context of Nishnaabeg political and ethical systems?
How do I ensure my nationhood and relationship to land on the
north shore of Lake Ontario do not replicate systems that restrict Black spatialities or replicate geographies of domination?
As Katherine McKittrick in her brilliant *Demonic Grounds:
Black Women and the Cartographies of Struggle* writes, "Black
matters are spatial matters. And while we all produce, know,
and negotiate space—albeit on different terms—geographies
in the diaspora are accentuated by racist paradigms of the past
and their ongoing hierarchical patterns."[23] Within Nishnaabeg
political thought, we have practices of sharing space with other
nations and communities of peoples and respecting their autonomy to govern themselves over those lands.

In September 2015, when asked why violence against wom-
en remains a problem with young men today, Trudeau said music lyrics, pornography, and absentee fathers are factors in "a lot
of communities." Several Black activists responded on Twitter,
among them *Toronto Star* columnist Desmond Cole; one of his
tweets read, "Is it a coincidence that two of the three factors
Trudeau cited about violence against women are well-worn stereotypes about black people?"[24] A few months later, Trudeau an-
nounced the "most diverse cabinet in Canadian history," except
there were no Black cabinet ministers. What does it reveal when
the state seemingly holds Indigenous peoples issues in high regard while replicating anti-Blackness? What does it reveal about
us when we are silent? You can't engage the Indigenous community with one hand and continue to erase Black Canadians with
the other. It matters to me profoundly how change is achieved
and with whom we achieve it.

Within Nishnaabewin, I have ethical obligations to the
Black community. My people and the Wendat shared land and
then respected each other's self-determination and jurisdiction,

and I believe Nishnaabeg political practices compel me to do the same. I think then we would have to figure out political mechanisms to respect each other's governance, sovereignty, and jurisdiction while committing to taking care of our shared ecosystem. I think we would have to figure out how we can support each other so both of our peoples could live free on the north shore of Lake Ontario. To me that's what solidarity could look like under grounded normativity. That's what a constellation of coresistance and freedom could look like under radical resurgence. That's a future I'm interested in building.

The creation of a radical resurgence practice seems critical to me, and we are in a stage of building a movement that rejects state recognition at its core and is committed to sacrificing and doing the hard and long work of rebuilding Indigenous nationhood one system at a time. We need to collectively figure out how to instigate and sustain mass resurgent mobilizations within nation-based grounded normativities. We need to radically uncouple ourselves from the state political and education system. We need to be willing to take on white supremacy, gender violence, heteropatriarchy, and anti-Blackness within our movement. We need to be willing to develop personal relationships with other communities of coresistors beyond white allies. We need to develop these as place-based constellations of theory and practice because when we put our energy into building constellations of coresistance within grounded normativity that refuse to center whiteness, our real white allies show up in solidarity anyway.

CONCLUSION
TOWARD RADICAL RESURGENT STRUGGLE

I AM WRITING THIS FINAL SECTION in Tio'tia:ke/Montreal in April. This place holds meaning for me as a Michi Saagiig Nishnaabeg because my people came here often to trade, to visit, and to maintain diplomatic ties with the Kanien'kehá:ka. It is also in some ways the birthplace of my own politicization, witnessing the mobilization and resistance at Kanehsatà:ke during the summer of 1990. Yesterday, Ellen Gabriel drove me around her community, past the golf course and through those glorious Kanien'kehá:ka Pines—the magnificent trees of peace that used to exist all over her territory and mine and now only barely exist in small stands. I'm not sure I've ever seen trees this size in my territory. The Pines are peace. They are full of quiet beauty. To me, the Pines themselves are generative refusal. They refused the golf course, and within their roots, barks, needles, and spirit, they continue to generate peace as they have always done. The Kanien'kehá:ka people that protected this place in 1990 are also generative refusal. Looking back, I remember this now as both an intense sacrifice and a resurgent mobilization, based on

Kanien'kehá:ka political processes, analysis, strategies, action, and love.

This Kanien'kehá:ka resurgence is also a spectacular echo of Kanien'kehá:ka intelligence, and it compels me to think more deeply about our approaches to organizing and mobilization. Indigenous peoples with radical imaginations and desires for freedom must create collective, private physical spaces where we can come together and think very long and hard about how to organize and build resurgent movements, about how we move beyond everyday acts of resurgence to collective actions in the short and long term, and about how to create community that embodies and practices our nation-based processes in the present. How do we organize in the present to ensure we are creating a generation of Indigenous peoples who are intimately attached to their lands, skilled in the practices of grounded normativity, and have direct experience in building and maintaining our political processes, education systems, and wellness practices, for example?

I began to think more deeply about strategy and tactics during Idle No More when debates and differences of opinion emerged over tactics. Segments of the movement were decidedly against direct action because it makes Canadians angry—the assumption is that we lose their support—and in some cases because it was seen as incompatible with *Aboriginal culture*.[1] On one hand, they are right. It does make a segment of Canadian society very angry. On the other hand, this analysis has always bothered me because it centers the transformation of Canadians and of whiteness as the measure of a movement's success. More than that, it centers the politics of recognition and forces us to hand over our power to the white Canadian liberals we're trying to get onside. There is an assumption that if I act nicely, calmly, and happily, Canadians will support me because it is the right thing to do, because it feeds into Canada's international narrative of themselves as being a champion of human rights and the benevolent empathic state that cares about the oppressed. There is an assumption that if we behave as "good Indians" in the eyes of white liberals and even of what remains of the Canadian Left, we will be rewarded with rights and recognition. There is an assumption that I need to come at this from a place of pity, victimhood, and powerlessness. If this had been the starting point for the Kanien'kehá:ka, I wonder if their Pines would still exist.

I've tried to consider this in a less flippant and deeper manner because the white racism in the mainstream media and Canadian society, which fully erases Indigeneity and continually replaces it with stereotypes, means that our movements and actions will *always* be misrepresented. It means that *we* are *always* misrepresented. When we do something "nice," like hand out free coffee and donuts along with information flyers, racist Canadians might be taken aback because they are being confronted with the opposite of their assumptions about "Indians."[2] But there is also something that doesn't feel very authentic or genuine to me. I don't want my racist neighbors to like me because I gave them free Tim Hortons coffee, or because I have a PhD, or because they believe my education in their systems means "I'm a credit to my race." I actually don't care if they like me, nor do I care if they support me. That doesn't matter to me. It does, however, matter in a profound way what my immediate family and community think of me. It does, however, matter in a profound way that other communities of radical resistance see in me someone who has their backs because I have consistently acted in that manner. It does matter that the metaphorical pines in my territory exist for my children and for their children.

At the beginning of Idle No More, Dene scholar Glen Coulthard wrote:

> If history has shown us anything, it is this: if you want those in power to respond swiftly to Indigenous peoples' political efforts, start by placing Native bodies (with a few logs and tires thrown in for good measure) between settlers and their money, which in colonial contexts is generated by the ongoing theft and exploitation of our land and resource base. If this is true, then the long term efficacy of the #IdleNoMore movement would appear to hinge on its protest actions being distributed more

evenly between the malls and front lawns of legislatures on the one hand, and the logging roads, thoroughfares, and railways that are central to the accumulation of colonial capital on the other. For better and for worse, it was our peoples' challenge to these two pillars of colonial sovereignty that led to the recommendations of RCAP: the Canadian state's claim to hold a legitimate monopoly on use of violence and the conditions required for the ongoing accumulation of capital.[3]

If Idle No More had embraced placing Indigenous bodies between settlers and their money, in a coordinated, strategic, nation-based, and internationalist orientation connecting with movements globally, and if we had done the on-the-ground work of building a movement, we might have seen a mass mobilization based on a strengthened articulation of Indigenous nationhood, tighter alliances between movements, and an interruption in the material economic infrastructure of Canada in a way that we've seen only reactionary glimpses of in the past. Networks of planned, rotating actions can be organized to respect local self-determination but require face-to-face communication networks of trusted relationships, which Idle No More lacked. Bodies on the land within the context of grounded normativity also doesn't necessarily mean blockades and protests— it does mean thinking through new strategies and tactics and placing our action within the practices and ethics of grounded normativity.

It's also important we think through our conceptualization of direct action, from the so-called protest tactics of non-Indigenous social movements to ways of organizing and mobilizing that are inherently Indigenous. Placing Indigenous bodies on the land in *any* Indigenous context through engagement with Indigenous practices is direct action. Anything we do that affirms the bodies, minds, and experiences of Indigenous women and 2SQ people as the embodiment of Indigenous political orders is direct action. Everyday acts of resurgence are direct action. Resurgent organizing, mobilizing, and political action have the potential to change the framing of this conversation in a significant and powerful way. Organizing that is based on the critical animation and embodiment of Indigenous intelligence leads to place-based organizing, nation-based organizing, and organizing that illuminates Indigenous processes—the *how*. Resurgent organizing clearly lives out Indigenous values and ethics. It strengthens ties to Indigenous practices—ceremony, politics, decision making, leadership, language, gender, and land. It approaches the state from grounded normativity, from a reciprocal Indigenous recognition, from a place of strength. It comes at organizing from a completely different place: we are not begging the colonizer for attention, for money, for sympathy, for rights, for recognition, or for moral benevolence. There isn't necessarily a list of demands, because lists of demands are either ignored as being structurally impossible while maintaining the system of settler colonialism, or are absorbed into the neoliberal state to ensure real change doesn't occur. We don't need a list of demands, because we are the demand. We are the alternative. We are the solution, based on our own nation-based conceptualizations of ourselves. Our bodies and the political orders they house are the demand. Our embodied alternative is the solution. Building movements that embody the Indigenous alternative in structure, process, and formation that are brilliant expressions of international grounded normativities changes the game.

The seeds of this approach can be seen on microscales whether they present as a freedom school in Kanien'kehá:ka territory, a blockade against deforestation in Nishnaabeg territory, a bush university in Denendeh, an alternative justice system for sexual offenders in Hollow Water, a Cree language house in a city, Native youth providing peer-to-peer support related to sexuality, gender violence, and addictions, or thousands of moccasin vamps traveling Turtle Island. These are resurgent mobilizations because they are consistent with nation-enhancing processes and practices and because they are actions that are not recognition based or colonially reactive. There is no demand upon the state or its citizens other than to get out of the way and respect Indigenous self-determination and nationhood. What if we take their lead and stop begging the state to be accountable but shift our energy into building our nations on our own terms?

Refusing Victimhood

What happens when Indigenous peoples, particularly Indigenous women and 2SQ people, write ourselves, represent ourselves, and enact ourselves as revolutionaries fighting a transformative campaign against colonialism, white supremacy, heteropatriarchy, and capitalism through everyday acts of resistance and resurgence, rather than allowing ourselves to be framed and represented in ways that articulate and amplify us as helpless victims?[4] How does the state respond? How does this strengthen our nations?

Trauma-based mobilizations in Canada from the organizing that preceded the Truth and Reconciliation Commission to the decades of organizing that preceded the national Inquiry into Missing and Murdered Indigenous Women have been successful in at least one of their main goals: compelling the state into apologizing and setting up commissions and inquiries as a mechanism to account for past injustices. There is no doubt in my mind that this may bring healing and solace to some survivors and the families of those victimized. My comments here are not meant to diminish the anguish of survivors or their families nor the sacrifice, commitment, and struggle of the families and community organizations that have acted out of love to try to bring justice and healing to their own lives and to our communities. They have done this for decades without support, acknowledgment, or empathy from Canadians and oftentimes without support from mainstream male-dominated Indigenous political organizations. I worry, though, that Indigenous grief can be managed, exploited, and used by the state to placate Indigenous resistance. I worry that while these movements have been excellent at forcing the state to enact its own mechanisms for accountability, these mechanisms have never brought about accountability for Indigenous peoples because they are *processes* that are partly designed to uphold the structure of settler colonialism.

Those who are grieving are vulnerable, and being Indigenous

in Canada is to some extent a constant state of grieving because our losses of our own family members, lands, languages, etc., etc. are so immense. Canada has become very good at responding to our pain by deploying the politics of grief: a set of tools the state uses to avoid structural changes and accountability by focusing on individual trauma rather than collective, community, or nation-based loses, by truncating historical injustices from the current structure and the ongoing functioning of settler colonialism, by avoiding discussions about substantive changes involving land and dispossession in favor of superficial status quo ones, and by turning to "lifestyle choices" and victim blaming to further position the state as benevolent and caring. The state then manipulates and manages our collective grief into a series of processes that feeds into the structure of settler colonialism. The politics of grief are deployed to use our grief against us.[5]

The politics of grief place white Canada in a position of moral authority, a position they have not earned, particularly with regard to Indigenous peoples. There is an assumption on the part of grief- or trauma-based mobilization that if Canadians see and clearly understand Indigenous pain and anguish, they will act differently. Many of the individuals and families who are targets of violence either through individual sexual, physical, or emotional abuse or through the disappearance or murder of a loved one are placed in the position of grieving publically as a mechanism for sparking mobilization and change. We grieve. The state performs false pity. We have collectively responded to state violence with the strategy of appealing to the morals and benevolence of the colonizing state and to the empathy of citizens of that same state for action. This tactic has produced the Truth and Reconciliation Commission and the Inquiry into Missing and Murdered Indigenous Women, both of which are controlled entirely by the state and are being used for the state's purposes: to placate Indigenous resistance and to appease the moral concern of Canadians. The politics of grief can also so easily become the politics of distraction—a process, which as Corntassel reminds us (see chapter 11), moves us away from the renewal of place-based practices by distracting us with politics that are designed to reinforce the status quo rather than deconstruct it. Both the politics of distraction and the politics of grief are just enactments of the politics of recognition. And so I ask, while these state-run processes are taking place on their own terms, what happens if we refuse, turn inward, and in concert engage in large-scale resurgent organizing on our own terms? What does that look like?

The PKOLS Reclamation

On May 22, 2013, members of the Tsawout (SȾÁUTW) nation, with support from the Songhees and the other local WSÁNEĆ nations, including Tsartlip (WJOŁEŁP), Pauquachin (BOȻEĆEN), Tseycum (WSIKEM), and Malahat (MÁLEXE) and allied supporters from the Greater Victoria community in British Columbia, walked from the bottom of Mount Douglas and placed a sign that said "PKOLS" at the top. They did not ask the city of Victoria for permission. Their authority to do so came from the leaders of the SȾÁUTW nation.

Now to many non-Native people, Mount Douglas, or Mount Doug as it is affectionately known, is a prominent landmark and park in Victoria, a 263-meter hill named after the second governor of the colony of Victoria Island, Sir James Douglas. It's a municipal park with hiking trails through a mature second-growth forest.

To the SȾÁUTW nation, Mount Douglas isn't a municipal park. It isn't even Mount Douglas. To the SȾÁUTW, it has always been known as PKOLS. PKOLS is a significant place in the creation stories of the nation, and its name can be translated to mean "White head" referring to the white rocks their creator collected in Cordova Bay and used to make the surrounding mountains. PKOLS is and has always been a gathering place for families, communities, and nations.

When six hundred people, many of them non-Native allies, march up a mountain in a Canadian city and restore one of those original place-names under the leadership of Indigenous nations, the act then is extraordinarily significant. When this happens within Indigenous constructions of the world, it is a joyful, inclusive, celebratory occasion because beyond being a grounded, embodied expression and practice of Indigenous nationhood, sovereignty, and freedom, it is a collective and transformative direct act. It changes people in the present. It transforms our relationships to each other and to the land we share.

I live 3,400 kilometers from PKOLS, and I am not a part of the SȾÁUTW, Songhees, or the WSÁNEĆ nations. I watched the event unfold from the other side of Mikinakong, the place of the turtle, or Turtle Island. I was struck by the strength of the SȾÁUTW, Songhees of the WSÁNEĆ peoples. It was a brave thing to do. I was struck by how much we can influence how our actions are represented to the Canadian public when they are deliberate, planned actions rather than reactions to settler governments or industry. It was extraordinarily difficult for the mainstream media to misrepresent this action as an overly aggressive and angry action that threatened the safety of Canadians and Canada when the images on their cameras were of families laughing and celebrating together. These faces told me that everyone felt good—Indigenous peoples for obvious reasons, and non-Indigenous peoples, I can guess, because it feels good to finally be on the right side of history. It feels good to do the right thing.

PKOLS is significant to me in terms of resurgent struggle and mobilization in several ways. First, although it is a response to the colonial occupation and the erasure of Indigenous presence, it is not an immediate responsive action. That is, the response wasn't instigated by the state through the passing of legislation or the enacting of policy. It was initiated by Indigenous peoples on Indigenous terms. The process of organizing the event served to strengthen relationships between different Indigenous nations and peoples and their allies. The event was a collective, physical act of renewing relationships to land and territory using the mechanisms of the SȾÁUTW nation. There were responsibilities for the SȾÁUTW nation, Indigenous allies, and non-Indigenous allies. There was a ceremonial renewal of the Douglas treaty. There was Indigenous reciprocal recognition. The sign remains, and to me the success of the action is that even if the city of Victoria had removed the sign, they cannot remove the experience of hundreds of people coming together to support the reinsertion of the self-determination of the SṈÁUTW nation into the city of Victoria.

The PKOLS reclamation was not a victim narrative. No one was asking for white recognition. No one was putting pain and hurt on display as a mechanism to influence white decency. It wasn't a directly reactionary act. It was an insertion of Indigenous presence and power. PKOLS was an action of holding our heads up high and holding each other up in the warmth of the village, of coming at it with our best selves, of coming at it from a place of strength and knowing and grounded power. The PKOLS reclamation was a generative refusal. It is an example of radical resurgent organizing and mobilization.

It was a taking back of Indigenous space for Indigenous purposes that is echoed in land reclamation actions in ceremonial gatherings and in places like the Unist'o'ten camp and in the blockade at Grassy Narrows. While the mainstream media might focus on the blockade aspects of these actions, which are important in their own right, there is also a taking back of space in that the communities that maintain the blockades are often reinvigorating Indigenous governance, ceremony, economic systems, education, and systems of caring. These are bubbles of resurgent life. They are our first, or perhaps our latest, attempts at actualizing Indigenous alternatives. I dream of Kanehsatà:ke and PKOLS reclamations everywhere in a coordinated, strategic, constelled wave of resurgent organizing and mobilization.

Generative Refusal

I have visited and revisited the idea of generative refusal at various points in the Radical Resurgence Project because I think it is a very useful tool both conceptually and kinetically and because the more time I spend with generative refusal, the more powerful this idea becomes. Over the course of writing and editing this book, the term came up naturally in several instances in the text. I thought of consolidating this into a chapter or a section at the beginning, but that didn't seem right. What seemed right is what naturally happened: it came up, it deepened itself, and now at the end, it's the concept that encapsulates what I want to leave you with.

I used a deer story in chapter 4 to talk about Nishnaabeg internationalism. I often use this story to teach about Nishnaabeg political practices in general and about Nishnaabeg diplomacy and treaty making specifically. Over the years, this story has come to be a wider, theoretical intervention, at least for me personally, and it is relevant to how we collectively respond to injustice, violence, and aggression because it is ultimately a story of refusal. This, to me, makes the story especially relevant when considering what resurgent mobilizing might look like.

In this story, the deer, collectively, as a nation of people, are faced with wrongdoing in the form of physical violence and exploitation. Both the Nishnaabeg and the Waawaashkeshiwag live and interact in the spiritual world, and they interact with the physical world by spending time here in bodies—deer bodies or human bodies. The Nishnaabeg bodies are dependent upon the deer bodies, political orders in their own right, in the physical world for survival, and therefore, there is a negotiation that primarily takes place in the spirit world, where the deer decide which deer bodies are given up in the physical world to return to the spiritual world, so that the Nishnaabeg might survive. The Nishnaabeg are dependent and reliant upon the deer. The deer are not particularly reliant on the Nishnaabeg, although in a settler colonial reality, the deer perhaps become more reliant on the Nishnaabeg because we have a voice they do not. That is, we can speak back to the colonizers in a way the deer cannot. In the confines of this telling of the story, however, the deer hold a nonhierarchical power, like all the plants and animals, that the Nishnaabeg do not, and although I don't understand the Nishnaabeg world as one that is imbued with hierarchy, I do understand that in all of creation, human beings require the most help from the rest of creation to live, and in that sense, we have the least amount of grounded, spiritual power and influence.

When faced with injustice and violence, the deer chose to leave the relationship and withdrew from the territory they were sharing with the Nishnaabeg. I've thought a lot about this story and deer in general for the past decade because I am a mother to two Deer clan children. This means that I have a more intimate relationship with the Deer clan than I did previously. Children in particular like and understand this story in an intimate way. It makes complete sense to kids that the deer withdraw in the face of violence because of course children are often in the position in settler colonial society where they have no other choice in response to violence other than withdrawal. Adults, presumably, even occupied and oppressed ones, have a wider range of tactical responses.

The withdrawal of the deer is a pretty radical response in that they did not try initially to *engage* with the Nishnaabeg, who I think are loving, rational, just people. They did not try to talk to us or negotiate. They didn't explain to us how our actions were hurting their nation. They didn't appeal to us morally. They didn't look to the Nishnaabeg for recognition. They didn't display the grief or the outrage they must have felt for the devastation, trauma, and violence the Nishnaabeg had caused them. Their emotional response, their healing, was not up for public consumption or performance. They didn't protest or demonstrate the emotional cost to our neglect, despite the fact it must have been significant. After all, the Nishnaabeg were essentially murdering their citizens in direct violation of our grounded normativity. Instead, the deer withdrew and turned inward to rebuild themselves as a nation and a clan.

The deer refused. They enacted the politics of generative refusal—they refused the Nishnaabeg and then went and renewed themselves. They initially refused to come to the negotiating table, believing the Nishnaabeg would either not join them or the Nishnabeg would attempt to manipulate the process, or because the Nishnaabeg were not ready to feel the full weight of our wrongdoing. They refused to subject themselves to more violence. They refused to give the Nishnaabeg an opportunity to encode that violence into a structural negotiation process, and they refused to give power to the party that was abusing power in the first place.

This is instructive in terms of radical resurgent mobilizing. The deer refused and organized on their own terms. They didn't need the Nishnaabeg, just like the Nishnaabeg don't *need* settlers. It seems consistent with the concept of Biiskabiyang, a turning inward toward the essence of, in this case, the deer nation.[6] They retreated and focused on rebuilding and recovering first, shifting the power away from the Nishnaabeg. They made the Nishnaabeg recognize them and our own neglect. There is also a thread of flight, of fugitivity, in this narrative because in their refusal and flight out of violence they liberated themselves *into* a physical reality that was entirely consistent with the one they deserved and wanted for themselves. In their flight, they turned inward. This is consistent with the idea that focused rebuilding using Indigenous processes enacts an Indigenous presence that has the ability to give life to an Indigenous future and changes not only the actors involved in the focused rebuilding, but the power dynamics between the deer and the Nishnaabeg, or between the Nishnaabeg and the state.

Final Words

I began the Radical Resurgence Project by grounding radical resurgence in the theoretical home of Indigenous intelligence, grounded normativity, and Indigenous internationalism and by communicating the book itself through Nishnaabewin. I highlighted the importance of land and land restitution in radical resurgence. I used *kwe as method* to refuse and to analyze settler colonialism as a *structure of processes*. I put forth a more expansive nonhierarchical conceptualization of dispossession to include land and bodies as the meta-relationship Indigenous peoples have with the state. I then turned to another crucial intervention in resurgence theory with a consideration of Nishnaabeg practices of anticapitalism. I made the case for dismantling heteropatriarchy as an impediment to Indigenous nation building and radical resurgence and argued that queer Indigeneity is a crucial expression of Indigenous brilliance. I emphasized the importance of land-based resurgence education. I considered resurgent struggle and organizing in relation to the politics of recognition, the politics of distraction, and the politics of grief. The concepts of reciprocal recognition and generative refusal emerged at several points in the discussion of radical resurgence. I reflected on the importance of everyday acts of resurgence and constellating these actions in the present to bring forth futures that are profoundly *Indigenous* through resurgent struggle, organizing, and mobilization. I recognize that it is so easy to write about this, and even talk about this, and that it is so difficult to realize it in real life, especially because we are still building the individual and community capacity to do so. I recognize resurgence is messy and difficult and requires a great deal of sacrifice, persistence, failure, and sheer dedicated hard work. It is struggle—struggle where most of us are at the limit of our emotional capacity to struggle. I still think we have to do it.

This book cannot end with a section on future directions for this research that is counter to what I think is the central point of this book: Indigenous futures are entirely dependent upon what we *collectively* do now as diverse Indigenous nations, with our Ancestors and those yet unborn, to create Indigenous presences and to generate the conditions for Indigenous futures by deeply engaging in our nation-based grounded normativities. We must continuously build and rebuild Indigenous worlds. This work starts in motion, in decolonial love, in flight, in relationship, in biiskabiyang, in generosity, humility, and kindness, and this is where it also ends. I cannot be prescriptive here because these processes are profoundly intimate and emergent and are ultimately the *collective* responsibilities of those who belong to unique and diverse Indigenous nations. I don't want to imagine or dream futures. I want a better present.

In many ways, I feel confident and grounded in the concepts and ideas in this book, although resurgence is not a process that can come from any one person or any single set of ideas. My hope for this work is that readers consider my words along with the intentions they come with, not as those of an expert but as part of a much larger, Indigenous international relationship-building process about how to liberate ourselves from the grips of colonialism—an interaction that centers Indigenous nationhood instead of colonialism. I hope that this work in a small way is able to propel a formation of Indigenous thinkers on their own trajectories in the way that Indigenous makers and land users always do, in the way that the PKOLS reclamation and the Kanehsatà:ke or Gustafsen Lake resistances did for a generation of us, and in the way that *Mohawk Interruptus, Creative Combat,* and *Red Skin, White Masks* did for me this year. I hope this book creates more connection, more thinking through together, more endless unfolding of the past and the future into the present. Perhaps the Radical Resurgence Project can propel us even a little to grow multiple layered constellations of freedom, to light our seventh fires over and over and over again, with the love and persistence in spite of everything. Perhaps it can make a little more space and forge a little more strength for those doing this work on the ground every day without recognition. I look forward to the coming years, when I'll look back on this book and see the weakness of my arguments and how much my thinking has changed, and this will be a very good thing. I hope that this next generation will read this book and see how little I actually know about how to live Nishnaabewin compared to them. That is the real Radical Resurgence Project, and it isn't radical or even resurgence, it's just Indigenous life as it has always unfolded. Indeed, "revolution will come in a form we cannot yet imagine."[7] Our revolutions will be our new dawn, our biidaaban, with the past and the future collapsing in on the present, *as we have always done.*

ACKNOWLEDGMENTS

NOTHING IS EVER CREATED IN ISOLATION, and this book is no exception. It was made in a community of relationships within which I exist, and although I am responsible for the mistakes and missteps, I am not responsible for the insights and the brilliance: these come from the land, the nation, and the community of thinkers and makers of which I am a small part. I would simply not exist as Betasamosake without the continuous friendship and support of elder Doug Williams. He is one of the smartest people I have ever met. His continuing influence on me is tremendous, and I am grateful for the decade of time he has spent with me. I am also grateful for the influence of elder Edna Manitowabi; her intelligence continues to inform and breathe vitality into my work. I am very appreciative of the elders and land users I have met and worked alongside in Denendeh through the Dechinta Centre for Research and Learning, for their generosity and Dene intelligence: Ethel Lamothe, Jane Dragon, Therese and Modeste Sangris, Mary-Rose Sundberg, Paul Mackenzie, Melaw Nakehk'o, Mandee McDonald (Maskîkow-iskwiw intelligence), Amos Scott, Gordie Liske, and Siku Allooloo (Inuit/Taino intelligence).

I am indebted to the brilliance of my cherished comrades

Sarah Hunt, Jarrett Martineau, Glen Coulthard, and Daniel Heath Justice and for their deep engagement with my work and with this manuscript. Miigwech to Susan Blight, Erin Freeland Ballantyne, and Matt Hern, who read and provided feedback on previous drafts, and to Alex Wilson and Billy-Ray Belcourt, who read chapter 8. Miigwech to Minowewebeneshiinh Simpson for giving permission to share her story. Nia:wen to Ellen Gabriel, who helped me with her language, and miigwech to elder Shirley Williams, who helped me with the Nishnaabemowin. Miigwech to Lianne Charlie for the cover art. I also thank Robert Warrior and Jason Weidemann and the staff at the University of Minnesota Press for their attentive support.

The first draft of this manuscript was completed while I was a visiting scholar in Indigenous studies at McGill University, arranged and supported by Allan Downey. Miigwech Allan. A previous version of "Land as Pedagogy" was published by *Decolonization, Indigeneity, Education, and Society,* and short sections of the manuscript were published by various blogs (including the *Nations Rising* blog and my own blog) and were panel presentations at the Native American and Indigenous Studies Association and the American Studies Association annual meetings.

NOTES

Introduction

1. A previous version of the section "I Am Not a Nation-State" in this chapter was first published on the Indigenous Nationhood Movement's *Nations Rising* blog, which no longer exists, and was reposted at http://leannesimpson.ca/i-am-not-a-nation-state/.

2. Doug Williams is an elder from Curve Lake First Nation. The French explorer Samuel du Champlain was the first white explorer through our territory in 1615.

3. Leanne Simpson, *Dancing on Our Turtle's Back: Stories of Nishnaabeg Re-Creation, Resurgence and a New Emergence* (Winnipeg: ARP Books, 2011), 14.

4. Rotinonhseshá:ka and Haudenosaunee are both words for Iroquois peoples. Since I wrote part of this book in Montreal, I have used the Kanien'kehá:ka terminology in this manuscript. According to Ellen Gabriel, Rotinonhseshá:ka means "People of the Longhouse" in Kanien'kćha (language of the Kanien'kehá:ka or Mohawk people).

5. Alternatively rendered as Mishi-zaagiig, "People of the large river mouth," as shared with me by the editors Alan Corbiere, Deborah McGregor, and Crystal Migwans in the publication *Anishinaabewin Niswi: Deep Roots, New Growth* (M'Chigeeng, Ont.: Ojibwe Cultural Foundation, 2012), 42n4.

6. Leanne Simpson, "Looking after Gdoo-naaganinaa: Precolo-

nial Nishnaabeg Diplomatic and Treaty Relationships," *Wicazo Sa Review* 23, no. 2 (2008): 29–42.

7. See Champlain's journal of his 1615 voyage, entry 321, available at https://archive.org/stream/voyagessam00chamrich/voyagessam00chamrich_djvu.txt.

8. I am using the terms *sovereignty* and *self-determination* within the context of Nishnaabewin and Indigenous political theory and practices.

9. This first part of this section is based largely on oral tradition passed down to me from Doug Williams. Some of this is recorded in his new, unpublished manuscript, but the vast majority of it was learned within Michi Saagiig Nishnaabeg Knowledge system over a fifteen-year period, from 2000 to 2016.

10. For historical context, see Nick Este, "Fighting for Our Lives: #NoDAPL in Historical Context," *The Red Nation* (blog), September 18, 2016, https://therednation.org/2016/09/18/fighting-for-our-lives-nodapl-in-context/.

11. Throughout this book when I use "Idle No More," I am referring to the broad movement that took place during the winter of 2012–13, not the organization.

12. I first learned this in the late 1990s from Robin Greene-ba, a Treaty 3 elder from Shoal Lake.

13. I am grateful for the brilliant scholarship of Rinaldo Walcott, Katherine McKittrick, Christina Sharpe, Luam Kidane, Hawa Y. Mire, Fred Moten, Idil Abdillahi, and Robin D. G. Kelley; the poetics and scholarship of Dionne Brand, Claudia Rankine, Alexis Pauline Gumbs; and the actions of Black Lives Matter Toronto for challenging me to think about anti-Blackness, Black life, and Black futures alongside Michi Saagiig Nishnaabeg futures and for compelling me to begin to think about an Nishnaabeg presence that structurally detonates anti-Blackness from our radical alternatives. These ideas are far from complete, but I look forward to thinking through this together.

1. Nishnaabeg Brilliance as Radical Resurgence Theory

1. Leanne Simpson, *Islands of Decolonial Love: Stories and Songs* (Winnipeg: ARP Books 2013). The Nishnaabeg story is in Eddie Benton-Banai, *The Mishomis Book: The Voice of the Ojibway* (Hayward, Wis.: Indian Country Communications, 1988), 61–68.

2. The "Oka Crisis" took place during the summer of 1990 as a re-

sponse to the expansion of a nine-hole golf course into a sacred area of the Mohawk community of Kanesatake and involved a large-scale mobilization of land protectors with sites of physical resistance in Kanesatake and Kanawake and solidarity protests across Canada.

3. I heard Justice Murray Sinclair say this about residential schools in his capacity as a member of the Truth and Reconciliation Commission at Queens University on March 27, 2015.

4. I use the term *heteropatriarchy* as an umbrella term to mean the intertwined systems of patriarchy and heterosexism to include its manifestations as heteronormativity, transphobia, and cis-normativity.

5. Leanne Simpson, *Dancing on Our Turtle's Back: Stories of Nishnabeg Re-creation, Resurgence and a New Emergence* (Winnipeg: ARP Books, 2011); and Wendy Makoons Geniusz, *Our Knowledge Is Not Primitive: Decolonizing Botanical Anishinaabe Teachings* (Syracuse, N.Y.: Syracuse University Press, 2000), 9–10.

6. Neil Roberts, *Freedom as Marronage* (Chicago: University of Chicago Press, 2015), 1–15.

7. Retreating to the bush was a common practice to escape the control of Indian agents, residential schools, coerced farming practices, encroachment, and many of the other impositions of settler colonial society; Roberts, *Freedom as Marronage,* 4–5.

8. Ibid., 8–9.

9. Jessica Marie Johnson, "We Need Your Freedom: An Interview with Alexis Pauline Gumbs," December 13, 2016, http://www .aaihs.org/we-need-your-freedom-an-interview-with-alexis-pauline -gumbs/?utm_content=buffera2b87&utm_medium=social&utm _source=twitter.com&utm_campaign=buffer.

10. As with *Dancing on Our Turtle's Back*, this book is based on my own interpretations of Nishnaabeg thought. I do not speak for all Nishnaabeg people. I do not speak for anyone but myself. Like all nations and cultures, there are many different ways of understanding our stories, histories, theories, and intellectual traditions within our collective system of ethics. There always has been and is lots of healthy and robust conversation about these interpretations.

11. Michael Yellowbird's lecture "Decolonizing the Mind: Healing through Neurodecolonization and Mindfulness," January 24, 2015, Portland State University, Portland, Oregon, is an excellent exploration of how ceremonial practices generate or regenerate neuropathways that provide the capacity to uphold Indigenous ethics and operationalize Indigenous political systems.

12. Some of our people are already doing this, and many of our people have always done this, in particular, language speakers, hunters, trappers, fishers, and medicine people.

13. See chapter 2 in Simpson, *Dancing on Our Turtle's Back,* 31–49.

14. I learned this from Doug Williams; see endnote 60 in Simpson, *Dancing on Our Turtle's Back,* 46.

15. Audra Simpson, *Mohawk Interruptus: Political Life across the Borders of Settler States* (Durham, N.C.: Duke University Press, 2014).

16. Glen Coulthard, *Red Skin, White Masks: Rejecting the Colonial Politics of Recognition* (Minneapolis: University of Minnesota Press, 2014), 60.

2. Kwe as Resurgent Method

1. Leanne Simpson, *Dancing on Our Turtle's Back: Stories of Nishnabeg Re-creation, Resurgence and a New Emergence* (Winnipeg: ARP Books, 2011); Leanne Simpson, *Islands of Decolonial Love: Stories and Songs* (Winnipeg: ARP Books, 2013); Leanne Simpson, "Land as Pedagogy: Nishnaabeg Intelligence and Rebellious Transformation," *Decolonization, Indigeneity, Education and Society* 3, no. 3 (2014): 1–25.

2. *Aki* means land—place, power, relation; it is the opposite of land as commodity. Aki is not capital. Throughout this book I used land-based and place-based interchangeably to denote practices that comes from relational reciprocity with Aki.

3. See chapter 2, Simpson, *Dancing on Our Turtle's Back,* 31–49.

4. The Creator, the one who loves us unconditionally, according to Doug Williams; see endnote 60 in *Dancing on Our Turtle's Back,* 46.

5. See chapter 2, Simpson *Dancing on Our Turtle's Back,* 31–49.

6. This is actually something Indigenous scholars do, and I think have always done. I was reminded of it in reading Mishuana Goeman, *Mark My Words: Native Women Mapping Our Nations* (Minneapolis: University of Minnesota Press, 2013), when she talks about the mobility of her family causing her to pause at the dichotomy between urban/reservation and reflect more deeply on spatialities (7).

7. The Indigenous academic community, particularly PhD students, have been forced to justify the use of Indigenous methodologies, ethics, and theories and more broadly Indigenous ways of knowing for nearly three decades now. I'd encourage those who find this paragraph surprising to read Linda Tuhiwai Smith, *Decolonizing Methodologies: Research and Indigenous Peoples* (London: Zed Books, 1999) as a start-

ing point. We have nearly two decades of this work now. Kwagiulth (Kwakwaka'wakw) scholar Sarah Hunt, in her dissertation "Witnessing the Colonialscape: Lighting the Intimate Fires of Indigenous Legal Pluralism" (Simon Fraser University, 2014), makes a similar case for this from a slightly different theoretical frame (31–43).

8. I am using Two Spirit and queer (2SQ) as an umbrella term in this book to refer to all Indigenous Two Spirit, lesbian, gay, bisexual, pansexual, transgender, transsexual, queer, questioning, intersex, asexual, and gender-nonconforming people. See http://www.nativeyouth sexualhealth.com/ for more information. Hunt writes, "Two-Spirit is used by some Indigenous people to describe the diverse roles and identities of lesbian, gay, bisexual, queer, trans and/or gender-fluid Indigenous people in North America. At the 1990 Winnipeg gathering of the International Gathering of American Indian and First Nations Gays and Lesbians, 'Two- Spirit' was chosen as a term to move away from the anthropological term 'berdache' in describing Native queer identities and communities. Following this usage, and that of some recent Two-Spirit scholarship, I choose to capitalize this term"; "Witnessing the Colonialscape," xv. I include the term *queer* in 2SQ to recognize that not all Indigenous queer people use the term *Two Spirit* to identify themselves. Lesbian elder Ma-Nee Chacaby presents a different understanding of the term Two Spirit, which is explained in chapter 8.

9. Again, for those readers who find this idea new, I'd suggest beginning with Patricia Hill Collins, *Black Feminist Thought: Knowledge, Consciousness, and the Politics of Empowerment* (New York: Routledge, 1990).

10. Tuhiwai Smith, *Decolonizing Methodologies*.

11. Of course this is beginning to change with the swell of Indigenous scholarship, particularly by Indigenous women and the 2SQ community.

12. The idea of bodies as political orders I learned from Audra Simpson in her talk "The Chief's Two Bodies," keynote address, International R.A.C.E Conference, Edmonton, October 2014; available online https://vimeo.com/110948627. This is discussed further in chapter 8.

13. In *Dancing on Our Turtle's Back*, I talk about debwewin as the sound of my heart or the art of truth making; see chapter 1, endnote 17.

14. Tuhiwai Smith, *Decolonizing Methodologies*; Margaret Kovach, *Indigenous Methodologies: Characteristics, Conversations, and Contexts*

(Toronto: University of Toronto Press, 2010); Shawn Wilson, *Research Is Ceremony: Indigenous Research Methods* (Halifax: Fernwood Publishing, 2009); Leanne Simpson, "Decolonizing Our Processes: Indigenous Knowledge and Ways of Knowing," *Canadian Journal of Native Studies* 21, no. 1 (2001): 137–48; Leanne Simpson, "Anishinaabe Knowledge as Process," *Tribal College Journal* 11, no. 4 (2000): 26–30; Leanne Simpson, "Anishinaabe Ways of Knowing," in *Aboriginal Health, Identity and Resources,* ed. J. Oakes, R. Riewe, W. Koolage, L. R. Simpson, and N. Schuster, 165–86 (Winnipeg: Department of Native Studies, University of Manitoba, 2000).

15. Lee Maracle, *I Am Woman* (Vancouver: Press Gang, 2003).

16. Audra Simpson, "On Ethnographic Refusal: Indigeneity, 'Voice' and Colonial Citizenship," *Junctures* 9, no. 1 (2007): 67–80; and Audra Simpson, *Mohawk Interruptus: Political Life across the Borders of Settler States* (Durham, N.C.: Duke University Press, 2014). This concept is also reconsidered in the conclusion, this volume.

17. This is a Nishnaabeg story, and it is explored further in chapter 4 and the conclusion.

18. See Leanne Simpson, "Land and Reconciliation: Having the Right Conversations," March 5, 2016, *Electric City* magazine, http://www.electriccitymagazine.ca/2016/01/land-reconciliation/.

19. I've heard this story from Doug Williams several times—every time we pass Kiizhigo Island. There is a written version of it in Vanessa Watt's master's thesis, "Towards Anishnaabe Governance and Accountability: Reawakening Our Relationships and Sacred Bimaadiziwin" (Indigenous Governance Program, University of Victoria, 2010), http://dspace.library.uvic.ca/handle/1828/2222; see page 41. Her story also comes from Doug.

20. Jessica Marie Johnson, "We Need Your Freedom: An Interview with Alexis Pauline Gumbs," December 13, 2016, http://www.aaihs.org/we-need-your-freedom-an-interview-with-alexis-pauline-gumbs/?utm_content=buffera2b87&utm_medium=social&utm_source=twitter.com&utm_campaign=buffer.

21. Ibid.

3. The Attempted Dispossession of Kwe

1. *Anishinabek News,* http://anishinabeknews.ca/wp-content/uploads/2013/04/2012–12.pdf; also see Williams Treaties First Nations, http://www.williamstreatiesfirstnations.ca/.

2. Although the Ontario Federation of Hunters and Anglers have continued to intervene in our treaty matters.

3. See Peggy Blair, *Lament for a First Nation: The Williams Treaties of Southern Ontario* (Vancouver: UBC Press, 2008).

4. Julia Emberly calls for a complication of colonial dispossession that takes into account sexual violence and that recognizes the commodification of land and bodies as naturalized objects of exchange and exploitation. Julia Emberly, "To Spirit Walk the Letter and the Law: Gender, Race, and Representational Violence in Rudy Wiebe and Yvonne Johnson's *Stolen Life: The Journey of a Cree Woman*," in *Indigenous Women and Feminism: Politics, Activism, Culture*, ed. Cheryl Suzack, Shari M. Huhndorf, Jeanne Perreault, and Jean Barman (Vancouver: UBC Press, 2010), 236.

5. Audra Simpson, *Mohawk Interruptus: Political Life across the Borders of Settler States* (Durham, N.C.: Duke University Press, 2014), 156.

6. Ibid.

7. Much of this resistance is documented in our oral traditions; see also Doug Williams, "Who Depleted Our Fish Anyway?" *Curve Lake Newsletter,* June 24, 2011.

8. These ideas were developed over conversations that began between me and Glen Coulthard, and expanded to the students in the Indigenous governance program at the University of Victoria in the winter of 2015, and then to conversations between me and Sarah Hunt. The idea of bodies being taken from the land comes to me from Geraldine King.

9. Patrick Wolfe, "Settler Colonialism and the Elimination of the Native," *Journal of Genocide Research* 8, no. 4 (2006): 388.

10. Ibid.

11. In this way, resurgence has always been radical, whether you consider the concept within Indigenous thought systems, its relatively recent appearance in the academy, or how it is embodied in our communities. Countless Indigenous peoples conceptualize it to be concerned with the root.

12. I thought of this recently when the National Research Centre on Indian Residential Schools invited me to a roundtable of Indigenous and non-Indigenous academics discussing resurgence. I chose not to attend.

13. I dislike the term *culture* because as a category it is too small and too restrictive to mean the breadth of practices and knowledges contained within Indigenous intelligence.

14. Indigenous feminists have been fierce and principled in their work. I am here commenting on the fact that this work is often confined to courses on "Indigenous feminisms" or, worse, "Native Women of Canada," to women's organizations, and to women's publications rather than integrated in a substantial and theoretical way across all of our work. I believe this work should have far more influence than it has in Indigenous life.

15. Sarah Hunt, "Violence, Law and the Everyday Politics of Recognition: Comments on Glen Coulthard's *Red Skin, White Masks,*" available at https://www.academia.edu/12834803/Violence_Law_and_the_Everyday_Politics_of_Recognition_commentary_on_Red_Skin_White_Masks_; see p. 6 in particular.

4. Nishnaabeg Internationalism

1. This chapter and the concept of Nishnaabeg internationalism were influenced by a series of conversations with Glen Coulthard during 2015–16, from his own yet unpublished work on Dene internationalism.

2. Edward Benton-Banai, *The Mishomis Book: The Voice of the Ojibway* (St. Paul, Minn.: Red School House, 1988), 6–12. Nanabush is a being that is continually transforming. Nanabush appears in stories as all different genders, as particular plants and particular animals. I am using the pronouns they/their to acknowledge this variance.

3. This is an Nishnaabeg story, and several different versions have been published. This version is from my book *The Gift Is in the Making: Anishinaabeg Stories* (Winnipeg: HighWater Press, 2013), 9–13. Nishnaabemowin: waawaashkesh is deer; mooz is moose; adik is caribou; Gchi Nishnaabeg-ogamig is "the place we all live and work together," according to elder Doug Williams from Curve Lake First Nation; dawaagin is fall; bboon is winter; Amikwag is beavers; Moozoog are moose (plural); makwag are bears; jijaakwag (ajijaakwag) are cranes; migizig are bald eagles; zhigaagwag are skunks; semaa (asemaa) is tobacco; ziigwan is the early part of spring when the snow is melting, the ice is breaking up, and the sap is flowing; Niibin is summer; waawaashkeshiwag are deer (plural); adikwag are caribou (plural).

4. Compare with the stories and practices discussed in Brenda Child, *Holding Our World Together: Ojibwe Women and the Survival of Community* (New York: Viking, 2013), 16–18.

5. Janice Hill, Tyendinaga Turtle clan mother and director of

Four Directions Aboriginal Student Centre at Queens University, Kingston, Ontario, reminded me of this when I visited the centre on September 27, 2013.

6. See Audra Simpson and Andrea Smith's discussion in their introduction to *Theorizing Native Studies,* ed. Audra Simpson and Andrea Smith (Durham, N.C.: Duke University Press, 2014), 9–12.

7. There are lots of examples of relationships between Indigenous peoples and the Black Radical Tradition and Black feminism, from George Manual's work, to Lee Maracle, to the history of the Dene Nation; see Glen Coulthard, *Red Skin, White Masks: Rejecting the Colonial Politics of Recognition* (Minneapolis: University of Minnesota Press, 2014). It is our responsibility to continue to build these relationships in the present and to liberate ourselves rather than take from others. I am using the term *abolition* as in the abolition of slavery in its various manifestations, not in the anti–sex worker abolition sense.

8. This is a quote from Vijay Prashad's panel discussion "War, Peace and Global Justice" at the Black Radical Tradition's conference "Reclaiming Our Future: The Black Radical Tradition in Our Time," Temple University, Philadelphia, January 9, 2015. It's available online at http://www.theblackradicaltradition.org/livestream. The preceding paragraph was influenced by the full panel, which included George Ciccariello-Maher and Glen Ford.

9. Prior to the consolidation of the Indian Act in 1876, this policy was practiced indiscriminately in Ontario at the whim of Indian agents. Although a Christian women, Nahnebahnwequay was also a resistor and was targeted here strategically. Donald B. Smith, "Upright Woman: Catherine Sutton, or Nahnebahnwequay, 'Nahnee,'" in *Mississauga Portraits: Ojibwe Voices from Nineteenth-Century Canada* (Toronto: University of Toronto Press, 2013).

10. Ibid.

11. Smith's *Mississauga Portraits* profiles several of these people, including Kahkewaquonaby (Peter Jones), Shawundais (John Sunday), Maungudaus (George Henry), Kahgegahbown (George Copaway), Nawahjegezhegwab (Joseph Sawyer), and Pahtahsega (Peter Jacobs). With the exception of Maungudaus (discussed in the context of artist Robert Houle's *Paris/Ojibwa* later in this volume), it seems to me these figures were actively engaged in the politics of recognition (and were subsequently writers, Indian Act chiefs, preachers) as advocates for our people, particularly in terms of improving social conditions. My belief is that much of the resistance that went into

ensuring Nishnaabewin exists today is not recorded in the historical record of Canada but is in the minds and bodies of Nishnaabeg families and elders.

12. See also Glen Coulthard and Leanne Simpson, "Grounded Normativity/Place-Based Solidarity," *American Quarterly* 68, no. 2 (June 2016): 249–55.

13. Maungwudaus/George Henry, *An Account of the Chippewa Indians, Who Have Been Travelling among the Whites, in the United States, England, Ireland, Scotland, France and Belgium; With Very Interesting Incidents in Relation to the General Characteristics of the English, Irish, Scotch, French and Americans, with Regard to Their Hospitality, Peculiarities, etc.* (Boston: George Henry, 1848).

14. Dr. Masazumi Harada first visited the community in 1975, and the community continued to build this relationship and work with him until his death. There were several trips back and forth. See Anastasia M. Shkilnyk, *A Poison Stronger Than Love: The Destruction of an Ojibwa Community* (New Haven, Conn.: Yale University Press, 1985) for a consideration of the mercury crisis and for the beginnings of this relationship (194).

5. Nishnaabeg Anticapitalism

1. One of the places it is blogged is http://www.yesmagazine .org/peace-justice/dancing-the-world-into-being-a-conversation-with-idle-no-more-leanne-simpson.

2. I'd like to acknowledge the work of Glen Coulthard on capitalism and Indigenous peoples here. He uses Marxist categories of analysis, and he attributes his understandings and interventions to the practices of his own Dene people; see Andrew Bard Epstein, "The Colonialism of the Present: Scholar and Activist Glen Coulthard on the Connection between Indigenous and Anticapitalist Struggles," *Jacobin*, January 1, 2015, https://www.jacobinmag.com/2015/01/indigenous -left-glen-coulthard-interview/; and Glen Coulthard, "For Our Nations to Live, Capitalism Must Die," Rabble.ca, November 6, 2013, http:// rabble.ca/news/2013/11/our-nations-to-live-capitalism-must-die; in addition to Glen Coulthard, *Red Skin, White Masks: Rejecting the Colonial Politics of Recognition* (Minneapolis: University of Minnesota Press, 2014). There are also several other Indigenous organizers, writers, scholars, and activists who provide critiques of capitalism, includ-

ing Lee Maracle, Art Manual, Nick Estes, and Daniel T'selie, and many more on-the-ground critics in reserves, at blockades, and in the bush.

3. Naomi Klein, *This Changes Everything: Capitalism vs. the Climate* (Toronto: Knopf Canada, 2014), 169.

4. The interview is reprinted with Naomi Klein's permission.

5. "Dancing the World into Being: A Conversation with Idle No More's Leanne Simpson," by Naomi Klein, *Yes! Magazine,* March 5, 2013, http://www.yesmagazine.org/peace-justice/dancing-the-world -into-being-a-conversation-with-idle-no-more-leanne-simpson.

6. This occurs at 24:20 on the January 13, 2016, episode of season 5, *Redman Laughing,* a podcast by Ryan McMahon, http://www .redmanlaughing.com/listen/2016/1/red-man-laughing-rebuilding -community.

7. There are several examples of these stories in print and many, many more in the oral tradition. See Alan Corbiere, ed., *Gechi-Piitzijig Dbaajmowag: The Stories of Our Elders* (Manitoulin Island, ON: Ojibwe Cultural Foundation, 2011); Anton Treuer et al., *Awesiinyensag: Dibaajimowinan Ji gikinoo'amaageng* (Minneapolis: Birchbark House; Wiigwass Press, 2010.; http://nanabush.ca/; Basil Johnston, *Living in Harmony,* The Anishinaubaemowin Series (Cape Croker, ON: Kegedonce Press, 2011); Basil Johnston, *Ojibway Heritage: The Ceremonies, Rituals, Songs, Dances, Prayers and Legends of the Ojibway* (Toronto: Royal Ontario Museum, 1976); Basil Johnston, *Tales the Elders Told: Ojibway Legends* (Toronto: Royal Ontario Museum 1981); Daphne Odjig, The Nanabush Series (Manitoulin Island, ON: Odjig Arts, 2011; originally published in 1971); Joe McLellan, The Nanabosho Series (Winnipeg: Pemmican Publishing); *Stories from the Seventh Fire: The Four Seasons: Traditional Legends for Each Season* (Kelowna, BC: Filmwest Associates, 2000), DVD; Edward Benton-Banai, *The Mishomis Book: The Voice of the Ojibway* (St. Paul, Minn.: Red School House, 1988; Patronella Johnson, *Tales of Nokomis* (Toronto: Stoddard Kids, 1994); *The Adventures of Nanabush: Ojibway Indian Stories,* compiled by Emerson Coatsworth and David Coatsworth (Toronto: Doubleday Canada, 1979); and Dorothy M. Reid, *Tales of Nanabozho* (Toronto: Oxford University Press, 1963).

8. I first heard this story orally from Nishnaabeg educator Dr. Nicole Bell, in Peterborough as part of our language nest, Nishnaabemowin Saaswansing, in 2010, although there are versions of the story in print as well.

6. Endlessly Creating Our Indigenous Selves

1. I often use Nishnaabe feminist Dory Nason's "We Hold Our Hands Up" as a reading to follow up this discussion; see "We Hold Our Hands Up: On Indigenous Women's Love and Resistance," *Decolonization: Indigeneity, Education and Society* (blog), February 12, 2013, https://decolonization.wordpress.com/2013/02/12/we-hold-our-hands-up-on-indigenous-womens-love-and-resistance/.

2. I have used this exercise a number of times at Dechinta; this particular event took place in the fall of 2014.

3. This is explained fully in the next chapter of this volume.

4. Audra Simpson, *Mohawk Interruptus: Political Life across the Borders of Settler States* (Durham, N.C.: Duke University Press, 2014), 156; Jaskiran K. Dhillon, "Indigenous Girls and the Violence of Settler Colonial Policing," *Decolonization: Indigeneity, Education and Society* 4. no. 2 (2015): 1–31.

5. Shari M. Huhdorf and Cheryl Suzack, "Indigenous Feminism Theorizing the Issues," in *Indigenous Women and Feminism: Politics, Activism, Culture,* ed. Cheryl Suzack, Shari M. Huhndorf, Jeanne Perreault, and Jean Barman (Vancouver: UBC Press), 21–29.

6. "Sexual and Gender-Based Violence in Crisis Situations," United Nations Development Programme, http://www.undp.org/content/undp/en/home/ourwork/crisispreventionandrecovery/focus_areas/gender_equality_andwomensempowerment/sexual-violence-in-conflict.html.

7. This is well documented by several feminist historians studying Indigenous women and coloniality working in different time spans and regions in Canada. In my own community, the work of Robin Jarvis Brownlie and Joan Sangster do this, as evidenced in the next chapter of this volume.

8. Robin Jarvis Brownlie's archival work on the Indian Act and the regulation of Indigenous women's sexuality is critically important here; see Robin Jarvis Brownlie, "Intimate Surveillance: Indian Affairs, Colonization, and the Regulation of Aboriginal Women's Sexuality" in *Contact Zones: Aboriginal and Settler Women in Canada's Colonial Past,* ed. Katie Pickles and Myra Rutherdale (Vancouver: UBC Press, 2005), 160–78; as is Karen Stote's recent work on sterilization and genocide in Indigenous women in Canada; see Karen Stote, *An Act of Genocide: Colonialism and the Sterilization of Aboriginal Women* (Halifax: Fernwood, 2015); Sarah Carter, *The Importance of Being Mo-*

nogamous: Marriage and Nation Building in Western Canada to 1915 (Edmonton: University of Alberta Press, 2008); and Lesley Erickson, *Westward Bound: Sex, Violence, the Law and the Making of a Settler Society* (Vancouver: UBC Press, 2011).

9. For a particularly detailed treatment of this, see Sarah Carter, *Capturing Women: The Manipulation of Cultural Imagery in Canada's Prairie West* (Kingston, ON: McGill-Queens, 1997).

10. There are literally countless Indigenous women and organizations that I could cite here, but I will point readers in the direction of Bev Jacob and the Amnesty International report she wrote in 2004 called *Stolen Sisters: Discrimination and Violence against Native Women in Canada* (Ottawa: Amnesty International Canada, 2004); and the 2009 report *No More Stolen Sisters: The Need for a Comprehensive Response to Discrimination and Violence against Women in Canada* (Ottawa: Amnesty International Canada, 2009).

11. Gloria Galloway, "70 Per Cent of Murdered Aboriginal Women Killed by Indigenous Men: RCMP," *The Globe and Mail,* April 9, 2015, http://www.theglobeandmail.com/news/politics/70-percent -of-murdered-aboriginal-women-killed-by-indigenous-men-rcmp -confirms/article23868927/.

12. The evidence that sexualized and gender violence was a deliberate tool of genocide, assimilation, and settler colonialism is overwhelming. However, it in no way matters that it was deliberate or whether this occurred consciously and strategically or unconsciously. It in no way matters, because it is sheer violence, and within Indigenous legal systems, the magnitude of the damage caused to our nations can in no way be mitigated by a defense of unintention or the context of "not knowing."

13. A. Simpson, *Mohawk Interruptus,* 7–8.

14. I worked with Hollow Water First Nation in the late 1990s and had the opportunity to participate in and observe the Community Holistic Circle Healing project in action. See Berma Bushie, "Community Holistic Circle Healing," August 7, 1999, International Institute for Restorative Practices, http://www.iirp.edu/article_detail .php?article_id=NDc0.

7. The Sovereignty of Indigenous Peoples' Bodies

1. This paragraph is based on Doug William's oral history of our nation and is offered here as a sketch to set the context for the

rest of the chapter, rather than an exhaustive account of our history.

2. Neil Semple, *The Lord's Dominion: The History of Canadian Methodism* (Kingston, ON: McGill-Queens University Press, 1996), 161.

3. Susanna Moodie, *Roughing It in the Bush* (Toronto: McClelland and Stewart, 1989), 181.

4. Ibid., 301.

5. Ibid., 304, 305.

6. Ibid., 305.

7. Carole Gerson, "Nobler Savages: Representations of Native Women in the Writings of Susanna Moodie and Catherine Parr Traill," *Journal of Canadian Studies Summer* 32, no. 2 (1997): 5.

8. Ibid.

9. Ibid.,10.

10. See Joan Sangster, *Regulating Girls and Women: Sexuality, Family, and the Law in Ontario, 1920–1960* (Toronto: University of Toronto Press, 2001), particularly chapter 6; and Robin Jarvis Brownlie, "Intimate Surveillance: Indian Affairs, Colonization, and the Regulation of Aboriginal Women's Sexuality," in *Contact Zones: Aboriginal and Settler Women in Canada's Colonial Past*, ed. Katie Pickles and Myra Rutherdale (Vancouver: UBC Press, 2005), 160–78.

11. Sangster, *Regulating Girls and Women,* 169.

12. Brownlie, "Intimate Surveillance," 162.

13. For a complete discussion on the complexities of this in light of new legislation, see Pam Palmater's 2010 report to the Standing Senate Committee on Human Rights on Bill S-4, http://www.ryerson.ca/content/dam/chair-indigenous-governance/img/reports/senate-commitee-bill-s-4.pdf.

14. Brownlie, "Intimate Surveillance"; and Sangster, *Regulating Girls and Women.*

15. Sangster, *Regulating Girls and Women.*

16. Brownlie, "Intimate Surveillance," 160.

17. Ibid.

18. Ibid.

19. See Peggy Blair, *Lament of a First Nation: The Williams Treaties of Southern Ontario* (Vancouver: UBC Press, 2009); Doug Williams, Curve Lake First Nation, August 15, 2015.

20. Jean Barman, "Taming Aboriginal Sexuality: Gender, Power, and Race in British Columbia, 1850–1900," in *The Days of Our Grandmothers: A Reader in Aboriginal Women's History in Canada,* ed. Mary-

Ellen Kelm and Lorna Townsend (Toronto: University of Toronto Press, 2006), 270–91.

21. Ibid.

22. Yvonne Boyer, "First Nations Women's Contribution to Culture and Community through Canadian Law," in *Restoring the Balance: First Nations Women, Community, and Culture*, ed. Gail Valaskakis, Madeleine Dion Stout, and Eric Guimond (Winnipeg: University of Manitoba Press, 2009), 78.

23. I am using the term *prostitution* here instead of sex work because it is a concept at this point defined by the colonizers and includes all kinds of sexual agency and self-determination outside of what Indigenous sex workers now define as sex work.

24. Boyer, "First Nations Women's Contribution," 78. Also see the work of Nishnaabekwe writer Naomi Sayers, "Prostitution Laws: Protecting Canada's Crackers since 1867," *Tits and Sass* (blog), March 27, 2014, http://titsandsass.com/prostitution-laws-protecting-canadas-crackers-since-1867/.

25. Sayers, "Prostitution Laws."

26. Sangster, *Regulating Girls and Women*, 168.

27. Ibid., 182.

28. See Ma-Nee Chacaby, *A Two-Spirit Journey: The Autobiography of a Lesbian Ojibwa-Cree Elder* (Winnipeg: University of Manitoba Press, 2016), 64–66; Lesley Erickson, *Westward Bound: Sex, Violence, the Law and the Making of a Settler Society* (Vancouver: UBC Press, 2011); Sarah Carter, *The Importance of Being Monogamous: Marriage and Nation Building in Western Canada to 1915* (Edmonton: University of Alberta Press, 2008); and Sarah Carter, *Capturing Women: The Manipulation of Cultural Imagery in Canada's Prairie West* (Kingston, ON: McGill-Queens UP, 1997).

29. Carter, *The Importance of Being Monogamous*, 160.

30. Brownlie, "Intimate Surveillance," 162.

31. Ibid.

32. Joan Sangster, "Scales of Justice Don't Balance for Women," View from Trent, May 4, 2001, https://www.trentu.ca/news/view/justice.html.

33. Sangster, *Regulating Girls and Women*, 184.

34. Sangster, *Regulating Girls and Women*.

35. This was brought to my attention by Sarah Hunt in her comments on a previous draft of the manuscript.

36. "Centering the Voices of People Who Trade or Sell Sex in

Indigenous Anti-Violence Organizing: Statement from the Indigenous Sex Sovereignty Collective," Indigenous Sex Sovereignty Collective, http://indigenoussexsovereignty.tumblr.com/.

37. Joan Sangster "Domesticating Girls: The Sexual Regulation of Aboriginal and Working-Class Girls in Twentieth-Century Canada," in *Contact Zones: Aboriginal and Settler Women in Canada's Colonial Past,* ed. Katie Pickles and Myra Rutherdale (Vancouver: UBC Press, 2005), 184.

38. This was brought to my attention by Sarah Hunt in her comments on a previous draft of the manuscript.

39. Audra Simpson, "The Chief's Two Bodies," keynote address, International R.A.C.E Conference, Edmonton, Alberta, October 2014, available online https://vimeo.com/110948627.

40. Sally R. Wagner, *Sisters in Spirit: Haudenosaunee Influence on Early American Feminism* (Summertown, Tenn.: Native Voices, 2001).

41. Doug Williams, unpublished manuscript, 32.

42. Leanne Simpson, *Dancing on Our Turtle's Back: Stories of Nishnabeg Re-creation, Resurgence and a New Emergence* (Winnipeg: ARP Books, 2011).

8. Indigenous Queer Normativity

1. I share this story here with my daughter's permission, although this is my version of the events, not hers.

2. I would encourage readers to seek out the voices of queer Indigenous youth: the work of Dana Wesley, Billy-Ray Belcourt, the Native Youth Sexual Health Network, Erin Marie Konsovo, to name just a few. Gwen Benaway's blog on transitioning is also important reading: https://gilesbenaway.wordpress.com/.

3. I believe that not wearing a skirt, or sitting on a different side of the lodge, or helping fire keep does not cause harm to our spiritual community, because I have led countless ceremonies where this is the case, and because I believe my Ancestors uphold our values of consent.

4. Alex Wilson, as quoted in Native Youth Sexual Health Network and Women's Earth Alliance, *Violence on the Land, Violence on Our Bodies: Building an Indigenous Response to Environmental Violence,* http://landbodydefense.org/uploads/files/Violence%20on%20 the%20Land%20and%20Body%20Report%20and%20Toolkit%20 2016.pdf, 5.

5. Eddie Benton Banai, *The Mishomis Book: The Voice of the Ojibway*, 2nd ed. (Minneapolis: University of Minnesota Press, 2010).

6. Native Youth Sexual Health Network and Women's Earth Alliance, *Violence on the Land*, 5–6.

7. Bruce Bagemihl, *Biological Exuberance: Animal Homosexuality and Natural Diversity* (New York: St. Martin's Press, 1999).

8. Alex Wilson, "How We Find Ourselves: Identity Development and Two-Spirit People," *Harvard Educational Review* 66, no. 2 (1996): 305.

9. Qwo-Li Driskill, Chris Finely, Brian Joseph Gilley, and Scott Lauria Morgensen, eds., *Queer Indigenous Studies: Critical Interventions in Theory, Politics, and Literature* (Tucson: Arizona University Press, 2011); Kiera Ladner, "Women and Blackfoot Nationalism," *Journal of Canadian Studies* 35 no. 2 (2000): 35–60; Chris Finely, "Decolonizing the Queer Native Body (and Recovering the Native Bull-Dyke): Bringing 'Sexy Back' and Out of Native Studies' Closet," in *Queer Indigenous Studies,* ed. Driskill, Finely, Gilley, and Morgensen, 21–43; Andrea Smith, "Queer Theory and Native Studies: The Heteronormativity of Settler Colonialism," in *Queer Indigenous Studies,* ed. Driskill, Finely, Gilley, and Morgensen, 43–66.

10. J. Michael Thomas, "Leading an Extraordinary Life: Wise Practices for an HIV Prevention Campaign with Two-Spirit Men," prepared for 2-Spirited People of the First Nations, Toronto, 2007, http.//2spirits.com/PDFolder/Extraodinarylives.pdf; George Catlin, "The Dance of the Berdashe," *Letters and Notes on the Manners, Customs, and Conditions of North American Indians* (New York: Dover Publications, 1973; reprint of the 1844 ed. published by D. Bogue, London).

11. This is a different Yellowhead than the Odawa chief in Ontario.

12. Nishnaabe playwright Waawaate Fobister uses the term *agokwe* in a similar manner and translates it as "wise woman," "two spirit," "woman within a man."

13. John Tanner, *Narrative of the Captivity and Adventures of John Tanner during Thirty Years Residence among the Indians in the Interior of North America*, ed. Edwin James (New York: G. & C. & H. Carvill, 1800), 105.

14. Joseph-François Lafitau, *Customs of the American Indians Compared with the Customs of Primitive Times*, 1724, page 365, as quoted in Thomas, "Leading an Extraordinary Life"; also see Scott Lauria Morgensen, *Spaces between Us*: *Queer Settler Colonialism and*

Indigenous Decolonization (Minneapolis: University of Minnesota Press, 2011), 36–42.

15. See Thomas, "Leading an Extraordinary Life," 21.

16. Morgensen, *Spaces between Us,* 16–17, 38.

17. Ibid., 16–17.

18. Ibid., 38.

19. I haven't done this research—there very well may be.

20. I understand *ojiijaak* as meaning "aura." This comes from Doug Williams. So this word to me does not literally mean two spirits but means a person has two auras. In my discussions with Doug, he indicated he wasn't sure this interpretation was right, and needed more discussion with elders and fluent language speakers. I flag it here as an ongoing conversation within Nishnaabemowin and Nishnaabewin.

21. Ma-Nee Chacaby, *A Two-Spirit Journey: The Autobiography of a Lesbian Ojibwa-Cree Elder* (Winnipeg: University of Manitoba Press, 2016), 64–66.

22. See Anton Treuer, *The Assassination of Hole in the Day* (St. Paul: Borealis Books, 2011), 26–27.

23. Leanne Simpson, *Dancing on Our Turtle's Back: Stories of Nishnabeg Re-creation, Resurgence and a New Emergence* (Winnipeg: ARP Books, 2011); Tara Williamson, "Of Dogma and Ceremony," *Decolonization, Indigeneity and Society* (blog), August 16, 2013, http://decolonization.wordpress.com/2013/08/16/of-dogma-and-ceremony/.

24. I identify as queer and live embedded in a web of queer relationship. I have been in a long-term heterosexual relationship for nearly twenty years, meaning I also carry heterosexual privilege. In my work, I try to engage queerness in a meaningful way by centering the voices of 2SQ writers and scholars and continually critiquing my own heterosexual privilege.

25. Chacaby, *A Two Spirit Journey.*

26. CBC, *ReVision Quest,* July 20, 2011, starting at 7 minutes, http://www.cbc.ca/revisionquest/2011/2011/07/20/july-20-21-23-two-spirited-being-glbt-and-aboriginal/; Métis writer and thinker Chelsea Vowel has also considered this in Cree, "Language, Culture and Two-Spirit Identity," *âpihtawikosisân* (blog), March 29, 2012, http://apihtawikosisan.com/2012/03/language-culture-and-two-spirit-identity/. Nishnaabeg Two Spirit playwright Waawaate Fobister uses the term *agokwe* in his play of the same name. I transcribed the Nishnaabemowin words from the recording and then asked language expert and elder Shirley Williams for help with the spelling. She under-

stood many of Roulette's words, and as an alternative, she suggested "wiichi-ninoonmaagan" or " wiichi-ninoonmaaganimon" for the term *gay,* December 12, 2016, Peterborough, Ontario. I also consulted Anishinaabemowin language expert Patricia Ningewance (through Tara Williamson, on January 22, 2017). Patricia understood Roger's words and added that *wiidigemaagan* means "spouse."

27. CBC, *ReVision Quest,* July 20, 2011, starting at 8 minutes, http://www.cbc.ca/revisionquest/2011/2011/07/20/july-20-21-23 -two-spirited-being-glbt-and-aboriginal/.

28. Gitxsan journalist Angela Sterritt wrote a series of articles on culturally relevant sex education in Indigenous communities for the *Globe and Mail,* and her article "Indigenous Languages Recognize Gender States Not Even Named in English" explores these ideas in other Indigenous nations, http://www.theglobeandmail.com /life/health-and-fitness/health/indigenous-languages-recognize -gender-states-not-even-named-in-english/article29130778/.

29. Treuer, *The Assassination of Hole in the Day,* 27. After reading a previous version of this chapter, Billy-Ray Belcourt pointed out that Treuer's use of the word *sex* in this quote is problematic because "sex" is an impossible category, as anatomy fails to name any obdurate form of life.

30. See Waawaate's discussion of the play *Agokwe,* http://www .tedxtoronto.com/speakers/waawaate-fobister/. These translations occur widely in the media in multiple places in their discussion of the play.

31. Doris O'Brien Teengs, "Two Spirit Women," 2nd ed., written for 2 Spirited Peoples of the First Nations and the Ontario Aboriginal HIV/Aids Strategy, Toronto, 2008, http://www.2spirits.com/PD Folder/Two%20Spirit%20Women.pdf.

32. Louise Erdrich, *The Porcupine Year* (Toronto: Harper Collins, 2008), 1–30.

33. Ibid.

34. Dana Wesley, "Reimagining Two-Spirit Community: Critically Centering Narratives of Urban Two-Spirit Youth," (master's thesis, Gender Studies, Queens University, 2015), 102; https://qspace .library.queensu.ca/bitstream/1974/13024/1/Wesley_Dana_L_201 504_MA.pdf.

35. This paragraph is based on the feedback I received from Alex Wilson, January 20, 2017. I am grateful for her generosity and perspectives on this issue and Idle No More.

36. I used the word *protocols* in an interview with Lee Maracle

for the *Quill and Quire* regarding storytelling practices. She corrected me and said stories are our birthright: "We wouldn't call it protocol. Protocol to me is what you have with other nations. With your children it's their birthright. These stories are their birthright. In my community, the elders actually don't have the authority over how you work with the stories. That's why I've never asked them. I can still plow on if they don't say anything. But I wouldn't. I wouldn't step outside my family." This made me think about the idea of protocols in a bigger way in the context of ceremony. The interview is available at http://www.quillandquire.com/authors/lee-maracles-tale/1/#search.

37. Reproduced courtesy of Billy-Ray Belcourt, https://nakinisowin.wordpress.com/2016/02/26/sacred/.

---

9. Land as Pedagogy

1. A different version of this story is told by non-Native author C. B. Cook in *Maple Moon* (Markham, ON: Fitzhenry and Whiteside, 1999). There are several other maple sugar origin stories; see the title story in Leanne Simpson, *The Gift Is in the Making: Anishinaabeg Stories* (Winnipeg: HighWater Press, 2013); Leanne Simpson, *Dancing on Our Turtle's Back: Stories of Nishnaabeg Re-Creation, Resurgence and a New Emergence* (Winnipeg: ARP Books, 2011)); and Alan Corbiere, "The Socio-Cultural History of Ninaatigwaaboo Maple Water," *Ojibwe Cultural Foundation* 6, no. 4 (2011): 1, 4–9.

2. A similar version of this story is published in Simpson, *The Gift Is in the Making*, with the main character as a boy. Another version of this story was published in 2014 in Leanne Simpson, "Land as Pedagogy: Nishnaabeg Intelligence and Rebellious Transformation," *Decolonization, Indigeneity, Education and Society* 3, no. 3 (2014), with the main character as a girl, available online at http://decolonization.org/index.php/des/article/view/22170.

3. Ziigwan is the first part of spring when the ice is breaking up and the snow is melting. Doodoom is an older Michi Saagiig Nishnaabeg word that children use for their mothers. It means "my breastfeeder." I learned this word from Doug Williams. Ajidamoo is a red squirrel. Gaawiin mean "no." Semaa is tobacco. Miigwech means "thanks." Nishnaabekwewag means "Ojibwe women." A saasaakwe is a loud shout or vocalization of approval used to call in or acknowledge the spirits. Ninaatigoog are maple trees.

4. This subheading comes from the work of Nishnaabeg scholar

Wendy Makoons Geniusz and her translation of the Nishnaabeg word
gaa-izhi-zhaawendaagoziyaang; Wendy Makoons Geniusz *Our Knowledge Is Not Primitive: Decolonizing Botanical Anishinaabe Teachings*
(Syracuse: Syracuse University Press, 2009), 67.

5. Geniusz, *Our Knowledge Is Not Primitive*, 67, calls this process
of coming to know gaa-izhi-zhaawendaagoziyaang: "that which is giv-
en lovingly to us by the spirits."

6. Manulani Meyers, June 3, 2014.

7. Simpson, *Dancing on Our Turtle's Back,* 3–7; Jill Doerfler,
Niigaanwewidam James Sinclair, and Heidi Kiiwetinepinesiik Stark,
"Bagijige: Making an Offering," in *Centering Anishinaabeg Studies: Un-
derstanding the World through Stories,* ed. Jill Doerfler, Niigaanwewid-
am James Sinclair, and Heidi Kiiwetinepinesiik Stark (East Lansing:
Michigan State University Press, 2013), xv–xxvii.

8. Manulani Meyers, June 3, 2014.

9. Jarrett Martineau and Eric Ritskes, "Fugitive Indigeneity: Reclaiming the Terrain of Decolonial Struggle through Indigenous Art,"
Decolonization: Indigeneity, Education and Society 3 no. 1 (2014), II.

10. Vine Deloria Jr., "Traditional Technology," In *Power and
Place: Indian Education in America,* ed. Vine Deloria Jr. and Daniel R.
Wildcat (Golden, Colo.: Fulcrum Resources, 2001), 58–59.

11. Ibid., 60.

12. Geniusz, *Our Knowledge Is Not Primitive,* 11, defines
Nishnaabeg gikendaasowin as knowledge, information, and the syn-
thesis of our personal teachings; *Nishnaabeg-inaadisiwin* as Nishnaabeg psychology, way of being; *Nishnaabeg-izhitwaawin* as Nishnaabeg culture, teachings, customs, history; *aadizookaanan* as sacred
stories; and *dibaajimowinan* as personal stories and history. I include
all of these components in the term *Nishnaabewin.* Also see Geniusz,
Our Knowledge Is Not Primitive, 67.

13. This is a term used to refer to the spiritual world by Sákéj
Youngblood Henderson, *First Nations Jurisprudence and Aboriginal
Rights: Defining a Just Society* (Saskatoon: University of Saskatchewan,
Native Law Centre, 2006). Also see Sákéj Youngblood Henderson,
"Empowering Aboriginal Thought," in *Reclaiming Indigenous Voice
and Vision,* ed. Marie Battiste (Vancouver: UBC Press, 2000), 248–79.

14. Gregory Cajete, *Look to the Mountain: An Ecology of Indigenous Education* (Durango, Colo.: Kivaki Press, 1994).

15. John Borrows, "Fragile Freedoms: Indigenous Love, Law and
Land in Canada's Constitution," unpublished paper that formed the

basis of a CBC *Ideas* episode, "Fragile Freedoms: John Borrows, First Nations and Human Rights," March 5, 2014, http://www.cbc.ca/play er/Radio/Ideas/ID/2440345608/. Also see John Borrows, "Maajita-adaa: Nanaboozhoo and the Flood, Part 2," in *Centering Anishinaabeg Studies: Understanding the World through Stories,* ed. Jill Doerfler, Niigaanwewidam James Sinclair, and Heidi Kiiwetinepinesiik Stark (East Lansing: Michigan State University Press, 2013), ix–xv; and Simpson, *Dancing on Our Turtle's Back,* 37–41.

16. Simpson, *Dancing on Our Turtle's Back,* 11.

17. Doug Williams taught me this concept through the word *dnaagaa'aa* (my phonetic spelling) in the context of hunting. It means "don't hurt anything if you don't need to, because you are stopping their path in life, have total compassion for other living beings."

18. To me, this is actually a critical part of the system. Being accountable and self-aware of one's own flaws and now, in the context of settler colonialism, one's experience with trauma and violence become critical to operationalizing Nishnaabeg intelligence.

19. Simpson, *Dancing on Our Turtle's Back,* 58.

20. It is my understanding that there is a high degree of noninterference in the intimate truths of individuals, and also a collective high degree of noninterference for groups of people to hold different truths. There is respect for this diversity. This is balanced with collective processes—ceremony and political processes (in governance, the generation of consensus, for example) that move, for instance, seven collective truths into an eighth understanding, while still acknowledging and validating dissenting views. See Simpson, *Dancing on Our Turtle's Back,* 58, for a more detailed explanation.

21. I started to think about Nishnaabeg intelligence after several discussions with Hawaiian thinker Manulani Meyer between 2012 and 2014, in Peterborough, Ontario, and Vancouver. See Manulani Meyer, "Indigenous Epistemology: Spirit Revealed," in *Enhancing Mātauranga Māori and Global Indigenous Knowledge* (Wellington: New Zealand Qualifications Authority, 2014), 151–66.

22. This is a Michi Saagiig Nishnaabeg name for our territory or nation that means the place where we all live and work together, and emphasizes the relational aspect of our conceptualization of nationhood. It refers to the north shore of Lake Ontario. See Simpson, *Dancing on Our Turtle's Back,* 14, for a more detailed explanation.

23. Ibid.

24. Winona LaDuke, *All Our Relations: Struggles for Land and Life* (Cambridge, Mass.: South End Press, 1994), 4, 132.

25. Henderson, *First Nations Jurisprudence*; L. Little Bear, "Jagged Worldviews Colliding," in *Reclaiming Indigenous Voice and Vision,* ed. Marie Battiste (Vancouver: UBC Press, 2000), 77–86.

26. Borrows, "Fragile Freedoms," 10; also see Borrows, "Maajita-adaa," ix-xv.

27. Geniusz, *Our Knowledge Is Not Primitive.*

28. I would add that this context was one of real and symbolic normalized violence for many Indigenous women and queer scholars coming through the system between the 1960s and the 1990s. "Indigenizing the academy" at this stage meant individual sacrifice for Indigenous women in order to obtain the credentials necessary to make the academy less violent toward the next group of Indigenous people coming through this system. It saddens me that these individual sacrifices so often go unrecognized.

29. I began to think about this more clearly after a discussion with long-time organizer Jaggi Singh about tactics in social movements, in St. John's, NL, May 14, 2014.

30. This is another idea that I learned from Manulani Meyer between 2012 and 2014 in Peterborough, Ontario, and Vancouver.

31. See Borrows's conceptualization of Nanabush (Nanaboozhoo) in his story "Maajitaadaa."

32. Linda Tuhiwai Smith, *Decolonizing Methodologies: Research and Indigenous Peoples* (London: Zed Books, 2012).

33. Manulani Meyer came to a PhD class in Indigenous Studies at Trent University in 2012 that I was teaching on methodology and theory. She began by asking students not what their dissertation was about, or what their theoretical framework or methodological approach was, but instead what their practice was in the context of Indigenous Knowledge. This is a critical distinction.

34. Glen Coulthard, "#Idle No More in Historical Context," in *The Winter We Danced: Voices from the Past, the Future, and the Idle No More Movement*, ed. Kino-nda-niimi Collective (Winnipeg: ARP Books, 2014), 36.

35. Peggy Blair, *Lament of a First Nation: The Williams Treaties of Southern Ontario* (Vancouver, BC: UBC Press, 2008).

36. For one example, see Leanne Simpson, "Aambe! Maajaadaa! (What #IdleNoMore Means to Me)," *Decolonization: Indigeneity,*

Education and Society, December 21, 2012, http://decolonization
.wordpress.com/2012/12/21/aambe-maajaadaa-what-idlenomore
-means-to-me/.

37. The basket clause was a legal clause added after the treaty was
negotiated that negated all other treaties Michi Saagiig Nishnaabeg
had signed with the Crown. It is our belief that this clause was added
after negotiations were complete without the knowledge of our leaders. See Blair, *Lament of a First Nation.*

38. Doug Williams, interviewed, recorded, and transcribed by Leanne Simpson, July 4, 2013, Curve Lake First Nation.

39. Leanne Simpson, "Our Elder Brothers: The Lifeblood of Re-
surgence," in *Lighting the Eighth Fire: The Liberation, Resurgence, and
Protection of Indigenous Nations,* ed. Leanne Simpson (Winnipeg:
ARP Books, 2008), 73–89.

40. For a broader discussion, see Glen Coulthard, *Red Skin, White
Masks: Rejecting the Colonial Politics of Recognition* (Minneapolis:
University of Minnesota Press, 2014); Andrea Smith, "Queer Theory
and Native Studies: The Heteronormativity of Settler Colonialism," in
*Queer Indigenous Studies: Critical Interventions in Theory, Politics, and
Literature,* ed. Qwo-Li Driskill, Chris Finely, Brian Joseph Gilley, and
Scott Lauria Morgensen (Tucson: Arizona University Press, 2011),
43–66; and Paul Nadasdy, *Hunters and Bureaucrats: Power, Knowl-
edge, and Aboriginal-State Relations in the Southwest Yukon* (Vancouver: UBC Press, 2003).

41. For a discussion of Native Studies in the context of the academic industrial complex, see Smith, "Queer Theory and Native Studies."
For a broader discussion of Indigenous recognition in Canadian politics, see Coulthard *Red Skin, White Masks*; and for a discussion of the
politics of refusal, see Audra Simpson, *Mohawk Interruptus: Political
Life across the Borders of Settler States* (Durham, N.C.: Duke University
Press, 2014).

42. Martineau and Ritskes, "Fugitive Indigeneity."

43. Rubén Gaztambide-Fernández, "Decolonial Options and Ar-
tistic/AestheSic Entanglements: An Interview with Mignolo," *Decolonization: Indigeneity, Education and Society* 3, no.1 (2014): 196–212.

44. Martineau and Ritskes, "Fugitive Indigeneity," IV.

---

10. "I See Your Light"

1. In my mind two of the most important recent examples of this
are Glen Coulthard, *Red Skin, White Masks: Rejecting the Colonial*

Politics of Recognition (Minneapolis: University of Minnesota Press, 2014); and Audra Simpson, *Mohawk Interruptus: Political Life across the Borders of Settler States* (Durham, N.C.: Duke University Press, 2014).

2. Coulthard, *Red Skin, White Masks*.

3. Coulthard, *Red Skin, White Masks*, 69–71; A. Simpson, *Mohawk Interruptus*, 25.

4. "In particular Fanon emphasized the essentiality of *reciprocal recognition* for human life and relatedness. Without reciprocal recognition, there can be no identity, no self-worth, no dignity"; Hussein Abdilahi Bulhan, *Frantz Fanon and the Psychology of Oppression* (New York: Plenum Press, 1985), 114.

5. For a written version of this story, see Edward Benton-Banai, *The Mishomis Book: The Voice of the Ojibway* (St. Paul, Minn.: Red School House, 1988), 6–12.

6. I first heard this from Edna Manitowabi in 2005.

7. Leanne Simpson, *Dancing on Our Turtle's Back: Stories of Nishnaabeg Re-Creation, Resurgence and a New Emergence* (Winnipeg: ARP Books, 2011).

8. Simpson, *Dancing on Our Turtle's Back;* Winona LaDuke, *All Our Relations: Struggles for Land and Life* (Cambridge, Mass.: South End Press, 1994).

9. Basil H. Johnston, *Anishinaubae Thesaurus* (East Lansing: Michigan State University Press, 2007), 88.

10. When I say we are the land, I mean that we embody so profoundly the intelligence of the natural world that we are indistinguishable from it. I am conflating Indigenous bodies with land here at the same time as I'm refusing settler colonialism.

---

11. Embodied Resurgent Practice and Coded Disruption

1. Sarah Hunt and Cindy Holmes, "Everyday Decolonization: Living a Decolonizing Queer Politics," *Journal of Lesbian Studies* 19, no. 2 (2015): 154–72.

2. Jeff Corntassel, "Re-envisioning Resurgence: Indigenous Pathways to Decolonization and Sustainable Self-Determination," *Decolonization: Indigeneity, Education and Society*, 1 no.1 (2012): 86–101.

3. It is also important to acknowledge that many Indigenous peoples have always lived this way and continue to do so now, and they would neither frame their lives nor their practices in this manner. It is simply how they have always lived. Mahsi Cho to Daniel T'selie

(K'asho Got'ine Dene from Radili Ko/Fort Good Hope) for reminding me of this during the spring of 2015.

4. Susan Blight, panel presentation, Indigenous Writers Gathering, Toronto Reference Library, Toronto, June 9, 2016. This was confirmed with Susan in e-mail June 23, 2016, and is used here with her permission. Susan learned this from elder Alex McKay.

5. Leanne Betasamosake Simpson, "The Hōkūle'a: Indigenous Resurgence from Hawai'i to Mannahatta," talk given on March 31, 2016, The New School, New York.

6. This is a quote from the trailer, https://vimeo.com/51118047; also see http://www.hokulea.com.

7. For information about the organizations and their work mentioned here, see the following: http://christibelcourt.com/onamin-collective/, http://ogimaamikana.tumblr.com/, https://www.kwiaw tstelmexw.com/, http://nativeyouthsexualhealth.com/.

8. I'm thinking here of the wonderful women I've met through Dechinta, especially Melaw Nakehk'o (check her blog: https://melawnakehko.wordpress.com/) and Mandee McDonald.

9. For more information, see http://unistotencamp.com/ and http://freegrassy.net/.

10. Mishuana Goeman, *Mark My Words: Native Women Mapping Our Nations* (Minneapolis: University of Minnesota Press, 2013).

11. Ibid., 6–13.

12. Gerald Vizenor, *Manifest Manners: Narratives on Postindian Survivance* (Lincoln: University of Nebraska Press, 1999), vii.

13. Jarrett Martineau, "Creative Combat: Indigenous Art, Resurgence, and Decolonization" (PhD diss., School of Indigenous Governance, University of Victoria, 2015).

14. See http://postcommodity.com/; http://walkingwithoursis ters.ca/; and http://www.skookumsound.com/.

15. He does this is contrast to my own academic and nonfiction work, where I have purposefully and deliberately visibilized Nishnaabewin (to some degree) in *Dancing on Our Turtle's Back*. I understand and have a great deal of respect for his approach—an approach I take in my own creative work. The danger of Indigenous scholars and writers visibilizing Indigenous intelligence is that it sets it up for exploitation in the context of settler colonialism. This has happened with the release of *Dancing on Our Turtle's Back* to some degree. People can read the book and believe they have some grasp of Nishnaabewin without ever engaging any Nishnaabeg or learning these concepts in

the appropriate manner. The benefit of this approach is that many Indigenous people have told me it has inspired them to learn their own intelligence system on their own terms, in their own nations. The difference in approach ultimately comes from different but related guidance the two of us have received from our elders and our own spiritual communities.

16. Monique's talk was part of the *All in the Family Residency,* September/October 2011, Nozhem First Peoples Performance Space, Trent University, Peterborough, Ontario.

17. This section is from an interview I did with Jarrett Martineau for his dissertation and is originally published in Martineau, "Creative Combat," 106–7. It is edited slightly here.

18. See the Kaha:wi Dance Theatre's website: http://kahawid ance.org/feature/re-quickening.

19. This was Cherish Violet Blood, an actor, storyteller, comedian, activist, and Blackfoot woman.

20. A previous version of this section was published on my blog in July 2012, http://leannesimpson.ca/tag/rebecca-belmore/.

21. I'd like to acknowledge the curatorial work of Nishnaabekwe Wanda Nanibush in continually installing and exhibiting these artists and the very best of Indigenous performance art in particular.

22. There is a profound lack of work on Maungudaus by literary scholars, especially considering he wrote a few decades before Pauline Johnson. See Ojibwe writer Heid E. Erdrich's consideration of Maungudaus in "Name': Literary Ancestry as Presence," in *Centering Anishinaabeg Studies: Understanding the World through Stories,* ed. Jill Doerfler, Niigaanwewidam James Sinclair, and Heidi Kiiwetine-pinesiik Stark (East Lansing: Michigan State University Press, 2013), 13–34; and his journal Maungwudaus/George Henry, *An Account of the Chippewa Indians, Who Have Been Travelling among the Whites, in the United States, England, Ireland, Scotland, France and Belgium; With Very Interesting Incidents in Relation to the General Characteristics of the English, Irish, Scotch, French and Americans, with Regard to Their Hospitality, Peculiarities, etc.* (Boston: George Henry, 1848).

23. There are regional variations of this tradition, but Nishnaabeg practices concerning death involve not speaking the name of those who have passed for a certain period of time—sometimes four days, sometimes a year, sometimes forever—and some places don't carry these traditions at all. Houle and his family do carry these traditions, and rather than list the names of those who died, Houle cycled the

names, repeating them so the spirits would not feel "called back" to the physical world. Houle explained this to me at the opening of the exhibit in 2011.

24. Wanda Nanibush, "Contamination and Reclamation: Robert Houle's *Paris/Ojibwa*," review, *Fuse*, December 29, 2010, http://fuse magazine.org/2010/12/961.

25. See Nanibush's more detailed description of the work in ibid.

26. A previous version of this section was originally published as a review of the exhibit; see Leanne Simpson, "Robert Houle: Honouring Ojibwa History," *Canadian Art*, July 28, 2011, http://canadianart.ca /reviews/robert_houle/.

27. The video can be viewed at http://leannesimpson.ca/leaks -music-video/.

28. See Martineau's meticulous comprehensive discussion of opaqueness in Martineau, "Creative Combat," 46.

29. See Martineau, "Creative Combat," for his use of constellation. Houle told me at the opening at the Art Gallery of Peterborough in June 2010 that this transformation was jiibay to aandisoke.

12. Constellations of Coresistance

1. Leanne Simpson, *Dancing on Our Turtle's Back: Stories of Nishnabeg Re-creation, Resurgence and a New Emergence* (Winnipeg: ARP Books, 2011).

2. I was writing this section and ran into Lee Maracle at an International Women's Day event in Toronto, March 10, 2016. In the course of our conversation, Lee said, "sound holds the universe together" and talked about her daughter's powerful singing voice as an example of the sound.

3. These stories come from Doug Williams.

4. "Hole in the Sky or Pleiades," Annette S. Lee, William Wilson, Jeffrey Tibbetts, and Carl Gawboy, *Ojibwe Sky Star Map Constellation Guide: An Introduction to Ojibwe Star Knowledge* (Cloquet, Minn.: Native Skywatchers, 2014), 22; Michael Wassegijig Price, "Anishinaabe Star Knowledge," *Winds of Change*, 17, no. 3 (2002): 52–56; and http://www.michaelwassegijig.com/star-knowledge.html.

5. Lee, Wilson, Tibbetts, and Gawboy, *Ojibwe Sky Star Map Constellation Guide*.

6. Jarrett Martineau, "Creative Combat: Indigenous Art, Resur-

gence, and Decolonization" (PhD diss., School of Indigenous Governance, University of Victoria, 2015), 81.

7. "The purpose of fugitivity is to rupture the normative order of representation; 'to open the enclosure'"; Martineau, "Creative Combat," quoting Fred Moten and Stefano Harney, *The Undercommons: Fugitive Planning and Black Study* (New York: Autonomedia, 2013), 11.

8. Gchi Ojiig is "Big Fisher."

9. Origin stories about the creation of wolverine attach wolverines to the skyworld. I mention it here to demonstrate the code meanings, layering, and complexity of Nishnaabeg theory, but in the spirit of opacity and direct relevancy, I've chosen not to tell it.

10. Leanne Simpson, *The Gift Is in the Making: Anishinaabeg Stories* (Winnipeg: HighWater Press, 2013).

11. Lawrence Henry SittingEagle, no date, *Clan Responsibilities: Ojibwe Clan System, The Seven Original Clans,* Rousseau River Anishinaabe First Nations.

12. Jarrett Martineau has highly influenced my thinking in this regard both through his written work and as a colleague and friend. We've had countless conversations from 2012 to the present on the topics in this book, and while I've been careful to acknowledge concepts and ideas that came from him, there is a broader, more diffuse influence that I'd like to acknowledge here, although I remain solely responsible for how these ideas are presented in this work.

13. Martineau, "Creative Combat," 41.

14. Jarrett Martineau and Eric Ritskes, "Fugitive Indigeneity: Reclaiming the Terrain of Decolonial Struggle through Indigenous Art," *Decolonization: Indigeneity, Education and Society* 3 no.1 (2014): I–XIII.

15. *The Winter We Danced: Voices from the Past, the Future, and the Idle No More Movement* was edited by an editorial collective called the Kino-nda-niimi Collective comprised of Tanya Kappo, Wanda Nanibush, Hayden King, Niigaan Sinclair, and me. The book was published by ARP Books, Winnipeg, in 2014.

16. I am thinking here of the Nishiyuu walkers and their 1,600 kilometers from Whapmagoostui, Cree territory, to Ottawa; http://www.cbc.ca/news/aboriginal/quebec-cree-walkers-find-lasting-impact-in-trek-to-ottawa-1.2612958.

17. See elder Alo White's account of this in his "The Sucker Punch of January 11," in *The Winter We Danced,* ed. Kino-nda-niimi Collective, 160–63. Indian Act chiefs in the Assembly of First Nations agreed

to a high-level meeting with then prime minister Stephen Harper, which resulted in the ending of Spence's hunger strike and effectively the end of the movement.

18. Jarrett Martineau with Stephen Hui, "Give People a Hub," in *The Winter We Danced*, ed. Kino-nda-niimi Collective, 115–18.

19. Jarrett Martineau, personal communication, April 13, 2016, Toronto.

20. *Kinomagewapkong* means "the rocks that teach"; also known as the Peterborough Petroglyphs.

21. *Gchi Engiikaaying* is the word Doug Williams knows for Toronto and means "big bay."

22. I want to be careful here not to erase those Black and Indigenous community organizers who have been building relationships in Toronto for decades. There was recent evidence of this in the Black Lives Matter mobilizations and in the OccupyINAC actions of 2016. Also see Luam Kidane and Hawa Y. Mire, "Constellations of Black Radical Imagining: Black Arts and Popular Education," in *Our Schools/Our Selves* (The Canadian Centre for Policy Alternatives) 24, no. 3 (Spring 2015), 1–8.

23. Katherine McKittrick, *Demonic Grounds: Black Women and the Cartographies of Struggle* (Minneapolis: University of Minnesota Press, 2006), xii.

24. Robin Levinson King, "Justin Trudeau Called Out for Statements Made about Music Causing Violence against Women," *Toronto Star,* September 22, 2015, http://anti-Blackness.thestar.com/news/federal-election/2015/09/22/justin-trudeau-points-finger-at-communities-for-causing-violence-against-women.html.

Conclusion

1. See Jorge Barrera, "Idle No More, Defenders of the Land Form Alliance, Call for 'Sovereignty Summer,'" March 18, 2013, APTN National News, http://aptn.ca/news/2013/03/18/idle-no-more-defenders-of-the-land-form-alliance-call-for-sovereignty-summer/.

2. During Idle No More, there was an information blockade at Alderville First Nation where people handed out pamphlets and coffee, and I think this was a tremendously beautiful and generous act of resistance.

3. Glen Coulthard, "#IdleNoMore in Historical Context," *Decolonization: Indigeneity, Education and Society,* December 24, 2012,

https://decolonization.wordpress.com/2012/12/24/idlenomore-in
-historical-context/.

4. Vijay Prashad wrote this sentence with regard to Palestinian people in an interview he did with Daniel Whittall about his book *Letters to Palestine* on the *Red Pepper* blog, July 2, 2015; http://www.red pepper.org.uk/letters-to-palestine-an-interview-with-vijay-prashad/. I edited the sentence and placed it in an Indigenous context.

5. See Glen Coulthard, *Red Skin, White Masks: Rejecting the Colonial Politics of Recognition* (Minneapolis: University of Minnesota Press, 2014); and also Audra Simpson, "Reconciliation and Its Discontents: Reconciliation in the Age of Sorrow," video, March 22, 2016, https://www.youtube.com/watch?v=vGl9HkzQsGg.

6. Leanne Simpson, *Dancing on Our Turtle's Back: Stories of Nishnabeg Re-creation, Resurgence and a New Emergence* (Winnipeg: ARP Books, 2011).

7. Jack Halberstam, "The Wild Beyond: With and for the Undercommons," in *The Undercommons: Fugitive Plag and Black Study,* by Stefano Harney and Fred Moten (New York: Automedia, 2013), 11.

INDEX

Aaniin (Michi Saagiig Nishnaabeg greeting), 181
Abdillahi, Idil, 252n.13
Aborigines Protection Society, 68
abstraction, as aesthetic principle, 201–2
academy: bringing Indigenous Knowledge into, discussion in late 1990s on, 170–71; critical process of Indigenous academics, 63; gatekeeping by, 31, 37; importance of work as Indigenous scholars, 65–66; "Indigenizing" the, 159, 171, 273n.28; interventions in Indigenous scholarship dismantling colonial domination, 175–78; methodologies of, 13; methodologies of Indigenous scholars, 29–34, 254n.7; pressure on youth to gain Western academic credentials, 159–60, 162, 273n.28; proper context for Nishnaabeg intelligence, lack of, 164; using

conventions of, to critique system of settler colonialism, 31; Western liberatory theory, 56, 67. *See also* education; knowledge
accountability: alternative systems of, 92–93, 227; forcing state to enact its own mechanisms for, 238; politics of grief used by state to avoid, 239–40
Ace, Barry, 208, 209
Acevedo, Marina, 202
aesthetics, Indigenous: abstraction as, 201–2; coded disruption and affirmative refusal through use of, 171–72, 199, 200–10; duality as, 201; Kuna, 200; layering as, 202–3; multidimensionality as, 201; reenactment and presencing as, 203–10; repetition as, 200–201
affirmative refusal, 198, 199, 200–10; Belmore's performance art as, 206

81; ongoing blockade at, 81, 194, 242
Great Lakes, epic water walks around, 58
Greene-ba, Robin, 19, 252n.12
grief, Indigenous, 238–39; politics of grief and, 239–40
grounded normativity: artist collectives creating space for instantiating microcommunal forms of, 217; Cree, 122–23, 199; Dene, 199; dispossession from, 24–25, 106–7, 221–22; ethical systems of, 44, 78, 130; mobilization within, 178, 218–28, 236; organizing within nation-based, 178; productive place of refusal generating, 176; Seneca, 196. *See also* Nishnaabewin (grounded normativity)
Gumbs, Alexis Pauline, 18, 37, 252n.13
Gustafsen Lake resistance, 247
Gzhwe Manidoo (The Creator), 20, 28, 184, 254n.4; context for Nishnaabeg reality set up by, 160–61; Nanabush and, 57, 183, 184; stars as thoughts and ideas of, 211; story of Gchi Ojiig (Big Dipper) and, 214–15. *See also* creation story(ies)

Halberstam, Jack, 281n.7
Harada, Dr. Masazumi, 69, 260n.14
Harney, Stefano, 279n.7
Harper, Stephen, 47, 73, 74, 279n.17
Haudenosaunee, 77, 251n.4
Henderson, Sákéj Youngblood, 271n.13
Henry, Alexander, 124
heteronormativity, 130
heteropatriarchy, 10, 17, 21, 48, 144,

177, 205; centering gender in resurgence, 51–54, 94, 134; coded intervention disrupting, 206; as foundational dispossession force, 42, 51–52, 87–90, 93, 97, 127; gender binary and hierarchy of, rigid, 88–89, 97, 110–11, 123, 127, 129, 134; Indigenous men placed as agents of, 109–11; refusal of, 33, 34, 36; risk of replicating, 51, 52, 53, 89; sexual agency as threat to, 107–13; skirt-wearing and, 141, 142; systemic dismantling of, 52, 245; systemic dismantling of, as core project of Radical Resurgence Project, 82, 83–94, 118; systemic dismantling of, Indigenous men and, 93; use of term, 253n.4
heterosexism, 93, 130
Hill, Janice, 258n.5
Hōkūle'a, Polynesian Voyaging Society's journey of, 193
holism, 201
Hollow Water First Nation, 19, Community Holistic Circle Healing project in, 92, 263n.14
Holmes, Cindy, 36, 191–92, 275n.1
homophobia, 93, 130, 136
Hoof Nation, treaty with, 58–61, 77, 243–45
Houle, Robert, 7, 203, 277n.23; *Paris/Ojibwa*, 69, 206–10, 259n.11
Huhndorf, Shari M., 262n.5
Hui, Stephen, 280n.18
humor, resilience and, 169
Hunt, Sarah, 36, 53, 93, 191–92, 255n.7, 255n.8, 257n.8, 258n.15, 265n.35, 266n.38, 275n.1
hunter and gatherer societies: gender binary from within

necessary in, 226–28, 246; use
of term, 48–49. *See also* Radical
Resurgence Project
resurgent education, 80, 82, 166–73,
178, 245
retreating to the bush, 17, 253n.7
Revision Quest (CBC), 130–31,
268n.26
rice beds, wild, 3, 34; diversity of
ways to harvest and process, 129,
139; loss of, 4, 77, 99
rights-based approach to Indigenous politics, 219
Rings, Frances, 202
Ritskes, Eric, 171–72, 271n.9,
279n.14
rituals upon killing animals, 60–61.
See also ceremonial practices
Roberts, Neil, 17–18, 253n.6
Rotinonhseshá:ka, 2, 251n.4; political systems, 115, 117
Rotinonhseshá:ka Confederacy, 7;
diplomacy with, 2, 61–62
Rotinonhseshá:ka/Haudenosaunee,
77
Roughing It in the Bush (Moodie),
97–100
Roulette, Roger, 130–31, 137,
269n.26
Royal Canadian Mounted Police
(RCMP), 107, 112

sacred (Belcourt), 143–44
sacred places, 4; Oka Crisis and, 14,
33, 252n.2
salmon in Lake Ontario, 3; extinction of, 4, 74, 77, 99
Sangster, Joan, 111, 262n.7, 264n.10,
265n.32, 266n.37
Sayers, Naomi, 108, 265n.24
science fiction, 201
Scott, Amos, 186

Scott, Duncan Campbell, 106
self-actualization, responsibility for,
120–21, 133–34, 156, 158
self-determination, 3–4, 87; alternative systems of accountability
and, 92; Belmore's performance
art emanating, 203; of Indigenous women, Moodie's erasure
of, 97, 100; of Indigenous wom-
en, state regulatory mechanisms
to destroy, 107–13; individual,
106–7, 112–13, 116–17, 123, 130,
134; individual, gender and, 129;
mobility as expression of, 197;
Nishnaabeg society as society of
makers and, 80; return to, stories
relying on, 22. *See also* agency
self-recognition, 180; collective, 65;
reciprocal, 182–83
Semple, Neil, 264n.2
Seneca grounded normativity, 196
settler colonialism, 4–5, 7, 10, 15,
263n.12; biiskabiyang and flight
out of structure of, 17–21, 245;
commodification of land and
bodies under, 41, 43, 152, 198,
199, 254n.2, 257n.4; connecting
personal experiences to larger
structures and process of, 27,
45–46, 80, 81, 85–86; consensual engagement in context
of, 161–62; constellations as
opaque, fugitive theoretical
interventions in universe of,
216–18; cultural resurgence as
compatible with, 49, 50; destruction of, as response to, 44, 45, 47,
48, 49, 172; dispossession from
grounded normativities through,
25, 106–7, 221–22; flight paths
out of, 17, 36, 192, 193, 197,
203, 210, 213, 217–18; gendered

of women, replicating, 53, 89; Indian Act and, 101, 102, 103–14, 195, 262n.8; "Indigenizing the academy" and individual sacrifices for, 273n.28; inquiry into missing and murdered, 238, 239; as legal targets for death, disappearance, and elimination, 42, 89, 115, 195, 205; Methodist missions and dispossession of Nishnaabeg women, 96–100; Nahnebahnwequay as political order, 68; political influence of, 68, 97, 101, 105, 107, 220; raw truths coming out of intimate spaces created by, 202; regulation of menstruating women in ceremony, 141; sexual agency, as dilemma for colonizers, 107–13; stereotypes about, 83–84, 85, 89, 91–92, 102, 112, 205; truths about, 84, 85; urban activism of, 195; violence against (*see* gender

violence; sexual violence). *See also* bodies, Indigenous; gender
Women's Earth Alliance, 121, 266n.4
World Lacrosse League Championship tournament, Iroquois Nationals refusal to participate in, 177
WSÁNEĆ nations, PKOLS reclamation and, 240, 241

Yellowbird, Michael, 253n.11
Yellowknives Dene First Nation territory, 5
youth, Indigenous: listening to, resurgence and, 226–27; pressure on, to gain Western academic credentials, 159–60, 162, 273n.28. *See also* children, Indigenous; education

zhawenjige (to hunt), 156. *See also* hunting and fishing rights

Leanne Betasamosake Simpson is a Michi Saagiig Nishnaabeg scholar, writer, and artist. She is on the faculty at the Dechinta Centre for Research and Learning and a Distinguished Visiting Professor at Ryerson University in Toronto. She is author of *Dancing on Our Turtle's Back, The Gift Is in the Making, Islands of Decolonial Love,* and *This Accident of Being Lost,* and editor of *Lighting the Eighth Fire, This Is an Honour Song* (with Kiera Ladner), and *The Winter We Danced* (Kino-nda-niimi Collective). She is a member of Alderville First Nation, in Ontario, Canada.